THEATERS OF THE
AMERICAN REVOLUTION
Northern • Middle • Southern • Western • Naval

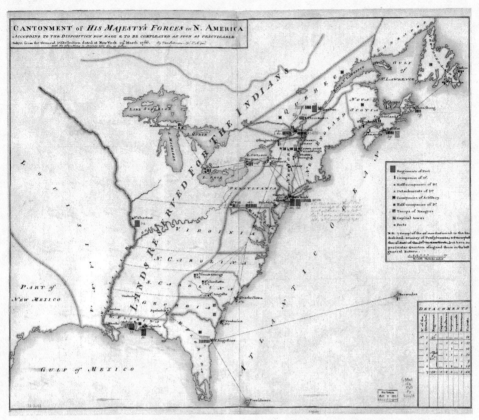

"Cantonment of His Majesty's forces in N. America according to the disposition now made & to be compleated as soon as practicable taken from the general distribution dated at New York 29th. March 1766." (*Library of Congress*)

THEATERS OF THE AMERICAN REVOLUTION

Northern · Middle · Southern · Western · Naval

James Kirby Martin and David L. Preston

EDITORS

WESTHOLME

Yardley

First Westholme paperback 2023

Introduction © 2017 David L. Preston and James Kirby Martin
The Northern Theater © 2017 James Kirby Martin
The Middle Theater © 2017 Edward G. Lengel and Mark Edward Lender
The Southern Theater © 2017 Jim Piecuch
The Western Theater © 2017 Mark Edward Lender
The Naval Theater © 2017 Charles Neimeyer
Maps by Paul Dangel. Maps © 2017 Westholme Publishing

Westholme Publishing, LLC
904 Edgewood Road
Yardley, Pennsylvania 19067
Visit our Web site at www.westholmepublishing.com

ISBN: 978-1-59416-391-3

Printed in the United States of America.

"May ample justice be done them here, and may the choicest of heaven's favours, both here and hereafter, attend those who, under the divine auspices, have secured innumerable blessings for others."
—George Washington, Farewell Orders to the Continental Army, November 2, 1783

A cartouche on a 1776 French map showing a loyalist attempting to replace a banner displaying a pine tree signifying America with a banner bearing the British lion; the patriot raises a knife to defend his banner. The cartouche reads in part, "Map of the port and harbor of Boston with the adjoining coasts, and the lines of the camps and intrenchments occupied by both the English and the Americans." (*Library of Congress*)

CONTENTS

Maps

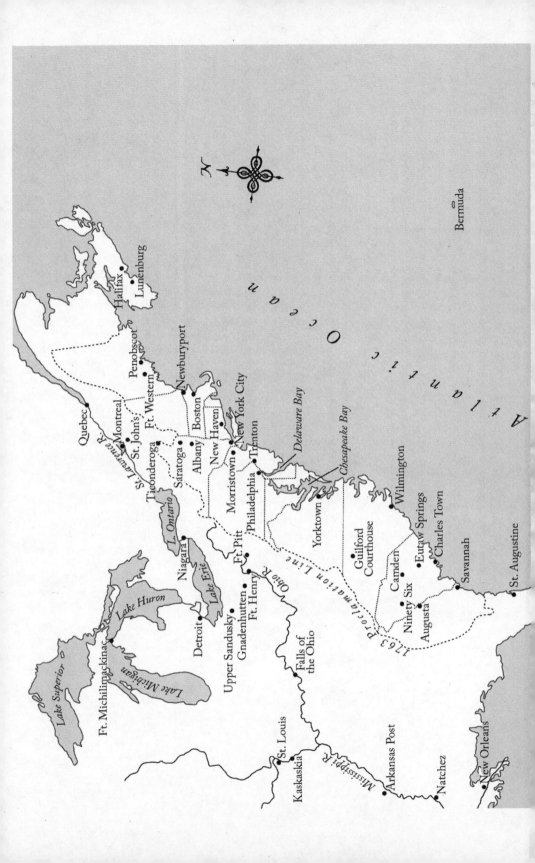

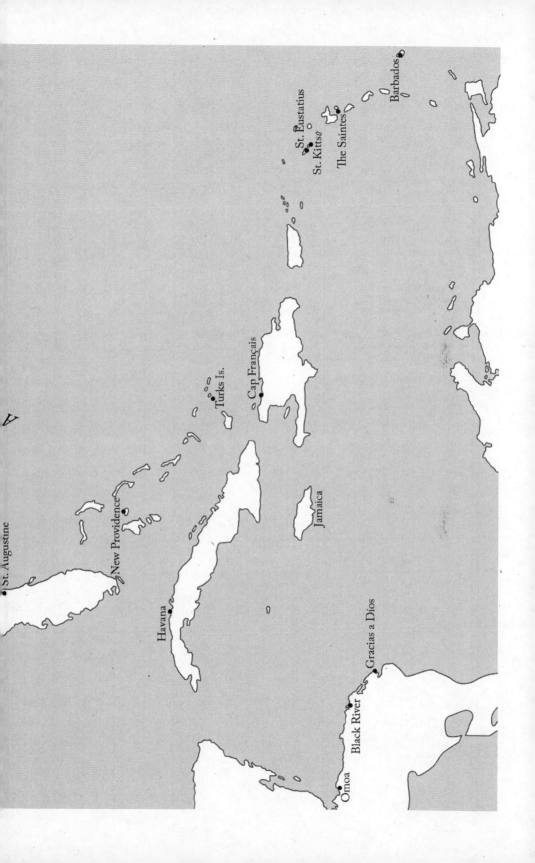

St. Augustine

New Providence

Havana

Turks Is.

Cap Français

Jamaica

Gracias a Dios

Black River

Omoa

St. Eustatius

St. Kitts

The Saintes

Barbados

INTRODUCTION

David L. Preston and James Kirby Martin

I t was a bleak December day in 1780 when Major General Nathanael Greene arrived at the American camp in Charlotte, North Carolina, to assume command of the Southern Department of the Continental Army. The Continental Congress, with General George Washington's blessing, had dispatched Greene from the main army in New York to redeem the perilous American situation in the Carolinas. Earlier that year, a British army and fleet had captured Charles Town, South Carolina, with stunning ease, bagging the entire southern Continental Army under General Benjamin Lincoln. British general Lord Cornwallis had similarly dispatched Greene's predecessor, Major General Horatio Gates, who had hastily advanced his makeshift army into South Carolina and into a pitched battle with Cornwallis. The Battle of Camden was among the greatest catastrophes that the Americans suffered during the entire war.

Reviewing the remains of Gates's shattered force, Greene despondently surveyed the insurmountable task that lay before him in the Southern Department—a theater of operations that was utterly foreign to this general of Quaker heritage from Rhode Island. He confided to General Henry Knox in New York that the "Difficulty of carrying on the war in this Department is much greater than my Imagination had extended to." His statement was remarkable, given that Greene was a veteran officer who had served well and faithfully for five years in Washington's army. He had seen action at the siege of Boston, the New York campaign, Trenton and Princeton, and the Philadelphia campaign. As the Continental Army's quartermaster general, he had helped to sustain the army through Valley Forge and onto its resurgence during the Monmouth campaign.[1]

Yet what Greene witnessed in the southern region was an entirely different kind of theater, one that staggered this otherwise unwavering veteran. He observed to Knox that even the word "Difficulty"—as both men had used it to describe the Northern Theater—"is almost without meaning" in a Southern Theater with such perverse character. Greene's letters during his first few weeks of command reveal that he had dutifully begun to survey the political, military, logistical, social, and geographical surroundings that would define his future operations. He recognized that civil authority in Georgia and the Carolinas was virtually nonexistent. The revolutionary governments were either in exile or ineffective in their ability to exert control, let alone provide supplies to his army. That lawless atmosphere led Greene to anticipate correctly that his would be "a kind of partizan war," with a small but mobile main army supported by militia drawn from the southern colonies and veteran guerilla fighters like Francis Marion. There would also be a stronger role for cavalry than in the Northern Theater.

Perhaps far better than any other American commander, Greene had a profound grasp of the political and social character of the Southern Department, one defined by a vicious civil war between Whigs and Tories "who pursue each other with as much relentless fury as beasts of prey." Greene had previously witnessed such internecine conflict in the northern colonies, but the scale and savagery of the civil war in the southern colonies utterly shocked him. He knew well that the southern population would be the center of gravity in the conflict, and took measures to appeal to the disaffected or neutral inhabitants. Greene the quartermaster also had the wisdom and foresight to study the varied terrain of the Carolinas. Countless rivers and rivulets wound their way southeast across the piedmont toward the coast, but there was no singular strategic river like the Hudson or Delaware that would control everything. Greene commissioned several subordinates, including the Polish engineer Colonel Thaddeus Kosciuszko, to survey those rivers with an eye toward transportation of supplies and troop crossings. Greene's early efforts to understand his operational environment would greatly contribute to his success in future campaigns in the Carolinas.[2]

Greene's experience—of discerning the differences between the Northern and Southern Theaters and their varied contexts—lies at the very heart of this collection and the symposium in which its essays were conceived. The presentations at the symposium, entitled "The Military Theaters of the Revolutionary War," which was held at The Citadel in Charleston, South Carolina, in April 2016, highlighted the breadth and the depth of the Revolutionary War's campaigns, beyond the narrow popular focus on Washington's main army operating in New York, New Jersey, and Pennsylvania. Military actions in all the various theaters of the war contributed to eventual American victory and British defeat. To study them in isolation risks losing a sense of their connectedness and the lines of influence that, for example, the Western and Naval Theaters had on operations in the northern states. A holistic understanding of the different theaters of the conflict also roots us in contemporary views of the war. Having been a part of a North American empire, most British colonists were conditioned to follow news of events in distant areas across the continent, and they intuitively grasped the connections and implications of developments outside of their own locales.

Contemporaries during the War for American Independence routinely used terms such as "theater of war," as "the Country or Place where a War is carry'd on," and a "theater of action," or "seat of war" to describe the presence of major field armies.[3] When George Washington arrived at Cambridge, Massachusetts, in July 1775 to take command of the Continental Army, he expressed "a thousand pities that such a Country should become the theatre of War." Following his victory at Dorchester Heights and the British army's evacuation of Boston, Washington remarked that people were "alarmed with the Apprehension of the Seat of War being removed to the Middle Colonies."[4] Washington's language hearkened back to that of classical antiquity and ultimately derived from translations of *Plutarch's Lives* and *Caesar's Commentaries* that eighteenth-century officers so eagerly absorbed. Caesar, for example, observed that Iberia "had been appointed the seat of war" during one of his many campaigns. By the nineteenth century, writers such as Carl von Clausewitz had firmly embedded the term "theater of operations" in the Western military vocabulary, defining it as "not just a part of the whole, but a subordinate entity in itself." That term became even more formalized by World War II with the use of acronyms such as ETO (European Theater of Operations) and PTO (Pacific Theater of Operations).[5]

Beginning in 1775, the Continental Congress gave definition to the broader American theater of war by creating territorial departments that were to be commanded by major generals. Congress's intent was that "the military operations of the colonies may be carried on in a regular and systematic manner" (and in interconnected fashion, the military departments dovetailed with the northern, middle, and southern departments for Indian diplomatic affairs that Congress had simultaneously created). Over time, a total of seven regional military departments were designated by the Congress: the Eastern (New England), Canadian (the St. Lawrence and lower Richelieu valleys), Northern (upper New York), Highland (West Point and its Hudson environs), Middle (New York City, New Jersey, Pennsylvania, Delaware, and Maryland), Southern (Virginia, the Carolinas, and Georgia), and Western (the Ohio Valley and Great Lakes east of the Mississippi River). Those military departments essentially constituted what would later be termed theaters of operations, and they also frame the geographical focus of the five essays that follow.[6]

This collection contributes to a greater appreciation of the military theaters of the Revolutionary War and fulfills a need for concise sketches of the events that unfolded within each geographic setting. James Kirby Martin's essay on the Northern Theater encompasses the Eastern, Canadian, Highland, and Northern departments. Edward Lengel and Mark Lender argue strongly for the centrality of the Middle Theater to American victory. Jim Piecuch recounts the decisive features of the war in the southern colonies, while Mark Edward Lender explores the violent reality of the Western Theater and the vicious fighting among diverse Indian nations, rebels, loyalists, Continentals, and British Regulars. To these we have added Charles Neimeyer's important contribution on the naval dimension of the war and crucial operations on the Atlantic Ocean ranging from American, West Indian, and British waters. It is the editors' hope that students, lay readers, and academic and military specialists will all profit from these engaging perspectives.

READER INVOLVEMENT AND INTERACTION

We invite readers of this collection to sift and evaluate the differences and similarities among the various theaters. Which theater or combination of theaters was most decisive in achieving American victory during the war? Which theater or combination of theaters was less decisive in contributing to American victory? What were the most important contributions within each theater to eventual American victory or British defeat? What military characteristics did various theaters have in common? How did operations in one theater affect those in another?

The United States Army, in its current training and doctrine, emphasizes eight variables that give shape to military operations within particular environments. Known by the acronym PMESII-PT, the variables include political, military, economic, and social-cultural considerations of combatants and non-combatants, information (military intelligence), infrastructure, the physical environment (including terrain and weather), and time available to the combatants. These variables, intended to aid commanders' decision-making within their operational environments, are useful in considering and evaluating the broader patterns involving people, issues, and events in the military theaters of the Revolutionary War (*Army Doctrine Reference Publication [ADRP5.0]—The Operations Process*. Department of the Army, 2012).

Readers who would like to express their thoughts, based on their analysis of these questions and variables, are welcome to send their conclusions and observations to editorial@westholmepublishing.com. They will then be shared with the contributors to this volume.

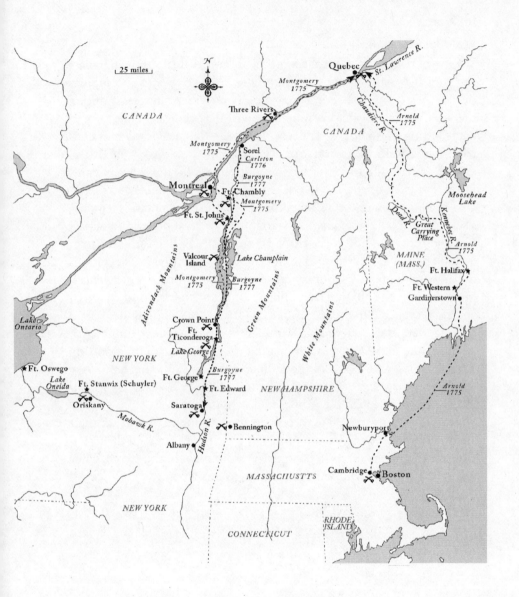

25 miles

N

CANADA

St. Lawrence R.

Quebec

Montgomery
1775

Three Rivers

Chaudière R.

Arnold
1775

CANADA

Montgomery
1775

Sorel
Carleton
1776

Burgoyne
1777

Moosehead
Lake

Montreal

Ft. Chambly

Montgomery
1775

Dead R.

Kennebec R.

Great
Carrying
Place

Arnold
1775

Ft. St. Johns

MAINE
(MASS.)

Ft. Halifax

Valcour
Island

Lake Champlain

Adirondack Mountains

Ft. Western

Gardinerstown

Montgomery
1775

Burgoyne
1777

Green Mountains

White Mountains

Lake
Ontario

Crown Point

Ft.
Ticonderoga

Lake George

NEW YORK

Ft. Oswego

Lake
Oneida

Ft. Stanwix (Schuyler)

Ft. George

Burgoyne
1777

Ft. Edward

NEW HAMPSHIRE

Arnold
1775

Oriskany

Mohawk R.

Saratoga

Hudson R.

Bennington

Newburyport

Albany

MASSACHUSTTS

Cambridge

Boston

NEW YORK

CONNECTICUT

RHODE
ISLAND

THE

NORTHERN THEATER

Setting the Stage for Victory

James Kirby Martin

Deadly shooting erupted early in the morning of April 19, 1775, on the Lexington, Massachusetts, village green. General Thomas Gage, serving as the military governor of Massachusetts, had received "secret orders" from the British home government. He was to stop whining about needing thousands of additional redcoats to put down the incipient rebellion; rather, he was to use the 3,000 or so troops at his disposal to demonstrate the futility of resisting massed British arms. After all, imperial leaders in England believed that the Massachusetts troublemakers were really nothing more than "a rude rabble without plan, without concert, and without conduct." They could easily be brought back to their senses with a flurry of muskets balls and a flash of bayonets, or by arresting "the principal actors and abettors" of rebellion. Whatever option Gage chose to pursue, he now had specific orders to act—and to act decisively.[1]

Gage's final operational plan focused on sending 700 redcoats twenty miles into the countryside from Boston to secure and destroy weapons

and gunpowder being gathered in and around the quaint village of Concord, five miles beyond Lexington. The eruption of gunfire and killing
that began on the Lexington green occurred when trained local militia,
calling themselves Minutemen, protested the presence of the British
troops entering their community. No one knows who fired the first shots,
but eight militiamen died in the brief encounter, with another ten
wounded. By day's end, fighting at places like Concord's North Bridge
and all along the road back toward Boston produced significant bloodshed in which the British suffered the most carnage. Including dead,
wounded, captured, and missing combatants, Gage's troops suffered 273
casualties as compared to 95 for the Americans.

The day of Lexington and Concord riled up the inhabitants of New
England, so much so that by the early May something like 15,000 militiamen had Gage and his redcoats entrapped on Boston peninsula.
Among those thousands rushing to the front were the Governor's 2d
Company of Footguards from New Haven, Connecticut, captained by
the prospering trading merchant Benedict Arnold. While marching along
the road to Boston, Arnold encountered prominent lawyer Samuel
Holden Parsons, then heading back home to Connecticut from Cambridge, Massachusetts, the headquarters of patriot resistance. Parsons
spoke about the need for artillery pieces to help keep Gage's minions
from breaking out of Boston. Arnold, based on his trading ventures in
Canada, indicated that dozens of ordnance pieces were located at Fort
Ticonderoga and Crown Point on Lake Champlain. With that exchange,
the two gentleman parted company, both thinking about how to secure
this cache of weaponry for the patriot cause.[2]

This chance meeting led to the opening salvo of what became the
Northern Theater military campaign that culminated more than two years
later in the climactic turning point American victory at Saratoga, New
York. As for Arnold, he proceeded to Cambridge, where he met with the
noted patriot Joseph Warren and other members of the Massachusetts
Committee of Safety. They gave him a colonel's commission with orders
to go west, recruit a regiment, and capture Fort Ticonderoga. Parsons,
meanwhile, rushed to Hartford, met with a rump group of assembly
leaders, secured £300 from the treasury, and hired local militia captain
Edward Mott to gather a force to attack the fort. Marching north, Mott
enlisted various characters from Massachusetts, including lawyer John

Brown, who had earlier traveled to Canada and reported back that Ticonderoga represented easy pickings. He also enlisted Vermont's controversial Ethan Allen and his motley following of Green Mountain Boys.

When Arnold, in turn, learned about the Mott-Allen party, he handed the task of recruiting a regiment to others. Then he rode hard to reach Bennington, Vermont, where Allen and the Boys based their vigilante activities in defying New York's claim to ownership of Vermont territory. Passing through Bennington to Zadock Remington's tavern in Castleton, he found out that Allen was now in command and was proceeding to Hand's Cove on the Vermont shoreline of Lake Champlain, where his column intended to cross to the New York side before attacking the fort. Arnold finally caught up with Allen and displayed his colonel's commission, but he had no troops, and the Boys alone numbered nearly two hundred. After much haggling, these two rivals agreed on a joint command.[3]

Taking the fort under cover of darkness early on he morning of May 10, 1775, was a bloodless event. Allen, Arnold, and some of the Boys rushed into the fort, where they caught the sleepy defenders completely off guard. In his fanciful *Narrative*, Allen bragged about how he rushed into the parade ground, marched over to the west side barracks, and informed the British commander, Captain William Delaplace, that he was taking command of the fort "in the name of the great Jehovah, and the Continental Congress." Other accounts noted that Allen's words were less prosaic, something like "Come out of there you damned old rat," or "old skunk," or "old bastard."[4]

That same day the Second Continental Congress began its deliberations in Philadelphia. Very few delegates, at least at this juncture, were in favor of declaring independence; rather, they wanted to reconcile their differences with King George III and Parliament. As such, they were not happy about the news that Fort Ticonderoga was now in patriot hands, or that Green Mountain Boy leader Seth Warner had overrun a small British contingent at Crown Point, which contained yet more artillery pieces. In facing reality, however, the delegates had to accept that war fever was spreading, as indicated by the bloody Battle of Bunker Hill (Breed's Hill) just north of Boston, on June 17, which was a factor in King George's decision to declare all the colonies to be in open rebellion on August 23. The home government's attitude was that treason had taken root in America and that the rebellious colonists had to either submit to imperial authority or face full-scale warfare.[5]

By mid-May the Green Mountain Boys, having drunk their fill of the ninety gallons of rum they found at Ticonderoga, were retreating back to Vermont. Arnold was now in command and thinking very seriously about what strategy the British would employ to regain control of their treasonous colonies. Having earlier traded as far north as Quebec City and Montreal, he appreciated how the rivers and lakes in the St. Lawrence watershed provided a natural geographic pathway for a sizable British force to invade the colonies through the hills and mountains of northern New York. Arnold could foresee one British army taking New York City and moving 150 miles up the Hudson to capture Albany. A second force, concentrated in Quebec Province, could travel south across Lake Champlain and the Hudson River to reach Albany, about 200 miles south of Montreal. Once united, these two forces could then sweep eastward through New England, wiping out patriot resistance in the region then at the center of the rebellion.[6]

Fort Ticonderoga and Crown Point represented locations from which Arnold could correctly predict British military strategy for ending the rebellion. He was so convinced that a martial assault would be forthcoming from Canada that he wrote the Continental Congress in mid-June 1775 suggesting a counter strategy. Arnold proposed that Congress think offensively, develop plans to invade Canada, and secure Quebec Province as the fourteenth colony in rebellion. Calling for the recruitment of a northern force of 2,000 troops, Arnold's "plan of operations" focused on first taking Montreal while securing supply lines back to Ticonderoga and Albany. With Montreal in the patriot fold, Quebec City was the next critical target. Once under patriot control, the province could serve as "an inexhaustible granary in case we are reduced to want" in the event of a lengthy war. Even more important, moving the patriot defensive line all the way north to Quebec City would greatly extend the geographic perimeter through which British forces would have to punch in efforts to reach Albany and reconquer the rebellion's vital center in New England. Overall, then, Arnold's vision was to "frustrate" England's "cruel and unjust plan of operation" to retake New York and New England by moving an army through Canada.[7]

Congressional delegates already had their eyes fixed on Quebec Province and had extended an invitation to have representatives from this colony join in their deliberations. No one appeared, however, a sure

George Washington called Benedict Arnold (1741–1801) his best fighting general, which Arnold proved in the Northern Theater at Valcour Island and Saratoga, among other places. However, he is known today today for his act of treason against the American cause. (*Private Collection*)

sign of scant enthusiasm about getting tangled up in the rebellion. At the same time, Quebec's governor-general Guy Carleton, much experienced in military matters, was doing what he could to organize regular troops and local militia to repel any attempted military incursion from the south. A determined servant of the empire, Carleton was not about to let his province fall into rebel hands.[8]

In mid-June Congress began to get serious about a well-organized military establishment. The initial step was to adopt the patriot force then enveloping General Gage's redcoats in Boston, thereby creating the Continental Army. Next the delegates put a command structure in place, first appointing George Washington as commander in chief, then naming additional general officers. One of those selected for high command, wealthy Philip Schuyler from the Albany region, received a commission as the army's third-ranking major general, to take command of what became the army's Northern Department.[9]

Overleaf: "A general map of the northern British colonies in America. Which comprehends the province of Quebec, the government of Newfoundland, Nova-Scotia, New-England and New-York. From the maps published by the Admiralty and Board of Trade, regulated by the astronomic and trigonometric observations of Major Holland and corrected from Governor Pownall's late map 1776." One of a series of maps dividing the British North American colonies into northern, middle, and southern sections. (*Library of Congress*)

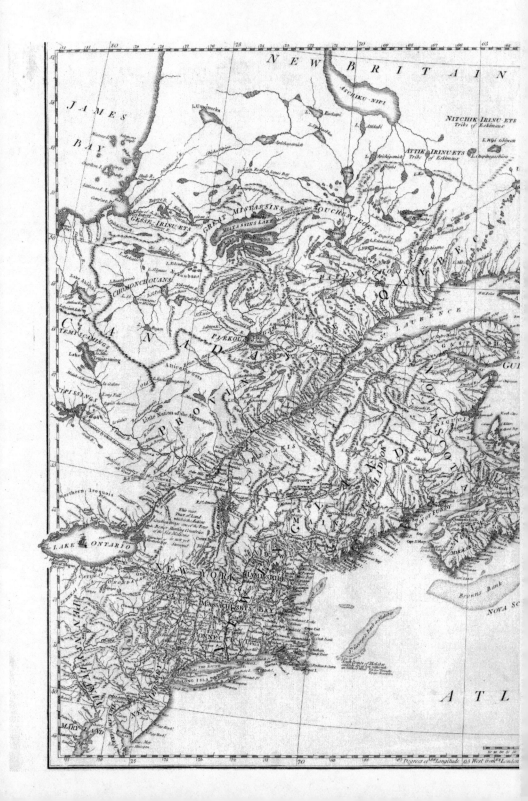

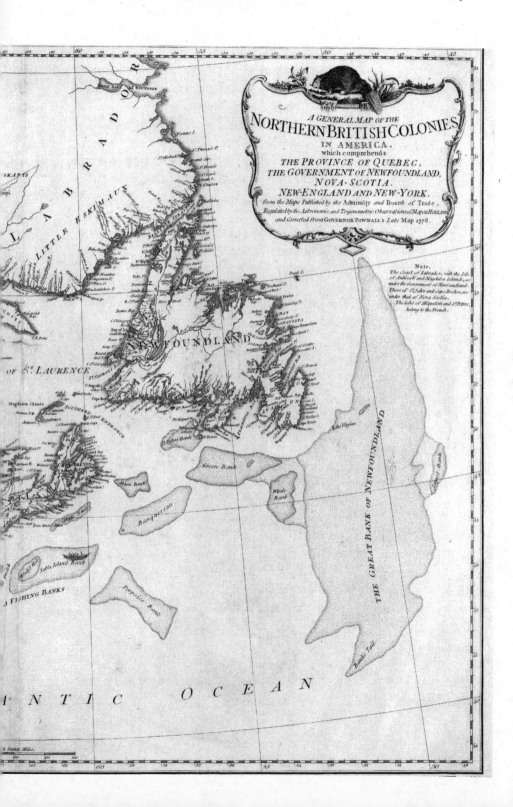

A few days later Congress ordered Schuyler to proceed to Fort Ticonderoga and Crown Point. There he was to determine whether it would be "practicable, and . . . not be disagreeable to the Canadians" to "immediately take possession of St. Johns, Montreal, and any other parts of the country, and pursue any other measures in Canada, which may have a tendency to promote the peace and security of these colonies." In issuing this order, Congress admitted, as Arnold and others had pointed out, that Quebec Province represented an exposed northern flank. Thus there was good reason to use military means to encourage this province to join the patriot rebellion.[10]

During July and August Schuyler worked closely with a recently retired British officer, Richard Montgomery, whom Congress had named a brigadier general back on June 22. Montgomery had moved to New York in 1772 to take up farming, then married into the prominent Livingston family in 1773. Having fought in the Champlain region during the French and Indian War, he was familiar with the region's geography. Also important, Montgomery felt an abiding commitment to defending American liberties against what he had concluded was England's oppressive rule. By August he and Schuyler were ready to move a sizable force northward across Lake Champlain and onto the Richelieu River with the initial objective of capturing Montreal.[11]

Meanwhile, back in early July, George Washington had ridden into Cambridge, Massachusetts, the headquarters of the patriot army. There he took command of what he described as "an exceeding dirty and nasty" gathering of undisciplined soldiers. While beginning the task of turning these newfound Continentals into something like real soldiers, he also maintained communications with Schuyler about the pending Canadian invasion. Before mid-August he started meeting with Benedict Arnold, now relieved of his command at Ticonderoga. With Schuyler's blessing Washington named Arnold a Continental Army colonel and placed him in charge of a second force charged with invading Canada. In this case, the target was Quebec City, which would involve moving a detachment through virtually uncharted backcountry Maine with the objective of capturing this walled capital city before it had its defenses in place.[12]

Back at Ticonderoga, Schuyler and Montgomery got off to a sluggish start. But by early September they had a force of some 2,000 troops from New York and New England assembled on Île aux Noix, a swampy island

A wealthy New York patrician, Philip Schuyler (1733–1804) was named by Congress as the first Northern Department commander in 1775. He was later removed in favor of Horatio Gates, despite mounting an effective resistance effort during the summer of 1777 against the invading army of John Burgoyne. (*New York Public Library*)

in the Richelieu River about twelve miles into Quebec Province. The main obstacle blocking them from gaining access to Montreal was Fort St. Johns (also rendered Fort St.-Jean), several miles farther downriver. Governor Carleton had assigned 750 regulars to defend this strongly rebuilt edifice. During the patriot advance Schuyler fell seriously ill and had to return to Ticonderoga. Montgomery, now in charge, persisted in what developed as extended siege operations (September 17 to November 3) before the defenders could no longer take the constant pounding of cannon fire. With Fort St. Johns captured, Montgomery marched his troops overland to Montreal, which surrendered without much resistance on November 13, 1775. So far so good for the patriot plan to conquer Quebec Province.[13]

Two months earlier, Arnold had taken charge of 1,100 volunteers and had them moving toward Fort Western on the Kennebec River in Maine. Just about everything that could go wrong was about to go wrong. Having a copy of a map drawn around 1760 by British engineer John Montresor, Arnold estimated the journey to Quebec City at 180 miles (actually closer to 350 miles) and calculated a twenty-day trip (took more than forty days). No well-defended obstacle like Fort St. Johns stood in the way of his detachment's forward movement, but the rugged terrain, rivers full of rapids, and even a likely late season hurricane kept challenging the endurance of his soldiers. One group, about 300 men under the command of faint-hearted Lieutenant Colonel Roger Enos of Connecticut, turned back and absconded with the bulk of dwindling food supplies. Before finally breaking through to Quebec City, a few of Arnold's soldiers even starved to death before provisions obtained in French settlements on the Chaudière River reached them. All told, Arnold was able to get 600 or more of his volunteers safely across the St. Lawrence River and onto the Plains of Abraham in front of the city's western walls by November 14; yet many of their muskets were lost or damaged, and they lacked cannons to attempt to breach the city's somewhat dilapidated but protective walls.[14]

Arnold had hoped to catch Quebec City in a defenseless state, unaware of the existence of his expeditionary force. Letters he addressed to a local merchant, however, ended up in the hands of Lieutenant Governor Hector Cramahé, and he had the city on full alert and preparing its defenses long before mid-November. Once on the Plains of Abraham, Arnold realized he had no hope of taking the city, so he marched his "famine proof veterans" twenty miles west to the village of Pointe aux Trembles overlooking the St. Lawrence River. There he wrote about the "brave men" under his command, "who were in want of everything but stout hearts." Arnold calculated that a force of 2,000 would be needed to take and hold the city, as he waited with "great anxiety" for the arrival of General Montgomery with whatever numbers of troops and artillery pieces he could bring forward from Montreal.[15]

Montgomery arrived at Pointe aux Trembles in early December with another 700 soldiers. Together the combined forces added up to some 1,325 troops, including a few Indians and Canadian volunteers. Montgomery assumed overall command with Arnold as his second. Together they discussed options for attacking Quebec City, knowing that Governor Carleton had returned there after his escape from Montreal just before that city fell to the patriots. Tactical choices included "siege, investment, or storm." Montgomery did bring captured artillery pieces with him in sailing down the St. Lawrence from Montreal, but they lacked the weight to break down the walls. The best alternative was "the storming plan," even if their small army lacked by many hundreds the numbers of troops Arnold believed they needed to conquer the city.[16]

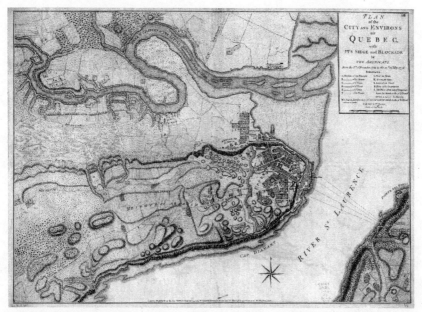

"Plan of the City and Environs of Quebec: With its Siege and Blockade by the Americans, from December 8, 1775, to May 13, 1776," by William Faden, London, 1776. The American batteries can be seen at the far right. (*Library of Congress*)

Soon the combined forces moved back to the Plains of Abraham and established themselves in the suburbs of St. John's and St. Roch. Their first storming plan involved sending a diversionary party into the Lower Town while Montgomery and Arnold would lead most of the troops in scaling the western walls to get into the Upper Town. They knew they had to act before January 1, since the enlistments of hundreds of troops ended that day, and many soldiers were threatening to return home. Late on the evening of December 27 Montgomery and Arnold were poised to attack using the cover of a heavy snowstorm, but the weather cleared suddenly, which nixed that effort.

Concerned that Carleton and the city's defenders, now on full alert and well organized, had gained intelligence about this plan's design, the two leaders reversed the arrangement of attacks. Diversionary parties now were to make lots of noise at points along the western wall, as if the major breakthrough attempt was to occur there. At the same time, Montgomery would lead about 300 New Yorkers along the narrow, icy road along the St. Lawrence River to break into the Lower Town while Arnold would approach along the other side with about 600 troops. Once the two forces came together, they would turn east and charge up Mountain Hill Street. And once they broke through a strong gate, hopefully lightly defended because of the diversion along the western wall, they would charge into the Upper Town with expectations of defeating any defender that had the temerity to challenge them.

This revised storming plan was born of desperation and fraught with large risks, especially since Montgomery and Arnold knew that Carleton had the Upper Town well defended. With time for action running out, a blinding snowstorm gave them the opening they wanted to launch their attack. Early on the morning of December 31, with darkness also covering their movements, the patriot force sprang into action, but everything seemed to go wrong. Carleton did not bite on the diversionary attacks; rather, he held his troops in assigned positions, waiting to determine where the major rebel thrust would come.[17]

Montgomery's column had to break through two strong wooden barricades to reach the Lower Town. When the general advanced through an opening in the second barrier, cannon fire erupted from a nearby log house that instantly killed him and two of his aides. His troops immediately retreated. As for Arnold, his column was approaching a well-placed barricade when a ricocheting musket ball, likely fired from the Upper Town, ripped into the lower part of his left leg. Stunned and bleeding profusely, Arnold reluctantly turned over command to the famous Virginia rifleman Daniel Morgan. Aides carried Arnold from the field. Morgan, in turn, charged ahead and breached his barrier, only to discover yet another barricade blocking his force from reaching Mountain Hill Street. As the storm subsided and early dawn approached, Morgan's troops found themselves trapped between the two barricades as Carleton's forces deployed to attack them. Some of the "famine proof veterans" were seriously wounded or shot dead, but around 400 of them surrendered, the last holdout being Morgan, who kept fighting until a priest convinced him to hand over his sword.[18]

Total defeat is the only way to characterize the patriot attempt to conquer Quebec City. Montgomery joined Dr. Joseph Warren of Massachusetts, killed at Bunker Hill, as an early patriot martyr who gave his all in support of the cause of liberty. Arnold, who lay seriously wounded, now in command of the remnant of troops trying to maintain a paper-like investment of the city, and Morgan, along with so many other patriot soldiers, were jailed prisoners. For his part, Governor Carleton refused to send a sizable force outside the protective walls to finish off the American resisters. He had taken part and suffered a head wound back in September 1759 on the Plains of Abraham when the French commander, the Marquis de Montcalm, led his troops out of the walled city for what was a climactic confrontation with British forces under General James Wolfe. Carleton was no risk taker. Having witnessed firsthand the mistake of taking on any enemy force outside the protective walls, he held to his strategy to remain on the defensive, however feeble the opponent's force, and wait for relief from the British Isles once winter snows melted during springtime.[19]

The Continental Congress, once apprised of the patriot disaster, worked diligently to pour hundreds of fresh patriot recruits into Canada. Arnold, now promoted to a brigadier general because of his heroic march through the Maine wilderness, advised the delegates that he lacked the depth of military experience to hold overall command. Congress first sent Major General John Thomas of Massachusetts north to bring order out of the growing chaos, but he succumbed to smallpox in early June 1776. Next appeared Brigadier General John Sullivan, who was helpless to resist what Carleton was counting on, the appearance of massive numbers of troops from Britain. The Crown's first relief vessels reached Quebec City on May 6, to be followed by dozens of additional ships carrying, in total, a force of some 10,000 redcoats and Hessians. They had one immediate mission: Drive the rebellious Americans out of Canada, which they accomplished by hammering at rebel troops now retreating or surrendering before them.[20]

By June 18, the patriot force, riddled by such killer diseases as smallpox, was struggling to get out of Quebec Province. Remnants of troops were bivouacking on Île aux Noix, waiting their turn to be evacuated up Lake Champlain to Crown Point and Ticonderoga. Benedict Arnold reached this island that same evening, aghast at what he saw regarding these fighting soldiers of the Northern Department army. A physician attending to the troops described how tents held "one or more [soldiers] in distress and continually groaning, and calling for relief, but in vain!" A large barn was "crowded full of men with this disorder [smallpox], many of which could not see, speak, or walk," even while allowing "large maggots" to eat away at their bodies. Hundreds of once proud patriot soldiers would die on Île aux Noix, which to this day has no marker memorializing their sacrifice or identifying the pits where their lifeless remains were piled one on top of another.[21]

The Canadian campaign had failed, miserably. The strategy of maintaining an extended defensive perimeter was no more. Realizing that British forces would eventually mount a major assault southward out of Canada, Benedict Arnold rushed southward from Île aux Noix, first up Lake Champlain and then down the Hudson River, all the way to Albany where he held meetings with General Schuyler. The question was how to best defend Lake Champlain in facing the expected onslaught. Their conclusion was to keep building a lake fleet of vessels that might somehow have enough fire power, or crew courage, to ward off the British advance. Arnold, because of his maritime experience as a merchant who had often captained his own vessels on trading ventures to the West Indies and Canada, agreed to assume overall responsibility in directing the construction of a patriot fleet. Schuyler now had a general officer who could effectively challenge British forces—both on land and on water.

Yet Schuyler still had to face a challenge regarding who actually was in charge of the Northern Department. On June 17, Congress, not well informed about the desperate state of the patriot retreat from Quebec Province, ordered Major General Horatio Gates to take command of all American forces in Canada. Unfortunately for Gates, a retired British field grade officer who had resettled in Virginia and served Washington as a ranking staff officer, the disease-ridden, exhausted patriot army was no longer in Canada. He and Schuyler squared off in less than friendly meetings in Albany. The ever ambitious Gates finally backed off his claim to be in charge of the army, whether or not it was in Canada, when Congress specifically stated that it had "no design to vest him with a superior command to General Schuyler, while the troops should be on this side of Canada."[22]

Congress expected Schuyler and Gates to act "with harmony" in warding off a British invasion, and they did—at least in 1776. Schuyler was in overall command while Gates took charge of the fixed line of defense at Fort Ticonderoga. Brigadier General Arnold, as events played themselves out, was a third partner in command, although subordinate to

James Peale's circa 1782 portrait of Horatio Gates (1727–1806). The so-called "Hero of
Saratoga" craved high field command in the Northern Theater, but his actual battlefield performance was commonplace at best. (*National Portrait Gallery*)

Schuyler and Gates. He not only provided overall guidance in the construction of the patriot Champlain fleet, but then served as the commodore of this flotilla of vessels. Before the middle of August thousands
of troops were strengthening the defensive works at Fort Ti, including a
key position on the east side of Lake Champlain known as Mount Independence. At the same time, workers at Skenesborough (modern-day
Whitehall, New York), about 30 miles to the south, were laboring day
and night to get enough vessels ready to give Arnold some semblance of
a fighting fleet.

As the patriot flotilla took shape, it consisted of sixteen vessels. Nine
were gundalows, sometimes rendered gondolas, best understood as over-
grown bateaux with flat bottoms, one fixed sail, space for up to 45 men,
and no capacity to sail into the wind. With such restricted maneuver-
ability, crew members could expect to pull on oars when moving to the
windward.[23]

Realizing how limited these gundalows were as war vessels, Arnold
pushed for the construction of row galleys, larger craft with two masts
carrying lateen sails that could swivel with changing winds. As such, they
could tack into the wind when necessary, making them much more ma-
neuverable. Three row galleys—the *Congress*, *Trumbull*, and *Washington*—joined the fleet. Once available, the *Congress* became Arnold's

flagship. He also had the sloop *Enterprise* and three schooners, including the *Royal Savage*, to complete the patriot fleet.

What the fleet represented was a mobile force designed to challenge the British long before they reached the fixed patriot defenses at Fort Ticonderoga. Gates, working closely with Arnold, prepared orders to guide the fleet's actions in its "momentous" objective of protecting "the northern entrance into this side of the continent." He expected his commodore to wage "defensive war," taking "no wanton risk" that would seriously damage the fleet. Yet Arnold was to demonstrate his "courage and abilities" in "preventing the enemy's invasion of our country." Without taking chances, Arnold was "to act with such cool, determined valor as will give them [the British] every reason to repent their temerity" as they sailed southward toward Fort Ticonderoga.[24]

Such orders placed Arnold between a rock and a hard place. He was to act boldly but cautiously—aggressively but defensively—against what he was sure was a decidedly superior enemy force. He understood that he had taken on a suicide mission of sorts, especially with crews of soldiers mostly lacking in sailing experience. The best strategy, he concluded, was to sail to the northern end of the lake with a portion of his vessels and wave them before the British, who were now assembling their fleet at St. John's. Arnold's objective was to create the impression that his vessels were ready and willing to fight, that they would not be swept aside easily, not without a major fight, regardless of the size and strength of the British naval force.

Governor Carleton, acting with his usual caution as he had when defending Quebec City, took the bait. He refused to sail his flotilla up the Richelieu River and onto Lake Champlain unless clearly holding every advantage in numbers of craft and firepower. For nearly a month he kept his fleet bottled up at St. John's until the sloop of war *Inflexible*, carrying eighteen 12-pounder cannons, was ready for service. Finally, on October 4, Carleton issued orders for his vessels to go after the patriot naval force waiting to engage them on Lake Champlain. Given the lateness in the campaign season, the governor's objective was to drive the rebels out of Crown Point and Fort Ticonderoga before winter weather halted his operations. Once overrun, Fort Ticonderoga would was to function as the new front line of British authority in the Northern Theater, as well as the launching point to continue their southward advance in 1777.[25]

Guy Carleton (1724–1808), governor-general of Quebec Province and determined opponent of the patriot invasion in 1775, was overly cautious in taking actions to drive the Americans out of Canada in 1776. (*New York Public Library*)

Commodore Arnold, meanwhile, had moved his fleet to a location on the east side of Valcour Island, some seventy miles north of Ticonderoga. Sailing south on a strong northerly breeze on the morning of October 11, the British fleet passed along the island's western shoreline before spying the patriot fleet, now anchored together in a semicircle defensive formation awaiting an attack. Arnold had chosen his position well. As he had hoped, the British fleet failed to form an organized battle line as they struggled to turn their vessels into the wind. He needed this kind of advantage, since his fifteen craft had to contend with the reality of a much more powerful British fleet. Carleton had thirty-six craft under his command, including twenty-eight gunboats that had one powerful cannon (12- to 24-pounders) mounted in each bow. All told, the British carried 417 artillery pieces with a more than four-to-one firepower advantage, since the patriot fleet had only 91 cannons, including small swivel guns.

Just as bad for the Americans, the British crews consisted of experienced mariners, not the kind of inexperienced landlubbers that formed Arnold's ranks. In addition, some 400 Indians followed along in canoes, and soldiers and marines were present on their larger craft, all ready to board the patriot vessels should close-order combat take place. By every measure, the patriot fleet should have been wiped out that day, but the.

British had failed to bag their prey by nightfall when the day's battle ended. The northerly wind kept them from forming an organized battle line that would let them shower the patriot craft with the full brunt of their superior firepower.

Carleton displayed his usual patience. Meeting with his fleet commander Thomas Pringle, they agreed to establish an east-west line from the southern tip of Valcour Island to close to the New York shoreline. Confident of victory, they would rest overnight, hope for a southerly breeze, then move forward and demand surrender, or crush the patriot fleet if Arnold and his officers refused to surrender.

As an early evening fog rolled over the bay, Arnold too knew that a shift in the wind would doom his craft, already battered and with one of the gundalows, the *Philadelphia*, slowly sinking. He called his captains together, and no one doubted they needed to escape from their pinned-in position. Their opening was along the New York shoreline, where the British had not placed any craft. The heavy nighttime fog gave enough cover so they could escape in single-file fashion through this gap. When the fog burned off the next morning, Carleton and Pringle could not believe what they beheld: The patriot vessels had disappeared, seemingly into thin air.

Arnold had his damaged fleet moving as fast as the wind would permit up the lake, hoping to reach Crown Point before the British caught up. His main objective was to save as many of the vessels as possible so they might be available to fight again another day. The problem was that when the wind shifted and started blowing in from the south, the gundalows could make little progress, even with the crews rowing as hard as their human energy would allow them. By October 13, the lead vessels of the British fleet were catching up.

Commodore Arnold now faced twin difficulties. First, his fleet was again facing capture or extermination. Second, he did not want to draw the British too quickly to Fort Ticonderoga, where he assumed that powder and ball were still in short supply, even if defending soldiers were not. He knew he had to do everything in his power to convince Carleton that patriot forces were ready to fight to the death, if need be, to halt the British vessels—and the large force following behind under the command of flamboyant General John Burgoyne—from reaching and attacking Fort Ticonderoga.

"The attack and defeat of the American fleet under Benedict Arnold by the King's fleet commanded by Sir Guy Carleton upon Lake Champlain, October 11, 1776." Valcour Island is at the far left. (*Library of Congress*)

What followed was an example of raw fighting courage in the face of overwhelming odds. At a land form called Split Rock, about thirty-five miles north of Ticonderoga, Arnold had his helmsman turn the *Congress* northward to engage the rapidly descending British craft. Four waterlogged gundalows stood by as he engaged three swarming enemy vessels having a fivefold firepower advantage. Soon four more British craft joined in like jackals taunting their prey while circling for the kill. For two hours or more, the commodore and his crew fought back as best they could, even as "the sails, rigging, and hull of the *Congress* were shattered and torn to pieces," Arnold later reported. Then unexpectedly, the *Congress* darted toward Ferris Bay (today called Arnold Bay) along the Vermont shoreline. The gundalows followed as the British kept firing round and grape shot at them. To leave nothing for the enemy Arnold ordered all five vessels burned before leading his surviving crew members overland back to Fort Ticonderoga.[26]

Seemingly, the patriot defense of Lake Champlain had failed. All told, only four patriot vessels had made their way back to Ticonderoga. Arnold estimated his casualties at 25 percent. Just as bad, for all the spilled blood, the British now were in full command of the lake, at least up to Crown

Point. While General Gates gratefully thanked "General Arnold, and the officers, seamen, and marines of the fleet for the gallant defense they made against the great superiority of the enemy's force," others were less kind. Brigadier General William Maxwell, another retired British officer who had settled in New Jersey and joined the patriot side, was present at Ticonderoga when the losses of the fleet became known. Wrote Maxwell, Arnold was now "our evil genius to the north," who "has, with a good deal of industry, got us clear of all of our fine fleet," which "by all impartial accounts, was by far the strongest."[27]

What Maxwell did not yet know was that Arnold's death-defying leadership and courage on the lake, both at Valcour and Split Rock, played a part in convincing Carleton to return to Canada before winter weather set in. Not an aggressive warrior, the governor was fretting about what kind of beating his forces would take in trying to capture Fort Ticonderoga. Marshaling his force on Crown Point, he refused to listen to Burgoyne, who urged him to attack or put the fort under siege. If all the Americans were like Arnold, willing to fight to virtual death, then pulling back to Canada and regrouping for another campaign in 1777 made the most sense to Carleton. On November 2, the British began their northward retreat. More then one hundred years later, the naval historian Alfred Thayer Mahan summarized matters this way: "The little American navy on Champlain was wiped out; but never had any force, big or small, lived to better purpose or died more gloriously, for it saved the Lake for that year."[28]

Arnold may have lost at Valcour Island, but he and his land-lubbing mariners, along with Schuyler, Gates, and the thousands of patriot soldiers gathering at Fort Ticonderoga, had actually won the campaign. They had held the line in the Northern Theater, which did not sit well with Burgoyne. Having to deal with his late wife's estate and not particularly liking American winters, he retreated to Quebec Province and soon arranged passage to England, arriving there in December. Meeting with Lord George Germain, the Secretary for American Affairs who played a pivotal part in overall campaign planning, Gentleman Johnny, known for his respectful treatment of troops, presented his operational plan for success in the northern region. Hardly surprising, Burgoyne modestly suggested that he should be in command, and Germain, who personally disliked Carleton, agreed, with King George's approval.[29]

Flamboyant British general John Burgoyne (1722–1792) determined to prove his brilliance as a commander in the field, but underrated his opponent and was forced to surrender his beleaguered army at Saratoga in October 1777. (*The Frick Collection*)

Burgoyne's plan had various key elements. Governor Carleton, faulted for not accomplishing a breakthrough in 1776, was to remain in Quebec Province with a defending force of 3,000 troops. In turn, Burgoyne's invading army was to consist of British regulars, Hessians, and loyalist troops along with Canadian laborers and boatmen, the latter to help move his troops southward across Lake Champlain. Burgoyne hoped to have a thousand or more Indians join his expeditionary force, but in the end the actual number was closer to 500, including Hurons (Wyandots) and additional warriors drawn from such native villages as St. Francis (Abenakis) and St. Regis (Mohawks).[30]

Burgoyne planned to ascend Lake Champlain, cross over to the Hudson River, and march southward toward Albany. There, theoretically, he expected "to effect a Junction with General [William] Howe," presumably to implement the northern strategy of reconquering New England, the original center of the rebellion. Not sure of Howe's plans, he expected no problems in breaking through to Albany, his primary target. What was obvious was that Burgoyne, along with Lord Germain and King George, had no clear idea of what they expected to gain from Burgoyne's expedition, except driving rebel resisters out of the Champlain region; and that more modest campaign objective depended on reaching Albany rather than getting entrapped in the northern wilderness.[31]

To avoid the unlikely prospect of getting hung up short of Albany, Germain and Burgoyne agreed to establish a diversionary force with a mission to confuse and divide the rebel opposition. This detachment, to consist of 675 British and loyalist troops, was to travel up the St. Lawrence River to Lake Ontario. Under the command of Lieutenant Colonel Barry St. Leger (breveted a brigadier for this mission), the column was then to rendezvous with hundreds of Iroquois Indians, mostly Mohawks and Senecas, at the mouth of the Oswego River. The first target, after moving southeast across Oneida Lake and Wood Creek, was Fort Schuyler (Stanwix), located at the western end of the Mohawk Valley. After reducing the fort and capturing or killing its defenders, the troops had as their next target the valley and its inhabitants, including farmers providing critically needed food supplies for Continental forces. Conducting his own operations in collaboration with St. Leger's detachment, Gentleman Johnny was sure that rebel resistance would collapse under the weight of both armies approaching Albany along two fronts. Divide and conquer the enemy was an essential characteristic of Burgoyne's strategy.[32]

On paper this operational plan, even if lacking in some climactic objective, seemed easily achievable. With necessary logistical support worked out and vessels ready to sail, the invasion force moved out from St. John's on June 15, 1777, sailing up the Richelieu River to Lake Champlain. Before the end of the month, Burgoyne's grand army of some 10,000 souls, including wives, consorts, and children of soldiers, had reached Crown Point, just twelve miles north of Ticonderoga. Burgoyne was jubilant. Intelligence reports indicated that rebel forces defending the patriot lines at Fort Ticonderoga were scant in numbers. At this juncture, he envisioned the first of many glorious victories that would ultimately frame him for all posterity as one of the great captains in British military history.[33]

Before departing Ticonderoga back in November 1776, Benedict Arnold had warned that the British were sure to launch an even more muscular invasion in 1777. Virtually no one seemed to listen. Rather, preparation for this onslaught lagged in the midst of steady rancor regarding who should be in command of the Northern Department. Put simply, the once harmonious team of Schuyler, Gates, and Arnold came apart. Mutual respect turned to backbiting and open contempt, leaving the department in a weakened state of defensive readiness even as Burgoyne's powerful army gathered at Crown Point before swooping down on Fort Ticonderoga.[34]

In many ways, the protagonist of discord was Horatio Gates. Still determined to have an independent command, and with support from such New England congressional delegates as Samuel Adams and James Lovell, he kept maneuvering to replace Schuyler, all the way into the summer of 1777. Just as bad, when General Washington, back in December 1776, named Arnold to a joint command in New England, Gates declared Arnold a threat to his own ambitions. After all, Arnold was inferior in rank to Gates but still had Washington's favor. At the time of action at Valcour Island and Split Rock, Gates had praised his newfound nemesis for his "gallant behavior and steady good conduct" in defending Lake Champlain. In January 1777, when Gates attended Congress, high on his list was bad-mouthing "that excellent officer" Arnold. In echoes of criticisms by William Maxwell and others, Gates was now sure that Arnold had wasted the fleet and certainly did not deserve a promotion to major general.[35]

In February Congress seemed to agree with Gates that the troublesome Arnold should remain a brigadier general—supposedly on the grounds that Connecticut already had too many major generals. The delegates voted to promote five officers below him in rank to major generalships. Ever deferential to civilian authority, Washington, wondering whether Congress had made some mistake, wrote his friend Richard Henry Lee, declaring that "Surely a more active—a more spirited, and Sensible Officer fills no department in your army." To Arnold, he asked for patience, hoping that he would "not take any hasty steps" like resigning from the service, despite such a major slight.[36]

Thoroughly insulted by this slap at his reputation and personal honor as a meritorious officer, Arnold threatened to resign unless he could get some explanation—as well as a promotion back over the five officers of junior rank elevated over him. Congress stood mute until late April when Washington's fighting general played a central part in driving a large British-loyalist raiding force out of eastern Connecticut. A red-faced Congress, learning that Arnold had two horses shot out from under him during two days of running combat, decided that he was now worthy of a major generalship but refused to restore his seniority in rank. Instead, the ever generous delegates voted to award him a fully caparisoned horse. Thoroughly frustrated, Arnold visited the delegates in Philadelphia but got nowhere. Reluctantly, he handed in his resignation on July 11, now wanting only to settle his financial accounts and return home to Connecticut. As Arnold stated, "honor is a sacrifice no man ought to make, as I received [it] so I wish to transmit [it] inviolate to posterity."[37]

General Schuyler, meanwhile, was having his own problems with Congress. He knew that many New England delegates, the same group that so admired Gates, were bad-mouthing him, in some cases just because he was a New Yorker. Schuyler first got himself elected to that body and then traveled to Philadelphia in April 1777 to defend his reputation and record. He was neither a war profiteer, nor solely responsible for losing Canada, as these critics charged. Despite the New England faction, Congress on May 22 voted to vindicate him from such damning accusations. The delegates then ordered Schuyler "to proceed to the northern department, and take upon him the command there."[38]

Wanting to begin preparations for the expected 1777 assault from Canada, Schuyler had earlier encouraged Congress to name a general officer to take charge of operations at Fort Ticonderoga. The New Englanders seized the opportunity and saw that Gates obtained that appointment, indicating on March 25 that their favored general "be directed immediately to repair to Ticonderoga, and take command of the army there." When Gates reached Albany, he found out that Schuyler was on his way to Congress, so he stayed there and began directing activities as the senior officer present in the Northern Department. Just to add to the confusion, on April 1 Congress instructed Arthur St. Clair, a Scotsman turned Pennsylvanian of undistinguished military accomplishments, "to repair to Ticonderoga, and serve under General Gates." Such wording appealed to the New Englanders in Congress, since they were hoping that Schuyler would not receive a favorable vote on vindication and would resign from the service.[39]

When Schuyler returned to Albany, he and Gates exchanged less than friendly words. Feeling betrayed by his admirers in Congress, Gates rushed back to Philadelphia. Through his New England admirers, he managed to get onto the floor of that body and launched into an ungentlemanly tirade about being jerked around over command assignments. Schuyler's supporters took offense, and a shouting match ensued.

Gates finally stormed out of the chamber but did not leave Philadelphia. Rather, he clung close to the New England friends, just waiting for some opportunity to find himself elevated to the Northern Department command.[40]

So the cooperating commanders of 1776 were now at complete loggerheads, even as Burgoyne's British-Hessian army was in position to launch a full-scale assault on Fort Ticonderoga. What Gates knew from his time in Albany was that Ticonderoga was totally unprepared to resist such an onslaught. When Arthur St.Clair, one of the five generals elevated over Arnold to a major generalship, arrived at Ticonderoga in mid-June, he realized the hopelessness of his position. He found about 2,200 troops, a portion of them sick and unfit for duty, and many hundreds short of the numbers needed to defend the fort's elaborate defenses. Food supplies, camp equipment, even cartridge paper were in scant supply. What was left of the 1776 patriot fleet was in wretched shape. Add inadequate intelligence reports about Burgoyne's movements, and St. Clair, never an innovator, was facing an impossible military assignment. As he wrote to a friend, he smelled an embarrassing defeat and could only hope that his "reputation" as a military leader would not "be murdered after having been sacrificed myself."[41]

As July began, Burgoyne's minions began to close in on Ticonderoga's defenders— British troops on the New York side, Hessians on the Vermont side, and even well-placed cannons within firing range looking down at the fort itself from Sugar Loaf Hill (today known as Mount Defiance). The patriots had left this position unprotected, thinking that no one would consider hauling large cannons up this mountainside. However, General William Phillips, Burgoyne's artillery chief, reportedly declared that "where a goat can go a man can go, and where a man can go he can drag a gun." The looming presence of these artillery pieces meant the British now had the capacity to obliterate the fort and all the other positions making up the Fort Ticonderoga complex.[42]

Facing a complete rout and the likely surrender of virtually all of his troops, St. Clair called a council of war, which voted that "a retreat ought to be undertaken as soon as possible." Before dawn on July 6, the patriot defenders were on the run, some sailing to the southern end of Lake Champlain. Others marched southeast through Vermont territory, where they engaged pursuing redcoats and Hessians in a bloody battle at Hubbardton before escaping over the mountains to fight another day. For his part, St. Clair had made the correct decision to retreat and save as many of his troops as possible from falling into enemy hands. A year later he faced court-martial proceedings regarding his decision to flee rather than defend the fort; and he retrieved his reputation when the court unanimously declared him innocent of cowardly behavior before the enemy.[43]

As for Gentleman Johnny, he was ebullient. Long brimming over with condescension toward the American colonists, he was convinced, after his success at Ticonderoga, that further campaign triumphs would come easily—all the way to Albany. Back in June, before launching his expedition, he had published a pompous-sounding manifesto; Burgoyne wanted everyone to know that he was leading "the military Servants of the Crown" on a specially anointed mission to bring an end to "the present unnatural Rebellion" by crushing the worst "system of Tyranny that ever God in his displeasure suffered for a time to be exercised over a forward and stubborn Generation." Grandly, he warned anyone foolish enough to stand in his army's triumphant pathway not to offer resistance—or suffer the consequences. For those with the temerity to do so, Burgoyne's "Messengers of justice and of wrath" would wreak "devastation, famine and every concomitant horror" in the days to come.[44]

For all of his calculated planning and grand pronouncements, the easy victory at Ticonderoga deceived Burgoyne about the obstacles ahead. One such reality related to the obstinate patriot resistance that his army faced as it traversed the twenty-plus miles of rugged ground lying between the southern ends of lakes Champlain and George and the Hudson River. This stretch of terrain in the northern wilderness slowed the British-Hessian advance to a crawl. Blocking the way were smatterings of patriot troops led by General Schuyler and, of all unexpected people, Benedict Arnold.

When Arnold resigned his commission back on July 11, he did not know that George Washington had just written Congress and asked for an "Active, spirited Officer" to help rally the New England militia in thwarting Burgoyne's invasion. The commander-in-chief wanted a proven fighter who could work with Schuyler "to check Genl. Burgoyne's progress or the most disagreeable consequences may be apprehended." To the surprise and chagrin of Gates and his civilian supporters in Congress, Washington called for Arnold's services, not only because of his proven fighting prowess but because he knew that Arnold would work harmoniously with Schuyler.[45]

Four days later Arnold was riding north from Philadelphia, but not before leaving his resignation on Congress's table and asking the delegates to resolve the seniority issue in his favor. Along the way he met with Washington and agreed to submit to the authority of officers recently elevated over him, most particularly Arthur St. Clair. On July 22 Arnold joined Schuyler at Fort Edward on the west side of the Hudson River, not quite fifty miles north of Albany. The two generals had about 4,400 Continentals and militia (some without weapons) ready to help in resisting Gentleman Johnny's much stronger force. With these troops, they continued to do everything possible to delay the British-Hessian southward drive to reach the Hudson River.[46]

Delay effectively they did, and Burgoyne admitted as much. "The toil of the march was great," he wrote to Lord Germain in late July, "the country being a Wilderness in almost every part of the passage." Patriot resisters littered the pathway with fallen trees and huge rocks, but also, Burgoyne estimated, his army had "above forty bridges to construct, and others to repair, one of which was of Log work over a morass two miles in extent." Completely outnumbered, Schuyler and Arnold kept pulling back, continuing to offer whatever resistance they could. By August 1, Burgoyne had his troops assembling at Fort Edward. There they regrouped, while waiting for the arrival of additional supplies and fifty-two artillery pieces being shipped southward over Lake George, then to be hauled overland to the Hudson River. In sum, nearly a month had passed since taking Ticonderoga. Burgoyne's minions, facing relentless patriot opposition, had moved less than a mile a day across the daunting backwoods terrain of hills, creeks, and swamps; and they still had to traverse close to fifty miles to reach Albany.[47]

As events developed, the land passage became a source of other unexpected difficulties for Burgoyne. He had promised in his manifesto to employ "every concomitant horror" against anyone who dared to challenge his pathway to Albany. Implied in this threat of "devastation" was the potential wrath of his Indian allies, some 500 of them traveling with his force. On July 26, when a firefight broke out near Fort Edward between retreating American pickets and Burgoyne's advancing regulars and Indians, some Wyandots entered a house and captured two loyalist women lodged there. Jane "Jenny" McCrea, described as a beautiful young woman in her early twenties, was waiting to meet Lieutenant David Jones, a loyalist officer in Burgoyne's army to whom she was betrothed. Two of the Indians began to argue over Jenny as their prize when someone shot her dead, at which point one of the Wyandots "scalped, stripped and Butchered" her remains "in the most shocking Manner."[48]

Soon news of Jenny's death, including exaggerated tales of merciless torture and rape, spread far and wide. As a result, some New England militiamen began to muster under arms. They were not about to let Burgoyne's "savages" attack their communities or harm and maim their families and friends. As for the British general, he demanded that Jenny's murderer be turned over for trial and possible execution, at which point his Indian allies said they would return to their Canadian villages unless Burgoyne backed off. He did so, but relations continued to deteriorate, to the point at which fewer than 100 Indians were still attached to his army at the end of August. The negative effect was twofold: Burgoyne was losing his best shock-and-awe allies in the task of driving back patriot resisters, whose numbers, in turn, were now beginning to grow in support of the Schuyler-Arnold delaying campaign.

Moving forward at a snail's pace while losing his most feared pickets was the bare tip of the problems now facing the ever-confident Burgoyne. He was not getting all the supplies he thought he needed, including horses for his mounted units. He thought he could reach Albany in three days of marching at a pace of about fifteen to sixteen miles a day, but he insisted on having thirty days of rations on hand before moving out from the Fort Edward area. In addition, heavy rains were turning roughhewn pathways into muck, making it difficult to move wagons full of necessary supplies, let alone available weaponry. So Gentleman Johnny sat with his army in place. According to the Baroness von Riedesel, the wife of Hessian commander General Friedrich Adolf von Riedesel, he was "having a jolly good time" by "spending half the night singing and drinking and amusing himself in the company of the wife of a commissary, who was his mistress and, like him, loved champagne."[49]

Outwardly Burgoyne projected complete confidence, even as he kept wasting valuable time. He wondered whether he should strike east into New England but shunned such thoughts as contrary to his orders. He now knew that he could not expect succor of any consequence from New

York City. Commander-in-chief William Howe had informed him that he was going after Washington's army, determined to destroy the main patriot force as it attempted to defend Philadelphia. As such, thousands of British regulars would not be moving northward toward Albany, as called for in the Hudson Highlands strategy. For all practical purposes, the army of Gentleman Johnny, now shrinking in size and stuck in the American backwoods, was on its own, hardly a testament to the kind of self-assured planning that denoted his preparations for the campaign.[50]

In early August, Burgoyne and Baron von Riedesel discussed conducting a limited plundering raid into Vermont territory. The German general preferred a sortie focused specifically on requisitioning much-needed horses for his dragoons. Gentleman Johnny, however, preferred a more grandiose operation—why not send out a substantial force to seize not just horses but anything and everything, including cattle and wagons, that would support the army as it conducted its final push to Albany? Riedesel reluctantly agreed. On August 9 Burgoyne ordered Lieutenant Colonel Friedrich Baum, commander of the Brunswick dragoons, to lead a force of 750 soldiers (Hessians, Canadians, and a smattering of loyalists and Indians) to seize whatever movable goods and animals they could find while intimidating local settlers into renouncing their revolutionary leanings.

The timing could not have been worse. Baum's detachment ran into some 1,500 New Hampshire militiamen under General John Stark moving forward to join in the harassment of Burgoyne's main army. The resulting Battle of Bennington on August 16 turned into a shattering defeat for Baum's raiders. The fighting was brutal, but Stark's force, supported by some 350 Green Mountain Boys under Colonel Seth Warner, prevailed with only 70 casualties. As for Baum's troops, even with the support of a relief column of 550 Hessians that appeared under Lieutenant Colonel Heinrich von Breymann, their losses included 207 killed, many more dozens wounded, and some 700 taken prisoner. Baum himself, seriously wounded when captured, died after the fighting was over. All told, Bennington was a major blow to the fighting strength of Burgoyne's army, now reduced by about 15 percent or roughly 1,000 soldiers.[51]

Still, Gentleman Johnny refused to admit that his was getting into serious trouble. He wrote confidently to Lord Germain on August 20 that "I yet do not despond." He declared that Vermont territory "now abounds in the . . . most rebellious race of the continent and hangs like a gathering storm upon my left."[52]

What Burgoyne did not yet know was that his divide-and-conquer strategy that featured St. Leger's diversionary force was on the verge of collapse to the west. Fort Schuyler proved to be an impregnable obstacle for St. Leger troops and Indian allies, some of the latter fighting under the famous Mohawk warrior Thayendanegea (Chief Joseph Brant). They had the fort, defended by some 750 Continentals, surrounded and under siege by early August. Then they defeated—some might say virtually annihilated—a militia relief column of some 800 local settlers at the Battle of Oriskany, six miles south of the fort, on August 6. Militia leader General Nicholas Herkimer suffered mortal wounds that day, and about 500 of his troops were killed, wounded, or captured, representing a casualty rate of about 60 percent.[53]

In terms of immediate impact, the defeat at Oriskany was a devastating blow for the American cause in the valley, just like the Bennington setback was for Burgoyne and his army. However, despite the human loss, the patriots could recover while Gentleman Johnny could not. When word reached General Schuyler about the Oriskany debacle, he called his ranking officers together and asked for one of them to lead a relief force of Continentals up the valley to link up with whatever militia were left and drive St. Leger's force out of the region. Benedict Arnold was the only volunteer, and he was soon on his way with 900 Continentals following along. Reaching Fort Dayton on the north side of the Mohawk River by August 21, Arnold's officers called a war council and refused to go any farther. They would not risk themselves in going up against St. Leger's force, as Herkimer had, until local militia and possibly Oneida and Tuscarora Indians significantly expanded their numbers.[54]

With thirty miles left to traverse before reaching Fort Schuyler, Arnold once again had to take innovative action to carry out his assignment. Good fortune turned out to be available in the form of a local loyalist of curious reputation named Hon Yost Schuyler. He had been captured trying to get local settlers to join St. Leger's ranks. His reputation was that of an odd fellow, perhaps dim-witted, but respected by area Indians with whom he occasionally lived. In exchange for his life, Hon Yost agreed to charge into St. Leger's camp and spread a tale among the Indians that Arnold, along with hundreds of soldiers, was about to descend on them.

The ruse worked; panic set in; and the Mohawks and Senecas were soon heading back toward Lake Ontario, much to the chagrin of St. Leger and his British-loyalist troops. They, too, were soon in retreat, thus lifting the siege before Arnold's slowly advancing column was within several miles of the fort.[55]

The threat posed by St. Leger's diversionary force was gone by August 23, another major blow to Burgoyne's campaign. Now seriously weakened on both his left and right flanks, and with knowledge that he could expect little support from British troops coming to his rescue up the Hudson River, Burgoyne knew he had to begin moving his army forward to Albany—either that or retreat in disgrace to Canada or remain stationary and rot in the New York wilderness. Intelligence reports were reaching him that American forces, supposedly up to twice his numbers, were waiting to challenge him. With ordnance pieces finally brought down from Lake George and with minimal rations in hand, Gentleman Johnny issued orders on September 12 to cross over the Hudson River to its west bank and move south on the road that would lead his beleaguered army directly to Albany.[56]

Congress, meanwhile, not knowing the deteriorating state of Burgoyne's position, decided to get involved. Once learning that poorly defended Fort Ticonderoga had fallen, the delegates needed a scapegoat. At the end of July Gates's adoring New Englanders pushed for the recall of both St. Clair and Schuyler from the Northern Department. They were to travel to General Washington's headquarters, there to explain in courts of inquiry their alleged failure in not properly defending the impregnable defensive works at Ticonderoga. Not having consulted their commander-in-chief before removing Schuyler and St. Clair, the delegates then directed him to name a new general officer to take charge. Washington knew who they wanted, but he demurred, hardly a testament to his opinion of Gates. Somewhat irritated, the New Englanders got what they wanted on August 4 when Congress named their favorite, Gates, to take command of the Northern Department.[57]

With a chip on his shoulder, Gates traveled north and met with Schuyler on August 19 on Van Schaick Island, about ten miles north of Albany. Rather than recognizing all the grueling labor and risky actions that were turning Burgoyne's army into a ripe candidate for total defeat, Gates rudely dismissed his rival. He was now in charge, acting like the savior sent from Congress, a body that in its apparent wisdom had ordered him to fix the mess that Schuyler had supposedly made in his efforts to resist, delay, and wear down Burgoyne's army. Seemingly, according to some admirers in the field who did not like Schuyler, Gates magically resolved everything. He had the patriot troops moving forward by September 8 to a location called Bemis Heights, where they dug in and awaited the appearance of the enemy.[58]

What transpired over the next month were the highly consequential battles of Saratoga. Burgoyne, moving his army southward along the west side of the Hudson River, reached Sword's Farm, about four miles north of Bemis Heights, on September 17. There he received intelligence about the American defensive position, running on an east-west line perpendicular to the river, and selected intentionally to stand between his army and Albany thirty miles away. The Americans had placed cannon batteries on the heights overlooking the river road with the potential to cause serious damage to his army, should he continue on that route. With hundreds of militiamen gathering along the Hudson River's east bank, the option of recrossing the river to effect a breakthrough there was fraught with prospects of a slaughter. The only option that gave Gentleman Johnny some faint glimmer of hope was to swing his troops westward onto higher ground and then attack his adversary's left flank. With enough martial force, his army could strike from the northwest and try to roll up the American line, ideally pinning Gates's troops up against the Hudson River. This kind of potential blow represented the only viable option in both breaking through the Bemis Heights defensive line while also potentially inflicting a significant defeat on the Northern Department army.[59]

In so many ways, from the point of view of military reality, Burgoyne never had a chance, not unless the Americans were too busy arguing among themselves to focus on the enemy challenging them. The focal point of patriot tension involved a form of divided command. Gates and Arnold, fellow warriors in 1776, had come to despise each other. The reasons were multifold, but one source was Arnold learning that Gates had demeaned him before Congress, thereby hurting his chances for a well-deserved promotion. As in December 1776 and as recently as July, Washington had favored Arnold with assignments while also doing virtually nothing to support Gates's relentless drive for an independent command. Further, Arnold had to wonder what role, if any, Gates had played in Congress's August 8 decision to deny his long-standing request for restoring his seniority in rank. So, from many angles, the real source of their differences involved both Washington and Congress, although too often interpreted as Arnold slighting Gates by naming two of Schuyler's staff officers—Richard Varick and Henry Brockholst Livingston—to serve in his military family at Saratoga.[60]

Beyond the intemperate feuding, what really affected the course of battle were the conflicting tactical approaches of Gates and Arnold. The new northern commander preferred to stay on the defensive—let Burgoyne's troops attack the Bemis Heights defenses, where he felt his protected troops would not run but stand and fight. Despite his reputation as a soldiers' general, Gates had little confidence in the fighting capacity of his Continentals, let alone poorly trained militia. Arnold, by comparison, in charge of the army's left wing, was offensive-minded. He had much greater faith in the courage of his Continental brethren. Nor had he shown any hesitancy, as demonstrated at Quebec City and on Lake Champlain, about providing leadership in the thick of combat, regardless of the personal consequences to his own life and limb. Gates, on the other hand, preferred to stay well back from the field of combat.

The first Saratoga battle occurred on September 19. Burgoyne marched his British regiments to the west, then turned southeast in aiming toward the American left flank. Arnold fairly begged Gates not to let his troops get bogged down just fighting to defend their own lines. Gates finally relented and allowed his second-in-command to test the advancing enemy's strength. While Gates stood by out of harm's way, Arnold acted as the commander in the field, first sending out Daniel Morgan's riflemen, then musket men under Joseph Cilley and Alexander Scammell, and eventually all the regiments in his immediate command.

A set-piece battle ensued around the open field of Freeman's Farm, a mile north of Bemis Heights. Back and forth the combatants swayed, with lingering questions to this day whether Arnold was only directing troops coming forward or actually in the thick of the fighting. To save his faltering position, Burgoyne called up Baron von Riedesel's Hessians from the river road where they were guarding his supply wagons. Their presence stabilized the British line. Gates, meanwhile, thought enough was enough and first called off Arnold, then his fighting regiments as daylight was beginning to fade into darkness.[61]

Because the British held Freeman's Farm when the battle ended, they were technically the victors. However, Burgoyne's casualties represented 22 percent of the estimated 2,500 Anglo-German soldiers engaged, a dear price to pay for an army that had already lost significant numbers back in August. Their losses had gained them very little, except a new position on which to dig in and wait while deciding how to break through the American position on Bemis Heights. As for the patriots, their casualties amounted to 310 losses, or about 56 percent of Burgoyne's total. However, as more and more militia units poured into the area, Gates's numbers were growing, and his army had not yet lost a foot of ground. The Americans still had every advantage. Gentleman Johnny later stated "that no Fruits, honor excepted, were attained" for his army that day.[62]

Both armies sat in place for the next several days. In Burgoyne's camp, the lone hope was for a sizable British force to drive up the Hudson River from New York City and draw off some of the ever-growing patriot strength aligned against Burgoyne's struggling army. Such a foray under General Henry Clinton did take place, beginning in early October, but this rather feeble martial demonstration happened too late and with not enough troop strength to have any positive effect.[63]

Meanwhile, the patriot camp found itself embroiled in a flurry of slurs and accusations passing between Gates and Arnold. Their smoldering differences finally resulted in verbal blows over a variety of matters, including the after action report Gates sent to Congress summarizing the September 19 battle. Giving himself most of the credit and also praising the soldiers, Gates mentioned neither Arnold nor the other officers who had actually been in the field directing those troops in the brunt of the fighting. Further, he did not state that all the troops engaged that day were from Arnold's left wing. As their tempers repeatedly flared, Gates gave his subordinate permission to leave and go to Congress with his complaints; he also stripped Arnold of his left wing command assignment by announcing that he would take charge of those soldiers that heretofore had been fighting under Arnold's direct authority. All but banished from camp, Arnold bluntly wrote Gates on October 1, stating that "I have every reason to believe your treatment proceeds from a spirit of jealousy." He wanted to make clear that his "wish" had never been "to command the army, or outshine you." Rather, Arnold's objective was to

Benedict Arnold was wounded in his attack on the British redoubt during the second Battle of Saratoga, October 7, 1777. (*New York Public Library*)

defeat the enemy while showing "my zeal for the cause of my country in which I expect to rise or fall." Gates did not relent or respond.[64]

Having resisted and fought against Gentleman Johnny's two armies since late July, Arnold refused to miss out on the final kill. That day came on October 7 when Burgoyne, running low on rations and not yet willing to retreat, sent out a reconnaissance force to gather grains from a local field while scouting the American lines on Bemis Heights. A recently discovered document suggests some sort of reconciliation between Gates and Arnold had taken place by October 7, suggesting they were now working together harmoniously. However, given the reality of their deep-seated differences, which had been building up over several months, the mass of contextual evidence suggests otherwise.[65]

No one can doubt that Arnold charged onto the field and led a stunning rally that drove Burgoyne's troops back behind the Freeman Farm defenses. Nor can anyone refute that Arnold, seeing a potential breach in the enemy's line, rode hard to his left and led a charge against Breymann's redoubt covering the right end of Burgoyne's defenses. Urging his soldiers forward, he charged into the redoubt and Hessian defenders shot down his horse, even as Arnold took a musket ball in his left leg, the same limb wounded at Quebec. The dying horse crashed down on him, further mangling his wounded left leg. In searing pain, Arnold had the satisfaction of witnessing the beginning of the collapse of the British line. In his "zeal for the cause of my country," he lay seriously wounded while, as time would tell, he would be questioning why he was giving everything short of life itself, for what he increasingly viewed as the ungrateful patriot cause.[66]

Once the Anglo-Hessian defensive line was broken, Burgoyne's only choice was to retreat, hounded northward for about ten miles by thousands of Continentals and militiamen to the village of Saratoga (today's Schuylerville, New York). Gentleman Johnny's once mighty army had suffered 698 casualties on October 7—American losses totaled 130 that day. Overall, for the whole campaign, Burgoyne reported that his campaign casualties totaled to 2,591, or roughly one third of the number of fighting troops he commanded when entering Lake Champlain back in June. He did not calculate the losses experienced by St. Leger's force, which brought the overall total to some 3,000 combatants serving in the two expeditionary forces.[67]

Finally accepting his entrapment, Burgoyne surrendered his battered and beaten army on October 17, 1777, a complete victory for Northern Department forces. In so doing, he met politely with his former British comrade Horatio Gates, but supposedly declared on one occasion that it was Arnold who had actually led the way in defeating his army at Saratoga. As for Arnold, he was not present at the surrender ceremonies, for he had been carted off to a military hospital in Albany writhing in horrible pain and acting peevishly toward doctors who feared the onset of gangrene and wanted to amputate his mangled limb.

In regard to Horatio Gates, he was never close to the battlefield on October 7, nor did he take any time to seek out Arnold and thank him personally for his death-defying combat performance. This time, however, in sending an after action report to Congress, Gates deigned to mention his suspended officer's "gallant" behavior in breaking through the British defenses. He more or less had no choice but to do so, since word was spreading far and wide about Arnold's heroics on the Saratoga battlefield. Leaders in Congress, more interested in patting themselves on the back for their presumed vision in removing Schuyler in favor of Gates, quickly voted to coin a gold medal to New England's darling general, one of only seven awarded during the whole Revolutionary War. Thus the Continental Congress declared Horatio Gates to be the hero of Saratoga, and so it has officially been ever since.[68]

Just as Congress maintained the right to rate the performance of its generals, so should all of us who seek to comprehend key historical confrontations. In reacting to the fall of Fort Ticonderoga and using that event as an excuse to change command leadership in the middle of a heated military campaign, Congress showed faulty judgment. To this point in the Revolutionary War, Gates had not established a line command record. Furthermore, Schuyler, with valuable assistance from Arnold, was slowly and surely—and luckily—wearing down Burgoyne's army.

In its rush to elevate Gates, Congress did not allow the generals in the field to finish the job. Whether Schuyler could have, we will never know—that is a hypothetical issue with no conclusive answer. Along the same line, whether Gates's presence was crucial to the victory at Saratoga is open for analysis, and fair-minded evaluators have differed in addressing this question. What can be stated is that Schuyler, with inferior numbers of troops, successfully directed the critical effort to keep delaying Burgoyne's slowly advancing army; that Arnold won the battlefield award for leading the Americans to victory in the two Saratoga engagements; and that Gates, while never getting near the actual combat, somehow walked away with the glory.

When one rates the generals, Gates contributed the least to the success of the more than two years of campaigning in the Northern Theater to block the two attempted British invasions from Canada. In many ways, his most valuable contribution was his handling of the defensive line at Fort Ticonderoga during the summer and fall of 1776. General Richard Montgomery certainly deserves mention; he went into battle fearlessly at Quebec City and died instantly, the price for wanting to make Quebec Province the fourteenth colony in rebellion. In turn, Philip Schuyler deserves more credit than historians have generally given him. Like Gates, he was more an organizer than a fighter, and he performed important service in repeatedly keeping necessary supplies flowing to the northern army. In addition, his delaying campaign after the fall of Fort Ticonderoga during the summer of 1777 set the stage for the final defeat of Burgoyne's army.

That leaves Benedict Arnold. Of all the commanders, he was the only one involved in the northern campaign from its beginning in 1775 up until the day he experienced a devastating wound while charging into Breymann's redoubt. Many historians since that time, looking backward through the prism of his treason that occurred three years later, have felt the need to downgrade, even belittle Arnold's Northern Theater performance. The usual explanation for his lack of importance invariably depends on conjuring up alleged character flaws, among them Arnold's "narcissistic self-confidence" and a "mercurial and impulsive" temperament. Even though he had the capacity to "seize the initiative when more cautious minds around him hesitated," the incriminating dark side was that Washington's fighting general was always dismissive of "any authority, but his own."[69]

Arnold certainly did not live his life backward, nor did he spend his childhood and young adulthood plotting his apostasy in 1780 to the American cause. In 1775, when the fighting erupted at Lexington and Concord, he was an enthusiastic patriot who employed his natural leadership talents to serve the Northern Department campaigns. He provided bold and intelligent leadership both on land and on water as a general and a commodore. He was severely wounded twice and limped around with much pain the rest of his life as a personal reminder of his service and sacrifice. So if Gates was truly the hero of Saratoga, as Congress first declared and numerous historians have repeated since, then perhaps some equivalent honor should also be awarded Arnold for having given so much to the patriot cause even while small-minded bystanders referred to him, with General Maxwell, as the "evil genius to the north."

As for the British generals, they made numerous miscalculations that finally resulted in the surrender of Burgoyne's army. Governor Carleton's lack of aggressiveness in finally getting his fleet onto Lake Champlain in October 1776 greatly abetted the Americans in mounting their resistance effort. In turn, Burgoyne developed a flawed invasion plan with no apparent final goal, except reaching Albany. In his self-assured flamboyance and snobbish contempt for Americans, he neglected to take possible patriot resistance seriously; nor did he allow for the monumental logistical challenges of moving a sizable army through a rugged wilderness, once his army so easily overran Fort Ticonderoga. Just as bad for Gentleman Johnny, General Sir William Howe chose to go chasing after Washington's army rather than linking up with Burgoyne's force and proceeding with the northern strategy of reconquering New England, the initial cradle of the rebellion against the British empire.

In conclusion, even as we discuss the vast number of variables that shaped the outcome of the Northern Department campaigns of 1775–1777, there can be no denying that the unexpected patriot victory at Saratoga represented a major turning point in the War for Independence. Within a few months France, duly impressed with news of the capture of John Burgoyne's army, openly joined the American contest as a good and faithful ally. With the direct involvement of France, what began in 1775 as a civil war in the British empire would now become a world war. The Northern Theater thus played a crucial part in shaping conditions that pointed the American patriots toward overall victory in their Revolutionary War. By 1783, the result was the successful appearance of a new republican nation among the monarchical regimes then dominating the world.[70]

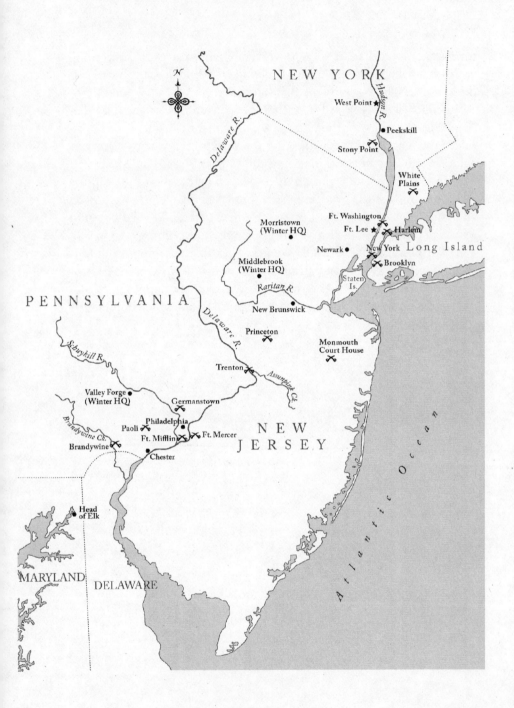

THE
MIDDLE THEATER

The Decisive Front of Independence

Edward G. Lengel and Mark Edward Lender

S oldiers and historians are alike in preferring victory to defeat. Military academies emphasize great generals and their triumphs over mediocrities, failures, and stalemates. Tourists prefer to visit battlefields where the "good" side won. Few indeed—and uniquely blessed—are those who ponder history's seemingly inconclusive periods instead of thrilling to the moments and decisions that changed the world in an instant. These facts help explain the relative neglect of the Revolutionary War's Middle Theater by historians and the general public. With one outstanding exception—the brief Trenton-Princeton campaign of 1776–1777—and leaving aside for a moment the siege of Yorktown, which many consider to have been an extension of the southern campaign, few of the military engagements that took place in this region seem of any particular strategic significance. Long Island, Brandywine, Germantown, Monmouth, Stony Point, Paulus Hook, and Springfield shine dimly in the war's military constellation. While they were surely dramatic and intrinsically interesting, none of these encounters—win, lose, or draw—proved decisive. Perhaps equally important, none—again with the exceptions of Trenton and Princeton, and perhaps Monmouth, for reasons more political than military—added any special luster to the commander-in-chief's reputation, at least as a battlefield leader.[1]

This last point is important, for the Middle Theater is for all intents and purposes synonymous with George Washington. With the exception of the 1775–1776 campaign when he was stationed outside Boston, and again in 1781 when he took the road to Yorktown, Washington spent the majority of his time in the vicinity of New York City, in New Jersey, and around Philadelphia. It is difficult to point to any one moment in which he "won" the war. Like events in the region in which he fought, however, it is Washington's deeds in the aggregate that ultimately counted the most and which, in the long run, made the Middle Theater (as we argue) the theater of decision.

DEFINITION AND TERRAIN

The definition of any military theater always contains an element of the arbitrary: Where, exactly, does "lower" New York State end and "upper" New York begin; where, precisely, was "western" as opposed to "eastern" Pennsylvania? But for the purposes of this essay the Middle Theater is taken to include Virginia, Maryland, Delaware, New Jersey, eastern Pennsylvania (the area approximately between the Delaware and Susquehanna rivers), and lower New York State (roughly between West Point and New York City). Admittedly, an argument may be made for considering the Yorktown campaign an extension of the Southern Theater. By any eighteenth-century or modern definition, indeed, the Old Dominion constituted part of the American South. Yet events at Yorktown were anything but purely "southern." The land forces that intervened so decisively at Yorktown marched there directly from the Middle Theater under the command of Washington, who managed to convince British commander-in-chief Sir Henry Clinton that he (Washington) was about to carry out his long-planned assault on New York City even as he began marching toward Virginia. The frustrated British efforts to come to Cornwallis's aid eventuated in New York City. Cornwallis's relocation to Virginia, moreover, had wholly separated him from the campaigning that continued below the Dan River in the Carolinas.[2] Thus the military context of the Yorktown campaign places it firmly in the Middle Theater.

Eighteenth-century Europeans who had yet to venture across the Atlantic often imagined America as a forlorn wilderness inhabited by "savages" and half-savage colonials. In the sparsely settled South, and along and beyond the Appalachian frontier, the image was not far from the truth (at least in European eyes). There white settlers were only beginning to make inroads into North America's vast virgin forest, and Native Americans remained dominant. Within what we have defined as the Middle Theater, however, terrain and climate did not differ widely from, say, that then prevailing in southern and central Europe. New York and Philadelphia did not approach London, Paris, or Vienna in size and magnificence, but they did resemble moderately prosperous European towns. Much of the forest had been cleared, and farms and crop-bearing fields were common.[3] European immigrants, especially Germans, carved out landscapes that resembled what they had remembered from their youth. Perhaps the largest difference between this region and Europe was that swamps and poor-to-middling quality land that would have been drained and cleared in the Old World remained untouched in the New, where farmers could more easily bypass obstacles and move on to clear new land. The eastern Virginia climate resembled that of the Mediterranean, but in the rest of the Middle Theater temperatures posed few undue challenges to Europeans used to the usual variations of cold and heat, although American swamps bred malaria and other diseases.

Terrain and climate, then, did nothing to hinder armies from operating in the Middle Theater according to prevalent European norms of linear warfare. This perfectly suited Washington, who for many reasons preferred to run traditional campaigns which the rugged terrain made difficult in upstate New York (which British general John Burgoyne learned the hard way) or in rural South Carolina (to which Nathanael Greene adapted so brilliantly). British and German forces also found the terrain and temperate climate mostly to their liking, although they complained to no end about towns and farms that were rustic and underde-

Overleaf: "A general map of the middle British colonies, in America. Containing Virginia, Maryland, the Delaware counties, Pennsylvania and New Jersey. With the addition of New York, and the greatest part of New England, as also of the bordering parts of the province of Quebec, improved from several surveys made after the late war, and corrected from Governor Pownall's late map 1776." (*Library of Congress*)

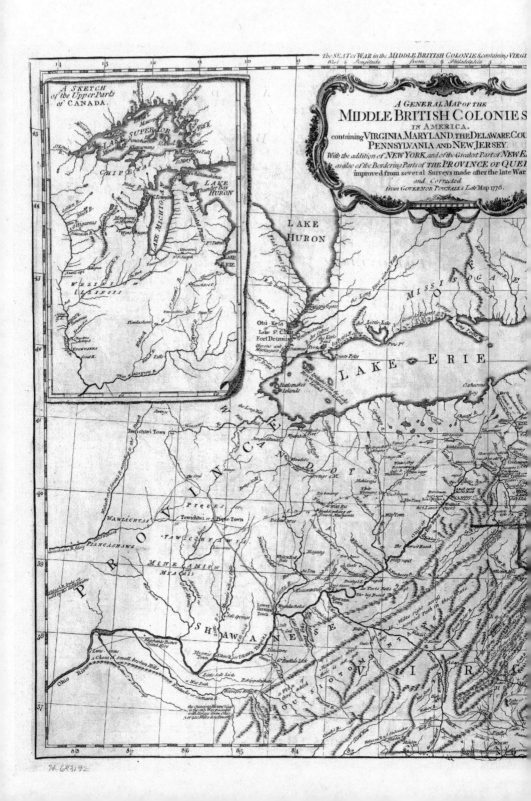

veloped by European standards.[4] In the West, of course, deployments on the European model made no sense to anyone. Thus, on balance, terrain in the Middle Theater weighed in favor of the better-trained and experienced Europeans, who did not have to make the adjustments in this theater that they would have to do elsewhere.

All this being said, the middle colonies were of course not as densely populated or economically developed as western Europe. Virginia and Maryland had a combined prewar population of about 649,600, but almost 250,000 of those were enslaved blacks. Tobacco and slavery largely defined the economies of those two colonies. Tobacco accounted for three-quarters of their exports—especially via the Chesapeake—although many planters such as Washington were switching over to wheat. As production and trade diversified over time, however, towns like Baltimore and Norfolk had become urbanized; and overall Virginia and Maryland were far less backward than the plantation-dominated Carolinas and Georgia.

Farther north, Delaware, Pennsylvania, New Jersey, and New York had a total population of about 555,900, largely white. They were economically more advanced than both their southern neighbors and New England. Philadelphia and New York had bypassed Boston in volume of trade and overall prosperity well before the Revolution. Commerce and entrepreneurship dominated the region's economy at the hands of New York's Dutch and Pennsylvania's Quakers. While the region still had many subsistence farmers and small shareholders, a diversified agricultural base sold crops, timber, livestock, and animal products to the colonial, Caribbean, and Atlantic markets. Ironically, though, the region's dependence on commerce and trade made it vulnerable to disruptions brought about by land war and naval blockade. Partly because of this, people from the middle colonies often proved less willing to endure protracted economic hardship, and more willing to trade with the British in times of stress, than did Americans from other regions.[5]

While the middle colonies boasted more professed patriots than did the Carolinas or Georgia, then, their dependence on commerce meant that their patriotism often lacked resiliency. American leaders sensed this and so did the British, who in 1777 would attempt to exploit it. George Washington recognized the permeability of the boundaries between patriots and loyalists better than perhaps any of his compatriots. Perhaps this was because he spent so much of his time in the Middle Theater. As late as 1781 he was still worried about "souring" the "tempers" and "alienating" the "affections" of local populations. In some areas, notably in parts of New Jersey and New York State close to the British garrison in New York City, communications and trade with the royal army, even among civilians otherwise professing the patriot cause, drove Washington and other senior revolutionaries to distraction.[6] In any event, this basic fact—those permeable loyalties—would influence the course of the war in this theater.

Native Americans, largely vanquished if not eradicated from this part of North America, played no significant military role in the Middle Theater. Free and enslaved blacks contributed, sometimes significantly, to the overall calculus in Virginia, but not in the remainder of the region—except for their service in the Continental and militia units of the New England and Middle States and Virginia, in which black troops were numerous.[7] White American settlers represented a varied cross-section of Europeans, with English and Scots-Irish prevalent overall but with significant pockets of German settlement in Pennsylvania and Maryland, and Dutch in New York and New Jersey. Culturally, they had more in common with the British and their German allies than the latter did with central, southern, or eastern European peoples. In many respects, the War for Independence was a civil war between peoples who had, at heart, much more in common than they liked to admit.

WAR'S OUTBREAK: 1775

No significant fighting occurred in any of the Middle Colonies in 1775, but they were far from inactive. As relations with the mother country frayed, extralegal patriot authorities gradually replaced royal governors and other officials; significantly, rebels also took control of regional militia organizations and began stockpiling arms and munitions. Militia began to train, and patriots at the local level, often acting without the prompting or approval of senior leaders, launched an active campaign of intimidation of loyalists, many of whom fled in dismay or even terror. By early 1775, in many areas it took a brave man to speak in favor of the king; indeed, historian T. H. Breen has traced what he termed a "popular insurgency" against imperial authority under way well before Lexington and Concord.[8] This fact would have a significant impact on the course of the war in the Middle Theater inasmuch as patriot authorities were in effective control from the first shot. Over the course of the war British operations from time to time would disrupt and even disperse rebel governments, but they could never do so permanently nor root out the rebel grip on localities beyond areas not actively garrisoned by royal troops. Thus, as he campaigned in the Middle Theater, Washington seldom had to worry about the counterrevolutionary tides that threatened the rebel cause in the South and upstate New York.

When the "shot heard round the world" rang out at Lexington, Massachusetts, on April 19, the revolution's most prominent leaders were gathering in Philadelphia to attend the Second Continental Congress. That body convened on May 10, and as militia drilled clumsily at every available open space in the city, the delegates took up military affairs as their first order of business. They had little choice: The aftermath of Lexington and Concord found the British army besieged in Boston by some 14,000 New England militia. On June 14, Congress, responding to desperate New England pleas, resolved to adopt the patriot army and asked other states to send troops. For all practical purposes, the delegates had resolved on war. It was a monumental decision. In assuming responsibility for an army—now the Continental Army—Congress had created America's first "national" institution and linked the success of the Whig cause to the success of patriot arms.[9] At the same time, Congress selected a commander-in-chief.

The man, of course, was the Virginian George Washington. Much has been made of Washington's appearance in Congress wearing a blue and buff uniform of the Fairfax County militia that he had designed himself in 1774. The uniform, some have thought, drew attention to his desire to be appointed commander-in-chief despite his unwillingness to openly ask for the position. But the delegates were not fools, and Washington was no hypocrite. In his mind and theirs, Congress constituted an assembly of patriots, and no one wanted to stand accused of grasping for honors. Rather, each individual should contribute to the cause in whatever means he was best suited, and Washington's uniform reminded his compatriots that he could best serve as a soldier. He would have done so at whatever rank the delegates chose to appoint him.[10]

As the new general set out to join the nascent army—really little more than a heterogeneous mob—at Cambridge, Massachusetts, Congress set

George Washington (1732–1799) by Charles Willson Peale. This is the "Valley Forge" portrait, painted during the winter encampment and as close a likeness to the commander-in-chief as we are likely to have during his years in the Middle Theater. (*National Park Service*)

to work in Philadelphia defining the army's size, organization, supply, financing, and recruitment mechanisms and drafting of articles of war that would help define military discipline throughout the war. Weaknesses of the Confederation system (which was only ratified in 1781), and sometimes congressional ineptitude, hampered this work; but it was nonetheless vital. Washington consistently deferred to congressional authority, no matter how much the assembly frustrated him. He could accomplish nothing of significance without Congress; and although it occasionally fled mouselike from the British broom, the body convened in the Middle Theater throughout the war (variously in Philadelphia, Baltimore, Lancaster and York, Pennsylvania). Wherever Congress convened, however, it was seldom more than a week's travel from the main army—which could be a blessing or a curse for the general.

DEFEAT AND REDEMPTION: 1776

As British forces departed Boston on March 17, 1776, Washington watched them go with mixed feelings. He had whipped his often truculent soldiers into a semblance of an army, and its morale had soared as it watched the British sail away. But the commander-in-chief's blood-soaked dreams of assaulting Boston frontally had (fortunately) dissipated in the face of well-founded opposition from his general officers; and he lamented the fact Howe had not attacked strong rebel fortifications. American propaganda and subsequent mythologizing aside, Washington and his forces had accomplished little of strategic or even tactical significance.[11] The war had not been decided; the British would be back.

The primary theater of war, Washington knew, would now shift to the mid-Atlantic and particularly to New York City. The place was a crucial commercial hub whose loss would have a pernicious ripple effect throughout the region, heartening loyalists and disrupting patriot authority. Moreover, every major road to New England ran through the city. British interest in New York derived not just from its commercial and political value, but from its position at the mouth of the Hudson River. Control of the city and the Hudson Highlands, especially West Point, would open the river route to Albany. With the river under their control, the British would in effect be fitting a noose around New England's neck. The Crown always had identified New England as the heart of the rebellion and hoped cutting it off would allow the revolution to whither in colonies to the south.[12] It took no military genius to recognize the significance of seizing New York.

If an inviting target for the British, New York City was in essence a trap for the Americans. Though extremely important, it was next to impossible to defend. General Charles Lee learned this when he scoped the area in early 1776. British command of the sea meant that the enemy could penetrate to and past Manhattan easily and land troops at any point to cut off the defenders. "What to do with the city, I own, puzzles me," Lee wrote Washington in February, "it is so encircle'd with deep navigable water, that whoever commands the Sea must command the Town."[13] Political exigency nevertheless made it essential to defend the city as vigorously as possible. Accordingly, and against his better judgment, Washington directed the construction of a series of fortifications and emplacements on Manhattan and Long Island that he hoped would force the enemy to pay a high price for conquest even if they could not actually preserve American control in the long run.[14] Then he waited for his opponents, British commander-in-chief lieutenant general William Howe and his brother Admiral Lord Richard Howe.

The British armada arrived off Sandy Hook in late June, and within six weeks about 25,000 British and German troops were ashore on Staten Island or bobbing in transports offshore. The deployment represented

The Battle of Long Island, August 27, 1776, also known as the Battle of Brooklyn, was the Continental Army's first major baptism by fire; it was a crushing rebel defeat that could have been an utter catastrophe if the British had exploited their victory with a prompt follow-up attack. (*New York Public Library*)

the largest overseas military effort in British history, and on August 22 General Howe moved. Lord Howe ferried 15,000 of his brother's troops to Long Island, where Washington stationed a fraction of his 20,000 widely detached troops within a feeble defensive system. General Howe took five days to reconnoiter the American lines and lay his plans, and on August 27 he struck. The ensuing Battle of Long Island was a patriot disaster. Command confusion and lack of training contributed heavily to the defeat, but failure to prevent a British flank attack led by Howe's subordinate, Major General Sir Henry Clinton, sealed the rebel defeat. Patriots fought hard but lost well over 1,000 killed, wounded, captured, or missing, against some 370 British casualties. The end of the fighting found the stunned rebels trapped on Brooklyn Heights, pinned against the waters of the East River.[15]

The war might easily have ended there, well before Saratoga or Yorktown. Howe had an opportunity to storm the vulnerable American fortifications and so capture Washington and the bulk of his high command. He did not. Instead, the British general held back and decided to open siege operations. Why? Some of Howe's key subordinates, including Henry Clinton, thought the American works ripe for the taking.[16] The decision remains inexplicable, although Howe may have been gun-shy of frontal assaults after the ghastly bloodletting at Bunker Hill. This was the gist of his explanation to Parliament in 1779: "The loss of 1,000, or perhaps 1,500 British troops, in carrying those lines, would have been but ill repaid by double that number of the enemy, could it have been supposed they would have suffered in that proportion."[17] If Howe actually believed this, he had seriously overestimated the number of rebels hunkered down on Brooklyn Heights. Given the respite, Washington acted quickly to get his men over the river to Manhattan; fog shrouded the nighttime withdrawal and the patriot troops were safe away before the Royal Navy, which had complete command of New York waters, was any the wiser. It would not be the last time a British general failed to finish off a seemingly helpless rebel command.

Howe was in no hurry to follow the Continental Army's remnants. In addition to his role as commander-in-chief, the general (and his admiral brother) was also tasked as a peace commissioner, and he spent two precious weeks fruitlessly trying to open peace negotiations. On September 15, Howe finally stirred and landed troops on Manhattan at Kip's Bay, north of Washington's main positions. It was a model amphibious operation, a demonstration of what professional soldiers and the Royal Navy could do. In the event, the surprised and disorganized Americans barely escaped destruction. The fiasco left the patriot chieftain furious with his soldiers, many of whom were militia who panicked at the redcoats' approach. Kip's Bay served only to confirm Washington's belief that only American regulars could successfully confront European professionals.[18]

The series of small engagements that followed as the Continentals fled from Manhattan and into New Jersey and finally Pennsylvania were not especially significant individually. But in aggregate the fighting in northern Manhattan and at Pell's Point, White Plains, and Fort Lee and the skirmishing during Washington's retreat across New Jersey did teach a significant lesson General Howe should have learned: British tactical prowess, such as Lord Cornwallis's scaling of the New Jersey Palisades to overrun Fort Lee, was never enough to land a decisive blow if the Americans refused a fight to the finish. Except at Fort Washington on northern Manhattan, when a rebel garrison was trapped against the Hudson, pa-

Knighted for his victory at Long Island, Lieutenant General William Howe (1729–1814), with his brother Admiral Lord Richard Howe, also was a royal peace commissioner. His efforts to arrange peace negotiations proved fruitless, and while he won his major battles, more than once Howe failed to land a decisive blow against defeated patriot forces. (*New York Public Library*)

triot officers were nimble enough to stay a step ahead of their opponents. Washington's army remained intact even in retreat.[19] While the patriot situation was dire, Washington began to contemplate a limited counterattack well before he sent his battered units across the Delaware River to safety in Pennsylvania on December 7–8.

None of this is to slight the fact that the patriot cause was in deep trouble. Patriot morale had plummeted, militia support melted away, the New Jersey government had dispersed, and thousands of New Jersey residents formally renewed their allegiance to George III.[20] Fearing Howe's onslaught, Congress decamped to Baltimore. There was even dissension within patriot ranks. Charles Lee was the chief critic. Disillusioned with the commander-in-chief's judgment after the disaster at Fort Washington, Lee shared his criticisms with Adjutant General Joseph Reed and Major General Horatio Gates, even telling Gates, "*Entre nous,* a certain great man is most damnably deficient."[21] Worse, in the face of orders to join Washington in Pennsylvania, Lee deliberately remained in New Jersey, thinking he could steady the militia and threaten Howe's rear. That Lee may have been right was no excuse for disobeying orders, and probably only Lee's capture near Basking Ridge by a British patrol on December 13 avoided a potentially disruptive breach with Washington. General John Sullivan then quickly led Lee's troops to Pennsylvania.

While his men shivered in the December cold, Washington assessed the situation. He had fewer than three thousand men, and many of their enlistments were expiring. The apparent collapse of popular support in New Jersey left the general outraged: "In short," he complained to his brother, John Augustine Washington, "the conduct of the Jersey's has been most infamous. Instead of turning out to defend their country and affording aid to our Army, they are making their submissions as fast as they can. If they [the Jerseys] had given us any support, we might have made a stand . . . but the few Militia that were in arms, disbanded themselves . . . and left the poor remains of our Army to make the best we could of it."[22] Unless he could reverse the tide of defeat, Washington knew, the Middle Theater would be the graveyard of the Revolution. This was truly a low point—perhaps *the* low point—of the American cause: the famous "times that tried men's souls."

While Howe knew of the desperate condition of the rebel army, he failed to appreciate its resiliency. Given a respite and competent leadership, and even minimal reinforcements and resupply, a battered army can heal. While Washington provided the leadership and went about frantic efforts to rally men and matériel, Howe provided the respite. The royal commander gave up the chase at the Delaware. He had the ability to cross the river and go after Washington in a winter campaign; instead, on December 13 (which ought to be an American national holiday) he issued orders to go into winter quarters. He considered the Americans all but beaten, and if any rebels survived the winter, he would clean up the remnants in the spring. Howe deployed his units in a string of outposts across central New Jersey stretching from New Brunswick, Princeton, Trenton, and on to Bordentown. He conceded that the posts were too far apart to offer ready mutual support, but trouble was the last thing he expected. Indeed, he returned to New York City (and his mistress) to spend a comfortable winter.[23] It was the worst decision of Howe's career.

Washington took full advantage of Howe's failure to pursue. He urged his men to extend expiring enlistments, sent subordinates to round up Pennsylvania militia, and combed the region for supplies. He gathered all available boats north and south of Trenton, hiding them on the Pennsylvania side in the event of any effort to return to New Jersey. The army gained another 2,600 Continentals with the arrival of Sullivan and regiments from the northern army under Horatio Gates (who departed for Baltimore pleading ill health). The patriot force was hardly formidable, but it was enough to set the commander-in-chief planning a counterattack.

As Washington's army healed, the British faced a deteriorating situation in New Jersey. As the shock of the British invasion wore off over late December, patriots maintained their grip on local affairs wherever the British failed to remain in strength. Moreover, the behavior of British troops was deplorable. Pillage and violence stoked popular fury and sparked a militia revival. Attacks on British units gathered tempo, and redcoats traveling in small groups did so at their peril; in fact, a popular insurgency was under way.[24] Here was a lesson from the Middle Theater repeated in every theater over the course of the struggle: Without the direct presence of British troops, and in force, no area, including those held by loyalists, was safe from patriot attack or actual control.

As events unfolded in New Jersey, Washington launched one of the most spectacular military adventures in American history. He was strong enough to mount a raid—certainly not a major offensive—if he could target an isolated enemy post. He chose Trenton. The garrison was mostly Hessians, some 1,400 men in all, and other British outposts were too far away to reinforce them quickly. Washington's plan was daring. North of Trenton, Washington would lead his main body across the Delaware at McKonkey's Ferry; he would then attack south. Poised opposite Trenton, Brigadier General James Ewing's Pennsylvania and New Jersey militia would cross directly into town. South of Trenton, militia brigadier general John Cadwalader would cross near Bordentown and delay any British attempt to move north to relieve the Hessians. The three assaulting columns would move simultaneously late on Christmas Day. The plan was complicated and fraught with risk, but they were risks the commander-in-chief felt compelled to take.

Events foiled the elaborate plan, but it made no difference. Ewing and Cadwalader never got across the Delaware, or failed to do so on time, victims of treacherous river conditions and miserable weather. Washington crossed with some 2,400 men, and although they advanced hours late, they were enough. The fighting lasted only some forty minutes as patriot artillery and musketry tore the surprised Hessians to pieces. When it was over, the overwhelmed garrison had lost 106 killed and wounded, including the mortally wounded Hessian commander, Colonel Johann Rall. About 900 were captured; only some 200 escaped.[25]

The Battle of Trenton was a dramatic victory, but it is well to remember it was only a raid; Washington had no intention of remaining in town. His little army was still outgunned and outnumbered by a vastly superior British army, and the American quickly got his troops and prisoners back into Pennsylvania. Seeking to maintain momentum, however, Washington gambled again. On December 31, reinforced and rested, he returned to Trenton hoping to exploit his earlier success. This time the gamble easily could have ended badly indeed—that it did not was another gift from British lethargy.

Enraged at the reverse at Trenton, Howe sent a strong detachment under Cornwallis to finish off the troublesome rebels. American skirmishing delayed the earl's arrival in front of Trenton until the evening of January 2, 1777. There he found Washington, his back to the Delaware, behind the Assunpink Creek. It was a poorly chosen position; a successful assault would have thrown the rebels into the river—game over. But when Washington's men fought off several British probes (this was Second Trenton), Cornwallis refused the entreaties of his subordinates to mount a full-fledged attack and finish the business. It was getting dark, and Cornwallis *supposedly* said he could "bag the fox" in the morning.[26] With his enemy seemingly trapped, Cornwallis had failed to administer the *coup de grace*. It was a mistake as monumental as Howe's hesitation in front of Brooklyn Heights or his decision not to pursue Washington across the Delaware: The British learning curve of 1776 was not the quickest.

The "fox" was not to be "bagged." Washington left his campfires burning and had a militia detail make enough noise to convince the British he was still behind the Assunpink; then he crept away along an unguarded road. With sunrise, duped and livid, Cornwallis gave chase, but too late to stop the elated patriots from colliding with an understrength British detachment at Princeton. The redcoats initially had the upper hand, but Washington, to the alarm of his officers, led a counterattack under direct fire that overwhelmed and finally broke the regulars. The Battle of Princeton was over in twenty minutes of brutal close com-

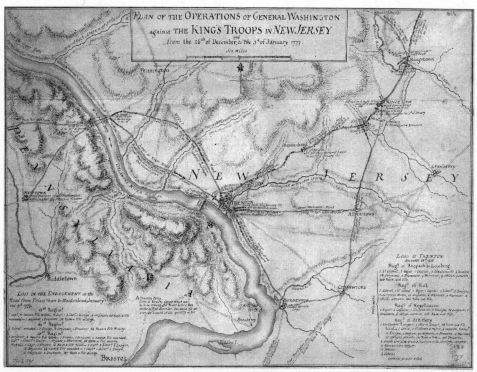

"Plan of the operations of General Washington, against the Kings troops in New Jersey, from the 26th. of December, 1776, to the 3d. January 1777" by William Faden, 1777. The Faden map traces British and American movements during the Trenton-Princeton campaign that saw Washington stun the British and largely reverse the impact of the rebel defeats of 1776. (*Library of Congress*)

bat. There was no time to celebrate, and the last rebels pulled out of Princeton with Cornwallis's leading elements in sight.

Washington's little army moved north, leaving Cornwallis to fume in Princeton. The troops moved to safety and winter quarters outside Morristown, a village of perhaps 350 residents, situated in strongly Whig territory behind the defensible Watchung Mountains. Washington made his headquarters in town while most of the army encamped in the nearby Loantaka Valley. (Morristown emerged as the Revolution's "military capital," hosting two major army winter encampments and support facilities and operations until the end of the war.)[27]

The revival of American fortunes at the battles of Trenton and Princeton rightly remains a staple of popular lore and children's textbooks. It does after all lend itself to storytelling. Washington displayed remarkable command ability in rallying his remaining troops under his personal leadership and leading them across the Delaware to pounce upon the German garrison at Trenton; and the Princeton operation, including his nighttime escape at Second Trenton, was one of the finest (if not *the* finest) tactical performances of his career.[28] Militarily, the Trenton-Princeton campaign was important in that it forced the British to abandon most of their gains of the autumn of 1776 in New Jersey, thus canceling part of Long Island's shameful aftermath. More important, Washington and his ragtag band had restored flagging public morale and demonstrated to all Americans that the Continental Army remained in the field and ready to fight. These brief engagements amply illustrated the resiliency of the patriot war effort; patriot arms in the theater were sometimes down, but never completely out. Of equal significance, they also may have preserved Congress from extended if not permanent dissolution.

Even so, Washington knew a difficult struggle lay ahead; he also understood that the Revolution lived only while *and because* the Continental Army lived. Thus, at least for the Americans, the tasks for the winter were clear: Rebuild the Continental Army and make ready for a spring campaign. Trenton and Princeton did not win the war, but for the moment they had saved the Revolution; and events in the Middle Theater, after a dark beginning, stood in stark contrast to the disasters of 1776 in Canada and the perilous situation in the Trans-Appalachian West.

THE YEAR OF THE HANGMAN: 1777

The Middle Theater saw a hiatus in major combat operations over the winter and early spring of 1777—but this hardly found the rival armies inactive. In January 1777 General Howe was no closer to defeating the rebels than he was in the spring of 1776. His troops were confined to a narrow strip of New Jersey between New Brunswick (just over thirty miles below Morristown) and Perth Amboy, as well as occupied Manhattan, Staten, and Long Islands. They also had garrisoned Newport, Rhode Island, as a Royal Navy base. Howe lacked the numbers and resources to secure additional territory, a quandary that would plague the royal commanders throughout the conflict. Insurgent militia moved freely in most of the countryside, and loyalists, many of whom had come out publicly for the Crown in late 1776, became targets for unforgiving patriots. Whig militia moved remorselessly against any signs of counter-revolution; tories were actively persecuted, frequently exiled, eventually stripped of their property, and some even killed. To his distress, Howe found loyalists seldom able to challenge rebels for control anywhere in the Middle Theater.

There were no major actions with the rebels, but redcoats and loyalist troops patrolled actively outside their winter garrisons in security and foraging operations. They tangled mostly with New York and New Jersey militia, and between January and March 1777 there were over fifty small-scale incidents; while there were relatively few casualties, the countryside outside occupied areas was dangerous enough.[29] As his men skirmished, Howe—knighted for Long Island, he was now "Sir William"—contemplated the coming spring. It was not an entirely happy prospect. For while Howe remained commander-in-chief, he knew his political masters wanted him to put right the reverses of Trenton and Princeton and polish off the politically troubling and expensive rebellion as soon as possible in 1777—the so-called "Year of the Hangman" (the three 7s reminding some of three gibbets).

At Morristown, Washington spent what was probably the busiest winter of his life. As the British clung to their strip of territory in central New Jersey, the American general undertook one of the most critical tasks of the war: Over the winter and spring of 1777 he built a new Continental Army. In September 1776 he had sent Congress his views on the best means to win what was probably going to be a long war. Militia, so dear to patriot hearts, but serving only briefly and indifferently trained, would not do. "I am persuaded and as fully convinced," he wrote, that the war would be lost if "left to any but a permanent, standing Army . . . I mean One to exist during the War." In December he struck the same note, bluntly telling Congress he needed "a respectable Army, and such as will be competent to every exigency." And by this he meant Continentals properly trained, disciplined, and equipped, with long-term enlistments—and able to confront European professionals on equal terms.[30] The gravity of the military situation convinced a majority of delegates to forego ideological objections to regular troops, and Congress voted an army of some 75,000 men. Troops would enlist for three years or "for the duration" of the war; recruits would receive bounties of $20, a clothing issue, and—"for the duration" men—one hundred acres of land after the war.[31] The rebels never met recruiting objectives and regiments were chronically understrength; the significant fact remains, however, that Washington would be able to shape the men he *could* get into a regular army.

The new army did not fit the image of the "embattled farmer" so dear to popular lore. Like their British counterparts, most recruits were rootless young men, often with little stake in civilian society; most generally came from the margins of colonial life.[32] For poor men in an overwhelmingly agricultural America, the promised bounty lands had real appeal. The Continental Line was racially integrated. All Northern states, as well as Maryland and Virginia, eventually allowed indentured servants and free blacks to enlist and permitted indentured servants and slaves to serve as substitutes for their masters. While regulations forbade the practice, recruiters often winked at enlistments of enemy deserters.[33]

Morristown was the crucible of the new regulars. Veterans of the 1776 campaign afforded the new regiments a core of vital experience; and as recruits, stores, and equipment converged on the encampment, Washington urged Congress, civil officials, and officers to muster financial and material support for the Continentals. The commander-in-chief was lucky: Howe remained leery of the New Jersey countryside and chose not to confront the rebels when they were most vulnerable. "As a result Washington had the Continental Line in reasonable condition as the winter faded; it was a signal achievement, important as any battlefield victory."[34] Indeed, the Middle Theater was the birthplace of the regular American army. These were the regiments that fought under Washington's personal command, and those he would send to other theaters later in the war, including the critical reinforcements that tipped the military balance to the patriots at Saratoga and eventually fenced with Cornwallis in Virginia.

In the spring Washington cautiously edged toward a new campaign. He sent parties of regulars south to work with local militia in central New Jersey. They challenged British foraging parties, who parried gamely. These small actions gave his men invaluable combat experience, taught them to work with militia, and kept the British on edge. But Washington

was not looking for a major fight; 1776 had proved the danger of confronting European professionals with an inexperienced army. Instead,
the commander-in-chief informed Congress he would wage a war of
"posts."[35] The Continentals would concentrate as a force in being, and
Howe's stronger army would have to guard against a patriot sally at an
isolated detachment (as at Trenton), while recognizing Washington
would refuse major combat except on his own terms. In the meantime
the rebels would continue chipping away at their adversary in a campaign
of attrition.

Not all patriots agreed with this strategy. Massachusetts radical Samuel
Adams, who wanted a quick showdown with the British, bemoaned "the
Fabian War in America." Adams, and others, saw in Washington's operations a reflection of Roman general Quintus Fabius Maximus Verruco-
sus, who fought a similar war against Hannibal's superior Carthaginian
army.[36] If Washington became, however temporarily, the American
Fabius, his tactics proved effective. British foraging parties required large
covering forces and casualties mounted. Redcoat frustration was real,
and the initiative in this "forage war" lay with the Americans.[37]

In late May talk of Washington as Fabius (if he ever had been) began
to fade. The appellation never really suited Washington anyway as his
instincts were offensive; given a reasonable opportunity, the general preferred to fight, and in mid-spring he was ready for bolder action.[38] He
moved his army south to the Watchung Mountains at Middlebrook, a
few miles above British-occupied New Brunswick. If they chose, the Continentals could challenge British moves deeper into the state; and they as
much as dared Howe to climb the Watchungs after them. It was quite an
accomplishment for a rebel army that had barely existed in January.

In the late spring General Howe belatedly attempted to make up for
his earlier failure to destroy Washington's army. He did so, however, in a
context radically different from the previous year. The imperial government had approved a new military plan for 1777. The scheme hinged
on an advance from Canada, down the traditional Lake Champlain and
Hudson River Valley corridor as far as Albany, New York. Lieutenant
General John Burgoyne would command this army.

Howe's forces would control the lower reaches of the Hudson and operate in support of the Canadian army; if necessary forces from the Middle Theater would move upriver as far as Albany. The objective was to

isolate New England and defeat the Revolution piecemeal. As they moved toward Albany the converging columns would destroy rebel forces encountered along the way. The plan had merit: Control of the Hudson would compromise patriot efforts to move troops and supplies between theaters, and it might encourage loyalists to rise in the less zealous colonies south of the Hudson.

If the plan looked good on paper, however, it was inherently flawed in practice. Neither generals Howe nor Burgoyne nor the secretary of state for America, Lord George Germain, ever clarified the meaning of "support." The term did *not* necessarily mean an action in direct cooperation with another force; it could also mean an independent operation preventing enemy forces from concentrating against a friendly unit. Indeed, Howe determined to go his own way; he would attack Philadelphia. Such an operation would tie up major patriot forces and prevent a concentration against Burgoyne—or so Howe hoped—thus indirectly supporting the northern venture. It would also let him even the score with Washington, hopefully in a decisive battle. In reality, however, given his commitments in Pennsylvania, Howe would have little or no time to mount a serious thrust up the Hudson. Burgoyne initially had no clear understanding of Sir William's intentions, and he learned only in early August that Howe would not be moving north in strength (alarming news that Burgoyne kept from his subordinates).[39] The generals would wage separate campaigns, and thus the British violated one of the cardinal principles of war: unity of command.

While Burgoyne prepared his army, Howe pondered operations against Philadelphia. His advanced post in New Jersey was New Brunswick, sixty-five miles from Philadelphia, perhaps four days' march. Yet he hesitated. The "forage war" had demonstrated a disturbing rebel aggressiveness, and he questioned what might happen if he marched west across the state. Could Washington fall on his rear or attack while the royal army was crossing the Delaware? Could the rebels turn on New York? There were too many risks, and Howe felt compelled to deal with Washington before marching on Philadelphia.

Sir William dismissed assaulting the Continental lair above Middlebrook; a direct attack up the Watchungs would have invited another Bunker Hill. The trick was to lure Washington to the plains below, and in June Howe maneuvered, hoping to draw Washington into a showdown fight. The American refused to take the bait and stayed put. In a final effort to bring the rebels to battle, the British commander feigned an evacuation of New Jersey. Washington cautiously sent detachments forward, and on June 26 Howe suddenly turned and struck. In a running action—variously called the Battle of Westfield, Metuchen Meeting-house, Flat Hills, or Short Hills—Continentals and militia avoided en-trapment and regained the heights above Middlebrook. Often overlooked, the battle reflected considerable Continental tactical agility.[40] Frustrated, on June 30 Howe quit the state; he would attack Philadel-phia, but his army would travel by sea.

The British armada, 270 ships strong, departed Sandy Hook on July 23. Howe first probed the Delaware River but decided (inaccurately) that it was too strongly defended. The fleet then sailed past the Virginia Capes and into the Chesapeake, reaching Head of Elk, Maryland, on August 22. Three days later debilitated British and German troops and animals began pouring ashore. Their thirty-two-day journey had sick-ened both men and horses in the sweltering August heat, and conditions were not much better on land. Fortunately for them, Washington's troops were in no position to offer significant opposition.

Howe's long sea journey should have given the Americans plenty of time to rest and prepare. The opposite was the case. A poor and largely still unformed intelligence-gathering apparatus left Washington entirely in the dark as to British intentions. Although he considered Philadelphia a possible target, he also thought Howe might strike up the Hudson to join Burgoyne. He "certainly ought now in good policy," Washington wrote of his rival, "to endeavor to Cooperate with Genl Burgoyne."[41] Initially unsure of where to post the Continentals, he dispatched strong detachments to the Hudson Highlands and, eventually, to the northern army confronting Burgoyne. In the meantime, rather than await solid news of Howe's location he exhausted his troops by rushing them to and fro according to intelligence that amounted to little better than hearsay. The American commander also neglected to order adequate scouting of terrain over which the British were likely to advance, leaving him essen-tially ignorant of the countryside in Delaware, Maryland, and southeast Pennsylvania. As Howe's troops landed all Washington could do was march his troops south at breakneck speed and then observe from a dis-tance as the enemy moved inland.[42]

Popular resistance to the British incursion was tepid at best. Militia in Maryland failed to turn out in significant numbers. The government of Delaware collapsed as British troops entered the state at the beginning of September and loyalists rose up in strength. After the desultory Battle of Cooch's Bridge, Delaware, on September 3, the British pushed into Pennsylvania, obviously making for Philadelphia. Contrary to Washington's reputation as a Fabian warrior determined to preserve his army, he placed his troops athwart the enemy advance only to be repeatedly outflanked before finally settling behind the Brandywine Creek at Chadds Ford. Here, determined to fight, he awaited Howe's next move.

That move was skillful and nearly devastating. On September 11, Howe out-generaled Washington at the Battle of Brandywine. The royal commander had Hessian lieutenant general Wilhelm von Knyphausen demonstrate across Chadds Ford, feigning an attack on the main patriot line. While the rebels watched Knyphausen, Howe accompanied a heavy column under Cornwallis upstream beyond the American right. The British crossed at two unguarded fords and bore down on the Continental flank, commanded by General John Sullivan. The attack took the Americans by surprise. (Perhaps it shouldn't have; the year before a similar flanking movement had defeated Washington at Long Island.) When Washington reinforced his hard-pressed right, Knyphausen stormed over Chadds Ford, fracturing the patriot left. A determined rear-guard action by Nathanael Greene probably saved the patriot cause from irrevocable ruin.[43]

Brandywine did not end the fighting. Fate, in the form of a sudden rainstorm, again played a hand by drenching the opposing armies' powder as they faced off on September 16 for another battle near Malvern, Pennsylvania. Washington's army remained between Howe and the city; but Congress decamped (again), ultimately to rustic York, a hundred miles west. On the night of September 20 redcoats under General Charles Grey surprised a laxly guarded Continental encampment at Paoli. Grey's men—their musket flints removed to avoid premature shooting—bore in with bayonets. It was a slaughter: The rebels lost 237 killed, wounded, or captured, Grey only 11; ever after the British general was "No Flint Grey."[44] After Paoli, Washington conceded Philadelphia, and Howe marched in unopposed on September 26.

Still the rebels refused to surrender the entire region. Undaunted, the Americans launched a surprise attack on British outposts at Germantown

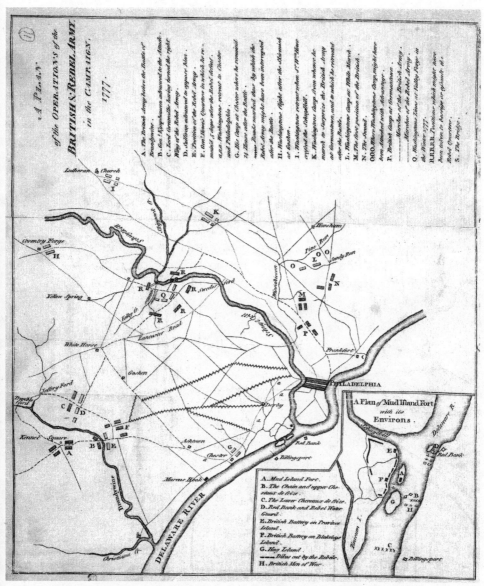

"A plan of the operations of the British & Rebel army in the Campaign, 1777." by John Lodge, 1779. The Lodge map depicts the series of hard-fought actions during the Philadelphia campaign, including the defense of the Delaware River approaches to the city that dragged on until late November. (*New York Public Library*)

on October 4. Properly executed, this battle might have resulted in a significant American victory; but the Continentals' confusion and British determination resulted in a victory for the latter. The Americans fought on. South of Philadelphia, on opposite banks of the Delaware, the guns of Forts Mifflin and Mercer closed the river to navigation. Unless the Royal Navy could supply the army in Philadelphia, Howe could not hold the city; if the forts held until the river froze, Howe was in real trouble. To break the impasse, Howe dispatched a strong Hessian column to New Jersey to take Fort Mercer. Their attack proved a miniature Bunker Hill; well-concealed Continentals decimated the Germans. Yet Sir William won through. Washington could send no relief, and by mid-November the heroic garrisons of both forts had pulled out, allowing the British to clear the river.[45]

Congress was appalled and urged a winter campaign to regain the de facto capital. The commander-in-chief's response was blunt: "It would give me infinite pleasure," he told South Carolina's Henry Laurens, to protect "every individual and . . . every Spot of Ground in the whole of the United States. Nothing is more my wish. But this is not possible with our present force."[46]

The rival forces skirmished inconclusively at White Marsh in early December, but on 19 December the Continentals moved to a winter encampment at Valley Forge, some twenty-five miles from the city. The Philadelphia campaign was over—as well as the Year of the Hangman.

For the British the 1777 campaign was a story of squandered potential. Howe had won his battles, but his decision to march for Philadelphia instead of supporting Burgoyne's descent of the Hudson played a substantial role in ensuring British defeat at Saratoga. Washington's detachment from his army of significant reinforcements, especially Daniel Morgan's riflemen, also proved of vital assistance to the army of Horatio Gates. Howe, meanwhile, had missed his opportunities to crush the main American army. He also found that Philadelphia—while undeniably an important objective, the loss of which was a blow to patriot morale—lacked the political or strategic significance of a European capital. Congress made no sign of surrender and Washington's army remained a credible force. Despite his defeats, Washington, like the best generals throughout history, was lucky.

TURNING POINT: 1778

Washington's decision, influenced by advice from Nathanael Greene, to encamp at Valley Forge was a brilliant strategic move. By remaining close to Philadelphia—but not so close as to endanger his main force—Washington was able to contest control of the countryside around the city for the duration of the winter. He thus denied the enemy the opportunity to spread their influence and trade without molestation. At the same time, American troops maintained a largely friendly intercourse with American civilians, thanks in part to Washington's refusal to countenance plunder or forced requisitions. Americans in the region were constantly reminded that the Continentals, and thus the Revolution, were alive (if not well).

Yet the long-term advantages of posting the army at Valley Forge were not immediately apparent. In fact, if Washington's central role in the eventual American victory is widely appreciated, never was his position more vulnerable than in the winter of 1777–1778. Over the early weeks in camp, the shivering regiments labored to build huts against the cold. But even with shelter secured, food, forage, and supplies quickly became scarce. The weather did not help. The winter was relatively mild compared to winters later in the war, but roads frequently alternated between snow and slush, impeding vital supply deliveries. Food shortages and near starvation were endemic and left the men surly and weakened; over the course of the winter some 1,900 men (and one assumes many camp followers) succumbed to camp diseases—usually typhoid, smallpox, other fevers, and malnutrition. Fearful of alienating public support, Washington had resisted impressing food and forage from local civilians; but scarcities became such that, at congressional urging, the general finally resorted to confiscations (farmers received promissory notes or receipts).[47]

This was tragic, as all too many wounds threatening the Whig cause were self-inflicted. Stores of necessities existed in scattered locations; the chief problem was maintaining transport and administrative operations enabling timely deliveries to the army. Poor record-keeping prevented a clear understanding of stores on hand or where they were, and bureaucratic bungling made things worse. Procurement personnel lacked funds to purchase supplies of all kinds, and in any case Pennsylvania farmers were reluctant to accept Continental currency or promissory notes for food and forage. When Quartermaster General Thomas Mifflin resigned pleading ill health (although he was fit enough to remain politically active), Congress, incredibly, showed no urgency in naming a replacement. "There was little Congress could do over financial woes," a 2016 study has noted. "There simply was too little money; but there was no excusing the lack of attention to the administrative mess. Valley Forge was not Congress's finest hour."[48]

For many men it was too much. They deserted in droves; desertion rates of 20 percent were common, and some regiments recorded losses of 50 percent. Nor were all officers dependable. Resignations, requests for leave, and unexcused absences drove Washington to distraction. The loss of good officers, he feared, "will shake the very existence of the Army." In November 1777 the general had 19,415 men present and fit for duty; by March 1778 there were only 7,316.[49] Alarmed visitors to camp noted the army's lack of discipline and withering morale. Without Burgoyne's defeat 1777 would have been utterly catastrophic for the patriot cause. In fact, other than Saratoga, the rebels had little reason to cheer. Thus, while the British reeled from the loss of an army, Washington struggled to keep his Continentals in the field. In late 1776 Thomas Paine had written eloquently of "the times that try men's souls"; he could easily have said the same of late 1777 and early 1778.

Finally Congress acted. In January it had named a "Committee at Camp" to visit Valley Forge and report on army problems and needs; until March the committee worked directly with Washington to resolve the crisis. Committee reports of bureaucratic mishaps, suffering soldiers, angry officers, and Washington's efforts to hold everything together appalled the delegates at York. Congressional surprise at the state of affairs at Valley Forge was inexcusable; but confronted with stark realities reported by its own committee, the delegates moved to remedy the situation with new money, appointments, and administrative changes.[50]

Significantly, Congress agreed to new appointments and funding for the Commissary and Quartermaster departments. In March 1778 Nathanael Greene agreed to serve as quartermaster general. Greene longed for martial glory, but Washington persuaded him to take the job. "No body ever heard of a quarter Master in History," he lamented.[51] Soon after, Connecticut's Jeremiah Wadsworth took over as commissary general of purchases. Greene and Wadsworth, spending freely, jump-started logistics operations. Improved transportation services enabled deliveries of food, clothing, forage, camp implements, and munitions. Over the early spring shipments of French supplies began arriving in camp, including enough excellent .69-caliber Charleville muskets to rearm most regiments. Greene and Wadsworth enjoyed considerable help and good fortune. Congress and Washington resolved many long-standing administrative bottlenecks, and the weather moderated after February 1778. Even Howe cooperated by not attacking Valley Forge. But the two department heads were diligent and competent, and they deserved much of the credit for the improved state of the army.[52]

As the army's distress gradually lifted, the war went on. Washington never enjoyed the luxury of simply holding his forces together; of necessity, he mounted foraging and security operations, probed British positions, and communicated with rebel commanders in other theaters. Even in a weakened state the rebels could still sting. In particular, Continental dragoons under Captain Henry "Light Horse Harry" Lee (father of Robert E. Lee) became the scourge of British foragers and patrols. Over February and March the army staged a "Grand Forage" as some 1,500 soldiers swept up desperately needed provisions in eastern Pennsylvania, Maryland, Delaware, and western New Jersey.[53] As logistics improved the commander-in-chief addressed the critical issues of recruiting, army reorganization, and training—especially training. Even a well-supplied army was useless unless it could perform in the field.

The Continentals had fought hard in 1777, but Washington understood his regulars lacked British tactical skills. The catalyst for change in this regard arrived at Valley Forge in February 1778 in the person of Friedrich Steuben. A pretended Prussian noble (although patriots never begrudged his assumed title of "Baron"), Steuben agreed to serve as voluntary inspector general, with the understanding that if he proved himself, appropriate rank and rewards would follow. The Prussian knew how to train and motivate soldiers, and he succeeded in part because he modified and simplified European drill for American use. The Continentals learned or relearned volley fire, movement from file into line and back again, skirmishing operations, and any number of other tactical evolutions. There was bayonet drill, teaching proficiency with the weapon the British used to such deadly effect.[54] Steuben taught a brutal trade, but the army was shaping up.

Steuben's success needs some context. In 1778 the Continental Army was not a mob. Veteran troops had a working knowledge of maneuver and weapons drill, and many officers were familiar with European military ideas; some were veterans of the French and Indian War and knew British drill. The army took tentative steps toward uniform drill in 1777, and only active operations had prevented Washington from implementing a standard system. Thus Steuben did not have to start from scratch. The commander-in-chief tolerated no deviations from Steuben's instruction; failure to conform, he warned, would "again plunge the Army into that Contrariety and Confusion from which it is endeavouring to emerge."[55] In great measure it did emerge, and with Washington's enthusiastic endorsement Congress confirmed Steuben's appointment as inspector general with the rank of major general.

As Steuben standardized training, Washington and his officers addressed other pressing issues. The commander-in-chief took a direct role in reorganizing the infantry. As in the British military, the foot regiments were the heart of the army; and Washington moved vigorously to replenish the depleted rank and file. With congressional authorization, he began reducing the number of regiments from 104 to 80, consolidating weaker units into fewer but stronger outfits. Even a goal of 80 regiments was ambitious, but at least it was more realistic. He pushed the states to pursue enlistments, and over the spring the recruiting machinery slowly responded. By May, Continental ranks counted over 15,000 men.[56] Brigadier General Henry Knox fostered a growing competence in the Continental artillery. He established armories and repair shops for his guns, and he carefully supervised the training of his gunners. He also reorganized and reequipped the artillery arm, making good use of imported French guns and pieces captured with Burgoyne. By late spring he had four well-trained regiments. Esprit among the artillerymen was among the highest in the army.[57] By spring 1778 the Continental Line was mending. The rebuilt regiments were still too thin, but they functioned in the face of impediments no European force could tolerate.

The improving circumstances of the army lifted morale to its highest levels in months—and morale soared higher still when the troops learned America no longer was fighting alone. News of the Franco-American alliance (negotiated in February 1778) reached Valley Forge on May 3, and Washington greeted it in terms of divine intervention. "The

Steuben drilling troops at Valley Forge. Steuben brought a uniform training regimen to the Continental Army. Starting with a model company (a detachment of which is pictured) he drilled personally, he contributed vitally to the improved tactical proficiency of the army's infantry regiments. (*Library of Congress*)

Almighty ruler of the Universe," he told the army, had favored America by "raising us up a powerful Friend among the Princes of the Earth to establish our liberty and Independence." The army paraded in honor of the alliance, cheered Louis XVI, fired repeated salutes, and (perhaps best of all for the rank and file) ended festivities with a special issue of rum.[58]

Valley Forge had changed the army, but it had changed Washington as well. The winter crisis saw the patriot chief at his administrative and inspirational best dealing with the army's maladies. He was at his diplomatic best in securing support from civil officials, Congressional delegates, and senior military personnel. He had done all of this in the face of daunting obstacles, not the least of which was heavy political fire from patriot critics. By June 1778 the so-called Conway Cabal had evaporated, but for several months the defeats of 1777 had raised serious questions about the commander-in-chief's ability to win the war. There is little question that there was sentiment in some quarters to replace Washington with Gates, the victor at Saratoga. This would have been an unmitigated disaster. Among other consequences, it would have quashed any prospect of a prosperous Franco-American alliance: Washington and his protégés Lafayette and Alexander Hamilton would prove essential to patching up the alliance when it verged on collapse on many occasions later in the war. Gates's success at Saratoga, subsequently challenged by many historians, hardly qualified him for the post of commander-in-chief (as his experience in the Southern Theater would prove in 1780). That he did not replace Washington was due to the latter's success in forging strong relations with civilian and military leaders throughout the country, as well as to the activity of men like Hamilton, Lafayette, and Greene in isolating disaffected elements in the army. Also, the example Washington set by working for the soldiers' welfare instead of posing or glory-seeking bound them to him as they had never been before. A Connecticut captain spoke for many when he wrote: "I am content should they remove almost any General Except his Excellency . . . Congress are not aware of the Confidence The Army Places in him or motions would never have been made for Gates to take Command."[59]

The Valley Forge winter of 1777–1778 was an epic of survival—but then, *revival*. As the 1778 campaign loomed, Washington commanded a much improved army, with the vast majority of his officers and men firmly attached to him. What remained, however, was to see how all of these changes might translate into success in the field, especially in the new context of an international conflict. War with France compelled a radical change in imperial strategy, which conceded that a military decision in the northern colonies was unlikely. Britain could not fight everywhere, so the ministry called for a redeployment to theaters more likely to produce results or to defend strategically and economically more important parts of the empire. That meant giving up Philadelphia and sending troops that had campaigned in the Middle Theater to the American South, including West Florida, and the sugar colonies in the Caribbean.[60] Accordingly, the main British army, now led by a new commander-in-chief, Lieutenant General Sir Henry Clinton, abandoned Philadelphia on June 18 and trekked slowly across central New Jersey toward Sandy Hook for transport to New York City.

Washington pursued. On June 28 the resulting Battle of Monmouth was a bitterly contested tactical draw, with both sides professing satisfaction with the results. Clinton, whose orders were to get his army back to New York for redeployment, did so without so much as losing a single wagon of a baggage train that sometimes extended over ten miles. He regretted only not being able to force a decisive battle and destroy at least a major part of the Continental Army. Washington had no regrets. His

Battle of Monmouth, New Jersey, June 28, 1778. The battle was a hard-fought tactical draw, but the performance of the Continental Army and Washington's sound leadership cemented his grip on his position as commander-in-chief. (*Library of Congress*)

regiments had fought well under tough conditions, inflicting considerable casualties on Clinton's regiments. It was enough to allow his army and political allies to "spin" a public relations account of a great victory. And that in turn was enough to further cement Washington's place as commander-in-chief.[61]

Monmouth was not the last major engagement in the Middle Theater or, for that matter, in the North. There would be serious fighting at Springfield, New Jersey, in 1780, and a savage British raid on New London, Connecticut, the following year. But Monmouth was the last time the main British and American armies, with their respective commanders-in-chief, confronted each other in the open field. (At Yorktown only Washington and Rochambeau had their main forces; Clinton still had the imperial main body in and around New York City.) Washington moved the Continentals into positions north of New York City on the Hudson River at White Plains, close to the old battlefield of 1776. In effect, the war had come full circle in the theater with the armies where they had been two years earlier—and with the conflict no closer to resolution. The difference, of course, was this time Washington had been

on the offensive. In the general's eyes it was a stunning turnabout in the
fortunes of war, even the military equivalent of divine intervention. "It
is not a little pleasing," he wrote fellow Virginian Thomas Nelson:

> nor less wonderful to contemplate, that after two long years Ma-
> noeuvring and undergoing the strangest vicissitudes that perhaps
> ever attended any one contest since the creation both Armies are
> brought back to the very point they set out from and, that that
> [sic], which was the offending party in the beginning is now re-
> duced to the use of the spade and pick axe for the defence. The
> hand of Providence has been so conspicuous in all this, that he
> must be worse than an infidel that lacks faith, and more than
> wicked, that has not gratitude enough to acknowledge his obli-
> gations, but, it will be time enough for me to turn preacher, when
> my present appointment ceases.[62]

In the summer of 1778, and in the afterglow of Monmouth, the commander-in-chief could not have predicted the duration of his "present
appointment"; in fact it would be quite some time.

THE WAR FOR NEW YORK AND THE ROAD TO YORKTOWN: 1779–1781

The years after Monmouth are typically regarded as insignificant for the
Middle Theater. Washington and the main army remained ensconced
around New York City while the arena of combat shifted southward. In
warfare, however, intensity of fighting and especially of movement is not
always the best indicator of a front's significance. Although the most outwardly exciting events in this period largely occurred south of the Dan
River, the bulk of American and British forces remained concentrated in
the Middle Theater. They were hardly inactive—combat remained a constant feature, if only on a smaller scale. This fighting held lessons of its
own. At Stony Point, New York (July 16, 1779), Brigadier General Anthony Wayne's command successfully stormed a British garrison in a bay-
onets-only assault. The feat was impressive enough to earn the respect
of Henry Clinton: "The success attending this bold and well-combined
attempt of the enemy procured very deservedly no small share of reputation and applause to the spirited officer (General Wayne) who conducted it, and was, I must confess, a very great affront to us."[63] A month
later at Paulus Hook, New Jersey (August 19), Major Henry Lee surprised another British outpost, killing some 50 troops and capturing

158. In June 1780 at Springfield, New Jersey, two weeks of combat frustrated a British effort to break through to Morristown. State militia and Continentals under Nathanael Greene gave Knyphausen's Hessians and redcoats all they could handle.[64] In aggregate these incidents demonstrated how well the patriot regulars had learned their trade, and how inhospitable seasoned local militia could make the American countryside.

These engagements also boosted rebel morale, and this was no small point as the war dragged on. In fact, there was plenty in the Middle Theater to test the spirit of the staunchest patriots. If there were no major battles, the civil war between patriots and loyalists raged with fierce intensity. There were places of relative calm. The British evacuation of Philadelphia had all but ended active loyalism in eastern Pennsylvania and western New Jersey. In August 1780 Delaware militia easily dispersed a Tory "rising," as much a tax revolt as it was a profession of support for the king; and Clinton was never sure of how much support the royal standard might raise in Maryland.[65] Without the cover of nearby redcoats, tories in these areas were virtually helpless. In areas contiguous to British-occupied New York City, however, civil strife became a dangerous, even deadly, norm.

Indeed, the Middle Theater *was* dangerous. Not counting actions in northern or western New York State (usually involving Indians), during 1779 and 1780 localities around the city saw at least fifteen clashes between rebels and British forces. The worst of the violence, however, was across the Hudson. Over the same period the eastern New Jersey counties experienced an astonishing 156 armed encounters (not counting naval actions off the state's immediate coast, which would have upped the total). Most of these incidents stemmed from loyalist or British foraging efforts; they were usually small actions with few if any casualties—but some were larger. As late as mid-May 1781, hundreds of militia struggled to oust a hundred tories from a blockhouse at Fort Lee, and only the evacuation of the loyalists prevented four hundred Continental light infantry from getting involved.[66] Notions of "fair play" seldom restrained combatants on either side. In response to loyalist activities in Monmouth County, patriots formed an extralegal militia (actually vigilantes), the Association for Retaliation; under militia general "Black" or "Devil" David Forman (whose nom de guerre said it all) the "retaliators" waged an anti-Tory campaign of such brutality as to alarm more conservative patriots.[67] That such constant strife at the local level over so long a period induced a profound war-weariness was no surprise.

Economic hardship also taxed morale. The rival armies consumed tons of food, forage, firewood, and other supplies weekly, and the constant demand for food and forage lay heavily on the regional agricultural economies. Virginia, largely untouched by major military operations until 1781, was able to send supplies to the Middle and Southern Theaters, and agriculture remained productive in Delaware, Maryland, and most of eastern Pennsylvania. The produce-growing areas of southern New York and most of New Jersey, however, were contested by British and American forces, as arable land was around Philadelphia during the British occupation. Normal markets were disrupted, and for hard-pressed farmers and merchants the temptation to trade with the British, who could offer hard cash, was frequently too great to resist. In fact, to the distress of Washington and senior patriot leaders, civilians traded actively with the enemy, sometimes with the connivance of patriot troops meant to stop them. "We find that our common Dragoons," Washington complained at Valley Forge, "are not proof agt the Bribes offered to them by the people who constantly are carrying provision to the City of Philada, so that instead of cutting off the intercourse they encourage it by suffering many to pass who pay them for it." Pennsylvania Quakers, extremely influential in the region, were inclined to work with whichever side had the upper hand, while Philadelphia businessmen yearned to renew the commercial activities upon which their prosperity ultimately depended.[68] Opposite New York City, New Jersey farmers and merchants, who otherwise considered themselves patriots, traded more or less openly with the British. Despite arrests, fines, and official denunciations—American pickets even killed the occasional farmer trying to reach British lines in Philadelphia—efforts to suppress illegal trade failed in the face of civilian demands for goods that only enemy sources could provide and hard money that offered a chance to avoid war-related economic hardship or even poverty.[69] Washington feared with good reason that this would in time rebuild a commonality of interest between Americans and the royal regime.

Hardship deeply affected army morale—almost fatally. The winter of 1779–1780 at Morristown was actually considerably worse than the ordeal at Valley Forge. Supply services were better organized than at Valley

Forge, but record cold and snowfalls—it snowed until April—crippled logistics. "The distress we feel," Washington recorded in his diary, "is chiefly owing to the early commencement and uncommon rigor of the Winter, which have greatly obstructed the transportation of our supplies."[70] The collapse of the Continental currency once again made living conditions almost intolerable, miserable service conditions and late pay brought the soldiery to the verge of mutiny, and in May several Connecticut regiments were barely persuaded to remain under orders. Desertion drained the ranks, and the resignations in the officer corps likewise bled the army of much of its veteran leadership. Again, Washington was the glue that held things together. He appealed to (and badgered) Congress and the states to forward supplies and reinforcements, and at times he dispersed his troops to put them closer to areas with available food and forage. Late 1780, however, despite his best efforts, saw the army near the breaking point. Benedict Arnold's treason had shaken morale and the men were simply tired and fed up with the seeming congressional and civilian indifference to their plight. The mutinies of the Pennsylvania and New Jersey regiments in early January 1781 were the result. While negotiations settled matters with the Pennsylvanians, Washington used force against the New Jersey mutineers, ordering the summary executions of the most serious offenders (two were shot) as an example to the rest of the army. The commander-in-chief was genuinely afraid the Continental Line he had labored to build, and on which the fate of the Revolution depended, would crumble under a wave of troop discontent and mutiny.[71] Had he not acted decisively, if brutally, the war may well have been lost without another battle—at least by the American regulars.

Yet all of this tumultuous military and economic activity—and they were hardly distinct—existed in a state of strategic stalemate. Washington lacked the resources to assault New York City, although Sir Henry Clinton correctly assumed his rival wanted to try. The rebel commander devoted considerable effort to divining his opponent's intentions and strength, and in so doing constructed the first organized military intelligence system in American history. He also worked heroically on army reform, seeking to keep his regiments in fighting trim even as the near collapse of rebel finances again posed severe logistical and supply problems. Such efforts, difficult as they were, would be crucial to future success. In New York, Clinton lacked the resources for the sort of campaigns the British had conducted in 1776 and 1777, and he worried constantly that (what he considered) his meager muster rolls left him vulnerable to the Continentals.[72]

Both sides, however, recognized the continuing strategic importance of the Hudson River. Washington was determined to fortify West Point, and to this end he employed the talents of French engineer Louis Duportail and of Thaddeus Kosciuszko, two of the more useful Europeans to serve in Continental uniforms. Though the British probed the Hudson—and the possibility that they might renew their efforts of 1776–1777 in this region remained a constant threat—American determination to defend West Point thwarted them. The British welcomed Benedict Arnold's attempt to betray the fortress in September 1780 with good reason, and his failure was also theirs.[73]

Even as he worked to protect West Point and the Hudson River corridor, Washington became fixated on a prospective attack on New York City. Although fiscal and logistical difficulties left the Americans unable to accomplish this on their own, the commander-in-chief was certain that each month that passed would further weaken the national infrastructure and incapacitate the Continental Army. Time also did not appear to favor the continuance of the French alliance. Winning the war quickly, preferably by means of a single devastating blow to British military power in North America, seemed imperative. Washington therefore worked assiduously to bring about the concordance of a French fleet bottling up New York harbor while a Franco-American army assaulted the city from the landward. This imperative was what fueled his creation of an intelligence network within the city.

By the spring of 1781, all the key elements seemed to be in place, or nearly so. The general had worked hard to gather regiments from what he considered peripheral commands, and he had reinforced other theaters only sparely. In early 1781, Washington had sent Lafayette to Virginia with Continental light infantry to confront the British invasion of the Old Dominion, and he followed by dispatching Anthony Wayne with another contingent of regulars. Beyond this, however, he would not go, candidly explaining to officers and political leaders in the Southern, Western, and Northern Theaters that he would not be sending them reinforcements.[74] The New York operation was more important. General Rochambeau, whose strong relationship with Washington via intermediaries such as the Comte de Chastellux and Alexander Hamilton was so critical to the American cause, stood ready with a French army several thousand strong. A French fleet under Admiral de Grasse was on its way to the coast of North America. Stretching his logistical resources to the limit, Washington assembled an American army around New York that would be capable—he hoped—of storming the British fortifications.

Fortunately for the future of the United States (an assault on New York City almost certainly would have failed disastrously), this vision was not to be. Instead of appearing off New York the French fleet materialized off the Virginia Capes, near Yorktown where Lord Cornwallis's army had taken post. Cornwallis was himself a refugee from the Southern Theater, out-generaled in a campaign conducted so brilliantly by Greene and others. The appearance of the French fleet, and its almost providential victory over the Royal Navy at the Battle of the Virginia Capes, changed everything. Urged by Rochambeau, Washington ordered a decisive move to seize upon these circumstances and march south. The stage was set for the war's end game in Virginia.

Whether or not one considers Yorktown part of the Middle Theater, the campaign that led to Cornwallis's surrender was conceived and began on the outskirts of New York City. Washington had followed events in Virginia closely. The war had largely spared the state. There had been fighting in 1775, but it ended quickly with the defeat and departure of the last royal governor, Lord Dunmore. Without British support, Virginia loyalists had been generally quiescent, and did not emerge in force even after Benedict Arnold, and then Lord Cornwallis, brought the war to the state in early 1781.[75] As Lafayette, with Wayne, fenced with Cornwallis over the spring and summer, the commander-in-chief monitored the situation, exchanging frequent correspondence with the young Frenchman. Now, however, he hoped Lafayette could keep Cornwallis occupied at Yorktown while he brought the main army south.

Washington and Rochambeau worked together brilliantly to deceive Clinton about their intentions until it was too late, and then conducted a remarkably efficient and rapid march to Virginia. Cornwallis's strangely halfhearted defense of Yorktown, and Clinton's failure to send aid in time, also contributed to the British defeat and surrender on October 19, 1781.[76] Ultimately, though, the decisive victory was won by a Franco-American army that had been assembled in the Middle Theater.

IN RETROSPECT

The fate of the Revolutionary War was decided in the Middle Theater. It was the site of the war's largest forces, most significant battles in the aggregate, and most important opportunities for victory or defeat. Washington's centrality is beyond question, and except for the winter of 1775–1776 he spent the war's entire duration in the Middle Theater; and it was from there that he directed much of the course of the war in other theaters (which included decisions to let those theaters look after themselves as he tried to concentrate his forces in the Middle Theater). It is true that he lost more battles than he won. The army's survival and national unity, however, ultimately depended on him. Had the British taken advantage of multiple opportunities to destroy the main American army and capture or kill Washington in 1776–1777, it is arguable that they would either have won the war outright or made total American victory impossible.

The alliance with France that was announced in the spring of 1778 was of course central to the ultimate American success, and it is generally regarded as having resulted in large part from the victory at Saratoga. It was not, however, fated to ensure Great Britain's defeat. In fact, in the end everywhere except in North America the French fared badly against their adversaries, just as they had in the past and would again in the future. Franco-American campaigns against Rhode Island and Savannah in 1778–1779 were such dismal failures that they threatened to split the alliance asunder, and many men on both sides of the Atlantic assumed with good reason that it was doomed to fail. Success ultimately depended on the ability of two men—Washington and Rochambeau—to work in tandem. No one else could have accomplished the same.

Except for Yorktown, Saratoga—really a series of battles—is arguably the war's most important military engagement. It did play a vital role in securing the French alliance. After Saratoga little happened in New England of strategic importance. Events in the Southern Theater, meanwhile, however dramatic, impacted the fate of that region but never came close to deciding the victor in the Revolutionary War. The war at sea was a key element at Yorktown and influenced logistics throughout the war, but it did not determine the future of North America any more than did the important but desultory and brutal conflict in the West.

The British might have won the Revolutionary War in the Middle Theater. The Americans did win the war there. Events in that theater never achieved the glamour of Saratoga, Kings Mountain, or Cowpens; but it was in and from the Middle Theater that Washington managed the war. That is, he exercised his function as commander-in-chief to the fullest extent. It was in this theater he built the Continental Army and undertook the complex and delicate political and administrative tasks necessary to keep it in the field. From here he sent north the regiments so critical to success at Saratoga; from here he dispatched Greene to retrieve the American cause in the Carolinas, and then Lafayette, Wayne, and their troops to confront Cornwallis in Virginia. And, of course, it was from the Middle Theater that the Franco-American allies marched to victory at Yorktown. Altogether, these decisions and actions were decisive.

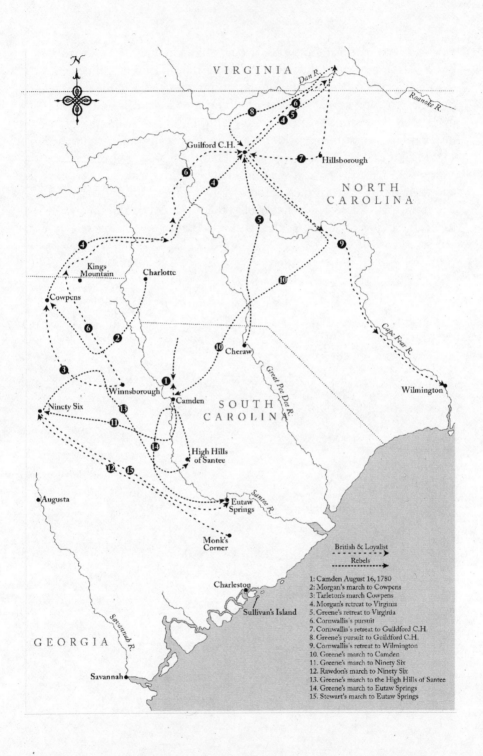

N

VIRGINIA

Dan R.

Roanoke R.

Guilford C.H.

NORTH
CAROLINA

Hillsborough

Cape Fear R.

Kings
Mountain

Charlotte

Cowpens

Cheraw

Great Pee Dee R.

Wilmington

Winnsborough

Camden

SOUTH
CAROLINA

Ninety Six

High Hills
of Santee

Augusta

Santee R.

Monk's
Corner

Eutaw
Springs

Charleston

Sullivan's Island

GEORGIA

Savannah R.

Savannah

British & Loyalist
Rebels

1: Camden August 16, 1780
2: Morgan's march to Cowpens
3: Tarleton's march Cowpens
4: Morgan's retreat to Virginia
5: Greene's retreat to Virginia
6: Cornwallis's pursuit
7: Cornwallis's retreat to Guildford C.H.
8: Greene's pursuit to Guildford C.H.
9: Cornwallis's retreat to Wilmington
10. Greene's march to Camden
11. Greene's march to Ninety Six
12. Rawdon's march to Ninety Six
13. Greene's march to the High Hills of Santee
14. Greene's march to Eutaw Springs
15. Stewart's march to Eutaw Springs

THE
SOUTHERN THEATER

Britain's Last Chance for Victory

Jim Piecuch

B y the spring of 1778, the British government's strategy for suppressing the rebellion in the American colonies had utterly collapsed. General Sir William Howe had occupied Philadelphia and twice defeated General George Washington's Continental Army the previous autumn, but these successes had not proven decisive. Instead, while Washington and Howe battled in Pennsylvania, Major General Horatio Gates and American forces in New York won a resounding victory, halting British lieutenant general John Burgoyne's southward advance in heavy fighting near Saratoga and forcing Burgoyne to surrender his entire army on October 17. This defeat was followed by repercussions even worse than the loss of so many British soldiers; in March 1778 France entered the war as an ally of the United States. British leaders could no longer focus their full attention on subduing the colonies, since troops had to be diverted from that theater to defend other imperial possessions against the French and to prepare for likely Spanish intervention.[1]

Despite these complications, King George III and the secretary of state for the American Department, Lord George Germain, were determined to continue offensive operations against the American rebels, albeit on a more limited scale. Germain, who was responsible for directing the war, decided that the best opportunity to conduct such a campaign would be found in the southern colonies. Lieutenant General Sir Henry Clinton had replaced Howe as commander-in-chief in America in February 1778, and after Clinton had evacuated Philadelphia in accordance with Germain's instructions, the general received a letter reiterating a point that the minister had been emphasizing since Clinton assumed command. "The Recovery of South Carolina and Georgia in the Winter, or even the latter Province, if the Other requires a greater Force than can be spared, is an Object of so much Importance," Germain declared.[2] Having exhausted their military options in the northern and middle colonies, the British government had decided to make a final bid for victory in the Southern Theater. The situation in that region appeared to offer a strong prospect of success, but only if General Clinton and his subordinates were able to capitalize on their advantages.

Germain's decision to focus British efforts in the South was not a new idea. His predecessor as secretary of state for the colonies, William Legge, the Earl of Dartmouth, had begun contemplating what came to be known as the "southern strategy" in 1775, and Germain had embraced the concept when he succeeded Dartmouth that November. Although most officials in London believed that New England was the center of the rebellion and that military efforts should target that region, there were also compelling reasons to undertake operations in the southern colonies, and both Dartmouth and Germain attempted to do so.[3]

The southern strategy rested on three pillars of expected support—from loyalists who maintained their allegiance to the Crown, from Indians anxious to protect their land from settlers and avenge past injustices suffered at the hands of the colonists, and from slaves eager for a chance to obtain freedom—that would together enable the British army to secure the southern colonies with a relatively small force. Georgia's royal governor, Sir James Wright, had informed Dartmouth on June 9, 1775, that "there are still many friends to government here," but warned that without British military support loyalists would succumb to rebel intimidation.[4] Lord William Campbell, royal governor of South Carolina, re-

General Henry Clinton (1730–1795) commanded British land forces during the unsuccessful effort to capture Charleston in 1776. He returned to South Carolina in 1780 with a large force and captured the city and its entire garrison. (*New York Public Library*)

layed a report from Thomas Fletchall, a militia colonel in the colony's backcountry, that 4,000 loyalists were ready to take up arms. The same estimate was given to Campbell by Moses Kirkland, another prominent backcountry loyalist, who added that the loyalists were ready to cooperate with British troops once they were provided with arms and experienced officers.[5] From North Carolina, royal governor Josiah Martin predicted in 1775 that 20,000 loyalists were ready to take up arms to uphold British authority, although by early 1776 he had reduced that estimate to 9,000 men.[6] There were far fewer loyalists in Virginia, yet that colony's royal governor, John Murray, Earl of Dunmore, had other plans in mind to check the rebels in his province.[7]

Both Dartmouth and Germain welcomed the possibility of loyalist support and intended to utilize the loyalists to help topple the rebel governments in the southern colonies and then secure the territory while British troops expanded their conquests. The king's ministers, however, along with many members of Parliament, had serious qualms about what role, if any, to assign to the Crown's Indian allies. Powerful Native nations bordered the rebellious colonies from New York to Georgia, but in the South the Indians were more numerous in proportion to the neighboring colonists. Together, the four major southern nations—Cherokees, Creeks, Choctaws, and Chickasaws—could field a total of some 14,000 warriors, and John Stuart, the superintendent of Indian affairs for the region south of the Ohio River, informed General Thomas Gage in March 1775 that the Chickasaws and Choctaws were "in the most friendly Disposition towards us," and later reported that the Cherokees and Creeks also remained favorable toward the British but lacked arms and ammunition. Gage was willing to employ the Indians and advised Dartmouth in June that "we must not be tender of calling upon the Savages" for assistance.[8]

Other officials agreed with Gage, including General James Grant, who declared that "a few scalps taken by Indians . . . would operate more upon the minds" of the rebels "than any other Loss they can sustain." East Florida governor Patrick Tonyn insisted that "the Americans are a thousand times more in dread of the Savages than of any European troops."[9] Dartmouth had been uncertain about whether or not to involve Britain's Native allies against the rebels, but Germain recognized the Indians' potential value. He also knew that calling upon the Indians for military assistance was "a measure of a very delicate nature," because many members of Parliament were staunchly opposed to employing Indians to fight against people whom they considered fellow Britons. Germain therefore hesitated to order his generals in America to seek aid from the Natives.[10]

While Germain pondered whether to utilize the Crown's Indian allies, he also grappled with the even more troublesome question of if and how slaves might be employed in the war. The large slave population in the four southernmost colonies represented what was perhaps the region's greatest weakness. Of the approximately 500,000 slaves in the thirteen colonies at the start to the war, the vast majority labored on southern plantations. Georgia was home to nearly 25,000 slaves, a number almost equal to the colony's white population. South Carolina's slaves outnumbered its white inhabitants by a margin of 104,000 to 70,000. The more than 200,000 slaves in Virginia constituted 40 percent of that colony's population, and there were approximately 75,000 slaves in North Carolina.[11] Rebel leaders in the South recognized that the large slave population there made them particularly vulnerable. Archibald Bulloch and John Houstoun, representing Georgia in the Second Continental Congress, told John Adams in September 1775 "that if 1000 regular Troops should land in Georgia and their commander be provided with Arms and Cloaths enough, and proclaim Freedom to all the Negroes who would join his Camp, 20,000 Negroes" from Georgia and South Carolina would join the British force within two weeks. The only reason the British were unlikely to do so, the Georgians believed, was "that all the Kings Friends and Tools of Government have large Plantations and Property in Negroes" and would lose their slaves as well.[12]

The fear of alienating loyalists was only one reason why British officials showed great reluctance in developing a policy to take advantage of the South's slaves. Petitions from British merchants and from several cities urged King George III not to employ slaves against the rebels, asserting that such a plan was horrific. Similar denunciations appeared in the press, and members of Parliament also voiced opposition. Edmund Burke, who clearly did not understand southern colonists' views on slavery, argued that if the British attempted to arm the slaves, the rebels would do the same thing and field armed slaves against the king's troops. When William Lyttelton, a former royal governor of South Carolina, introduced a measure in the House of Commons in October proposing to send "a few regiments" to the South so that "the negroes would rise, and embrue their hands in the blood of their masters," the proposal was defeated by a vote of 278–108.[13]

Nevertheless, many British officials favored arming slaves, including generals Thomas Gage and John Burgoyne. A captain in the 20th Regiment of Foot proposed that the army enlist 2,000 Catholics in Ireland and dispatch them to Chesapeake Bay, where they could be reinforced by "the bravest & most ingenious of the black Slaves." Another officer suggested that a regiment of slaves should be recruited in the British West Indies, with those who enlisted being granted their freedom after the war. Several plantation owners in the West Indies even offered to provide slaves for military service if the government requested them. Fearing the controversy this would create, the king's ministers took no action on these proposals.[14]

Overleaf: "A general map of the southern British colonies in America, comprehending North and South Carolina, Georgia, East and West Florida, with the neighboring Indian countries, from the modern surveys of Engineer de Brahm, Capt. Collet, Mouzon, & others, and from the large hydrographical survey of the coasts of East and West Florida," 1776. From late 1775 until 1782, fighting raged across the southern colonies. The most intense phase of the southern campaign was waged across the Carolinas in 1780 and 1781. (*Library of Congress*)

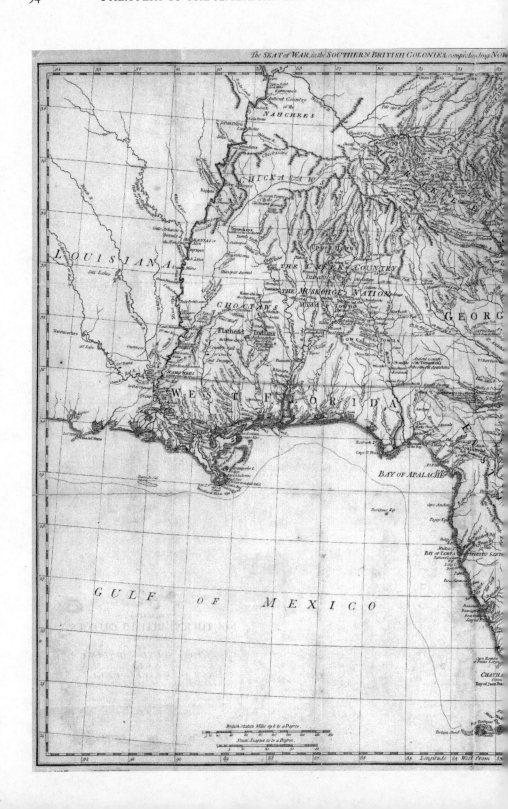

...being NORTH and SOUTH CAROLINA, GEORGIA, EAST and WEST FLORIDA, &c.

VIRGINIA

NORTH CAROLINA

SOUTH CAROLINA

GEORGIA

ATLANTIC or WESTERN OCEAN

PLAN OF CHARLESTOWN.

PLAN OF St. AUGUSTINE.

E. FLORIDA

GULF OF FLORIDA

GREAT BANK OF BAHAMA

THE FLORIDA STREAM

A GENERAL MAP OF THE
SOUTHERN BRITISH COLONIES
IN AMERICA,
comprehending
NORTH AND SOUTH CAROLINA,
GEORGIA,
EAST AND WEST FLORIDA,
with THE NEIGHBOURING INDIAN COUNTRIES,
From the Modern Surveys of
Engineer de Brahm, Capt. Collet, Mouzon & Others;
and from the Large Hydrographical Survey of the Coasts
of East and West Florida,
By B. ROMANS,
1776

Lord Dartmouth did decide to undertake a southern campaign, and ordered General Sir William Howe, who had replaced Gage as commander of the British army in America, to detach "a respectable force" to the South to support the loyalists. Howe's troops would be reinforced with additional units from Britain, and Dartmouth hoped that this force could "restore Order and Government" in Virginia, the Carolinas, and Georgia.[15] Howe protested that he preferred to focus his efforts on New York, but complied with the order, sending Major General Henry Clinton with more than 1,200 troops from Boston on January 20, 1776, to meet the force from Britain off the southern coast.[16] Dartmouth had informed Howe and Governor Martin of North Carolina that the reinforcements from Britain would sail from Cork in Ireland on December 1, 1775; by that time, Germain had succeeded Dartmouth and continued to pursue his predecessor's plan. Unfortunately for the British and the loyalists, delays disrupted Dartmouth and Germain's timetable and the fleet did not depart Cork until February 10, 1776. Shortly afterward, the ships were dispersed by bad weather, and the first vessels did not begin sailing into the mouth of the Cape Fear River in North Carolina until late April.[17]

Meanwhile, loyalists in the Carolinas and Governor Dunmore in Virginia took action on their own initiative. When it became apparent to the rebel council of safety in Charleston that much of the populace in the backcountry remained committed to the royal government, an attempt was made to persuade them to shift their allegiance to the revolutionary leaders. However, the trio of William Henry Drayton and the reverends William Tennent and Oliver Hart won few converts as they roved across the backcountry in August 1775. The rebels then resorted to economic pressure, announcing that anyone who did not sign an oath supporting the actions of the Continental Congress would be prohibited from conducting trade or using mills and ferries.[18] Tensions continued, and hostile actions by both sides provoked a confrontation at the town of Ninety Six, where some 2,000 loyalist militiamen surrounded a slightly smaller number of rebel militia in mid-November. After a brief siege the parties signed a treaty agreeing to end hostilities until the council of safety and Governor Campbell could settle the differences between the contending groups. In reality, the agreement was moot since the council refused to deal with Campbell. Ignorant of the situation in Charleston, both forces disbanded, but the loyalists had barely reached home when additional units of rebel militia from South and North Carolina marched through the backcountry, arrested loyalist leaders, and skirmished with and dispersed small groups of loyalists gathering in opposition. By the end of December, the loyalists in South Carolina had been neutralized.[19]

Unaware that the British force had not sailed from Cork on the scheduled date, Governor Martin and the loyalists in North Carolina also took action and were defeated. Martin had been forced to take refuge aboard a British warship in the Cape Fear River on July 18, 1775, but he remained confident that the colony's numerous loyalists, including some merchants and planters along with former Regulators from the piedmont region, who had opposed the colonial government before their defeat in 1771, and the large population of Highland Scots living in the vicinity of Cross Creek (present-day Fayetteville) could regain control of North Carolina with the aid of British troops. The governor appointed Allan MacDonald brigadier general of militia, and his wife, the charismatic Flora MacDonald, who had once been imprisoned in the Tower of London for her role in the unsuccessful effort in 1745–1746 to restore Prince Charles Edward of the deposed Stuart family to the British throne, raised a large number of recruits to serve under her husband. On January 10, 1776, believing that the arrival of the British fleet was imminent, Martin called upon the loyalists to take action. About 1,500 Highlanders assembled near Cross Creek and on February 18 began marching toward the coast to meet the British.[20]

North Carolina's rebel government learned of the Highlanders' activities and took steps to halt them, ordering Colonel James Moore's Continental regiment and militia under colonels Alexander Lillington, John Ashe, and Richard Caswell to Moore's Creek Bridge, less than twenty miles from Wilmington. The rebel soldiers dug in along the east side of the creek, removed the planks from the bridge, and greased the support timbers that remained. The loyalists attacked on February 27, suffering fifty casualties in a futile attempt to cross the slippery beams of the skeletal bridge. They decided to retreat, but nearly half of them, including General MacDonald, were captured by the pursuing Americans, who lost only one man killed and one wounded in the engagement.[21] The North Carolina rebels had put an end to the threat posed by the colony's loyalists, at least temporarily.

Virginia's royal governor John Murray, Earl of Dunmore, had been forced to flee the capital at Williamsburg in early June 1775 and take refuge aboard the British warship HMS *Fowey*. Although there were far fewer loyalists to assist him in Virginia than there were in the Carolinas, Dunmore offset the deficiency by taking more drastic actions. He assembled a small fleet in the James River, seized trading vessels and their cargoes, and launched raids against riverside plantations, where he took many slaves aboard his flotilla.[22] While officials in London dithered and agonized over how or even whether to employ slaves, Dunmore acted. He began arming the slaves who joined him during his raids, and on November 7, 1775, he made his policy official, issuing a proclamation summoning loyalists to the king's standard and announcing, "I do hereby further declare all indented servants, Negroes, or others, (appertaining to Rebels,) free, that are able and willing to bear arms, they joining His Majesty's Troops, as soon as may be."[23]

Rebel Virginians, and indeed people throughout the colonies, regardless of their political views, were horrified by Dunmore's proclamation, fearing that it might incite a general slave insurrection. Yet Dunmore had little choice if he wanted to conduct operations in Virginia; he was able to muster only 300 loyalists, sailors, and regular troops to man his fleet. An estimated 800 slaves joined Dunmore. The men, designated the Ethiopian Regiment, were armed and given uniforms with a sash proclaiming "Liberty to Slaves." On November 14, 1775, Dunmore's army defeated a force of rebel militia at Kemp's Landing on the Elizabeth River. However, on December 9, at Great Bridge on the Elizabeth River ten miles from Norfolk, Dunmore encountered a strong rebel force of over 1,000 men under Colonel William Woodford. The governor ordered his 600 "Ethiopians," sailors, loyalists, and handful of regulars to attack and dislodge the enemy, but the British could only advance with six men abreast across the narrow bridge against Americans protected by fortifications. Dunmore's force was repulsed after suffering 61 casualties. Only one American was wounded. The British vessels bombarded Norfolk on January 1, 1776, before resuming their raids in the Chesapeake Bay. These operations accomplished little. Many of the slaves who had joined Dunmore fell victim to smallpox, greatly reducing his strength, and on August 6 he abandoned his base on St. George's Island in the Potomac River, destroyed many of his small vessels, and sailed for New York with the 300 liberated slave soldiers healthy enough for duty.[24]

Lack of coordination had resulted in the loyalists of Virginia and the Carolinas fighting independently and unsupported, and in their subsequent defeat. The support that might have enabled them to succeed arrived too late. On March 12 Clinton's detachment from Boston reached Cape Fear, where he learned of the Highlanders' failure and found no sign of the fleet from Cork. As he waited for the ships to arrive, he considered his options. Admiral Sir Peter Parker urged an attack on Charleston, South Carolina, while Clinton, who had orders to join Howe's expedition against New York after concluding operations in the South, preferred to sail to the Chesapeake and assist Dunmore and then return to the North. Parker insisted on attacking Charleston, a measure that had been suggested earlier by both Dartmouth and Germain and backed strongly by deposed royal governor Lord William Campbell. Clinton reluctantly dropped his objection, and when the last ships from the scattered Cork fleet reached Cape Fear at the end of May, the combined force sailed south.[25]

The rebels in South Carolina had not remained idle after suppressing the loyalists in the backcountry. Concerned with the possibility of a British attack on Charleston, the South Carolina council of safety, acting as the executive authority for the rebel government, proposed fortifying the approaches to the city. As work began on the defenses, the Continental Congress appointed Major General Charles Lee to command the Southern Department, and Lee set out in March, gathering nearly 2,000 Continental troops from Virginia and North Carolina as he traveled to reinforce the nearly 2,000 South Carolina Continentals at Charleston. South Carolina's new governor, John Rutledge, had assembled an even greater number of militia, some 2,700 men, to aid in defending the city.[26]

Lee arrived on June 4, to the relief of Charleston's defenders and inhabitants, who had been thrown into a panic by the arrival of Parker's fleet outside the harbor earlier that day. Lee's cool demeanor calmed both troops and citizens, and he immediately set about inspecting the fortifications. He was not impressed. The key to Charleston's defense was a partially completed fort built of sand and palmetto logs at the southern end of Sullivan's Island. Lee described the post as a "slaughter pen" and demanded it be evacuated. Governor Rutledge and the ranking South Carolina Continental officer in Charleston, Colonel William Moultrie, refused, and Lee finally relented and did his best to see that the fort was strengthened. The Americans also fortified the northern end of Sullivan's Island and posted troops and militia to guard against an attack from the British forces that had landed on neighboring Long Island to the north.[27]

The British attacked on June 28. Parker planned to bombard Fort Sullivan, as it was then called (it was later renamed Fort Moultrie), while Clinton's infantry crossed Breach Inlet, the channel separating Sullivan's Island from Long Island, to assist in taking the fort. The ensuing battle was a fiasco for the British. Clinton had been informed by local inhabitants that the water's depth in Breach Inlet was only eighteen inches at low tide, which would enable his infantry to wade across easily. When Clinton went to verify the information, he found that it was incorrect; the water at low tide was seven feet deep. Unwilling to risk a piecemeal crossing in flatboats against an entrenched enemy, Clinton could only make a futile demonstration in hopes of distracting the American defenders across the inlet, doing nothing more than exchanging musket fire at a range too great to be effective.[28]

Parker's fleet moved against the American fort and its 31 guns, the heaviest firing twenty-six-pound shot. His nine warships included a "bomb ketch" that in addition to its artillery carried a large mortar capable of lobbing thirteen-inch shot over the fort's walls. Altogether, the British vessels mounted over 270 guns, while only between 12 and 15 of the fort's guns were in position to fire on the attacking ships. Parker positioned his vessels within four hundred yards of the fort and opened fire shortly before noon. The British barrage caused significant damage to some parts of the fort, but not enough to halt the rebels' fire. Most of the fleet's hits were absorbed by the spongy palmetto logs and the sand they enclosed, minimizing their effect. At about noon, Parker sent three frigates to enfilade Fort Sullivan's right wall; however, all three ran aground on a sandbar. Meanwhile the rebels, firing slowly and carefully to conserve their limited supply of gunpowder, inflicted serious damage on several British warships. As darkness approached, Parker broke off the engagement.[29]

The American defenders suffered losses of 12 killed and 25 wounded, while Parker's crews reported a total of 205 casualties. Among the wounded was Lord William Campbell, the colony's royal governor. His injury became infected, never healed, and ultimately caused Campbell's death in 1778. In addition to the human toll, the fort's guns had badly damaged several British ships, and the frigate HMS *Acteon*, unable to be freed from the sandbar, was burned by its crew the next day. The British lingered in the area for a few weeks, Clinton departing with his troops on July 21 and the navy leaving on August 2. The rebels had won their biggest victory of the war thus far.[30]

The failure to capture Charleston that marked the unsuccessful end of initial British operations in the South "in no way dampened Britain's optimistic view" of the potential for successful operations in the region.[31] Southern loyalists had openly demonstrated their adherence to the Crown by taking up arms, unsupported, against the rebels. Charleston remained vulnerable to naval assault, as did Savannah, Georgia, and as Dunmore had demonstrated, the Chesapeake Bay offered abundant opportunities for combined land and naval operations. Furthermore, the British colony of East Florida on Georgia's southern border remained staunchly loyal, and its determined, militarily experienced governor, Patrick Tonyn, provided land grants for a steady influx of loyalist refugees from the rebellious southern colonies. Tonyn also used his authority as commander-in-chief of his province's forces, excluding the regular troops assigned to garrison St. Augustine, to organize refugees into provincial military units with the intention of employing them offensively against the rebels.[32]

The opportunities for the British to operate along the coast and from their base in East Florida, however, were largely offset by the geography and settlement patterns in the interior of the southern colonies, which presented difficulties that would also trouble any large American force conducting an inland campaign. Rivers provided the primary means of transportation, with the few existing roads little more than sandy trails that turned to mud in rainy weather. Most of the rivers flowed northwest to southeast, could be crossed only at widely scattered fords or ferries, and rose rapidly during times of heavy rain. The bulk of the population lived on or near the rivers; American lieutenant colonel Henry "Light Horse Harry" Lee, who served in the Carolinas and Georgia throughout 1781, noted that "the settlements on the river are rich and populous. . . . Therefore the motions of the army must be from river to river" to procure supplies. However, rebels and loyalists alike destroyed crops or concealed livestock from their enemies, forcing troops to forage extensively in search of food. In addition to shortages of provisions, the troops also had to deal with mosquitoes and other bothersome insects, and in summer, the intense heat. One British soldier later described marching "under the rage of a burning sun . . . sinking under the most excessive fatigue, not only destitute of every comfort, but almost of every necessary" required for survival. In combination with diseases such as malaria and yellow fever, exhaustion and heat would render hundreds of soldiers on both sides unfit for duty when the South became the focal point of the war.[33]

Although the British temporarily abandoned major efforts in the South after their defeat at Charleston, fighting continued in the region. On July 1, Cherokee militants led by Dragging Canoe launched attacks across the southern frontier from Virginia to Georgia. John Stuart, Britain's superintendent of the Southern Indian Department, had tried to dissuade the Cherokees from going to war, as had most of the nation's more cautious leaders, including Dragging Canoe's father, Attakulla Kulla. The militants, angered by years of mistreatment by the colonists, ignored this advice. Aided by loyalist refugees who disguised themselves as Indians, the Cherokees achieved some initial success, but by mid-autumn militia from Virginia, the Carolinas, and Georgia had launched a counteroffensive that devastated Cherokee towns and crops and forced that nation's leaders to sue for peace. Undeterred by the defeat, Dragging Canoe and his followers moved farther west and continued to harass the frontier settlements.[34]

In Georgia, the revolutionary movement had advanced more slowly, due largely to the substantial number of loyalists there. One observer remarked in December 1775 that "in this province two out of three are friends to government, but as there is neither ships nor troops to protect them, they know it is in vain to oppose the current, as the Carolina people are all in arms."[35] When a British naval force anchored off Savannah in mid-January 1776 to procure rice for the British troops in Boston, the rebels took decisive action, including arresting the royal governor, Sir James Wright, and other prominent loyalists who were then released on parole. Wright violated his parole and escaped to the British fleet, and fighting between rebel Georgians and the Royal Navy broke out on March 3, after which the British, having secured a quantity of rice, sailed for Boston. Many loyalists also took the opportunity to escape, and the rebels assumed complete political control of the province.[36]

The rebel council of safety ordered Georgian troops to raid East Florida, and several incursions between May and July destroyed plantations along the St. Mary's River. Southern governors and Continental Army commander Charles Lee decided to follow up the raids with an invasion of East Florida. Lee assembled a force of Georgians, South Carolinians, and Virginians in August and marched southward, but got no farther than Sunbury, a Georgia port town forty miles south of Savannah, when supply shortages and widespread illness among the troops forced Lee to cancel the operation. Tonyn retaliated by dispatching loyalist rangers to raid southern Georgia; in October they burned plantations at Beard's Bluff and in the area south of the Altamaha River, meeting little opposition.[37]

Recognizing the weakness of the rebels along the East Florida border, Tonyn ordered another raid in February 1777 to harass the Americans and seize cattle to feed the troops and refugees in St. Augustine. Loyalist rangers and Creek and Seminole Indians captured Fort McIntosh and its garrison on February 18, and rounded up two thousand cattle before returning. A supporting force of British regulars skirmished with rebel troops at the Altamaha River and then it too withdrew.[38]

The successful British raid convinced Georgia's rebel leaders that it was necessary to invade and occupy East Florida to put an end to such threats. Major General Robert Howe, who had replaced Lee as Continental commander in the South, disapproved and declined to provide support, so the Georgians acted alone. After pushing aside sporadic resistance from small parties of Indians, the Georgians reached the St. Mary's River on May 12 but did not meet the expected naval force that had been sent to assist them. During the night of May 14, Indians attacked the Georgians' camp and captured about a hundred horses. The American commander, Colonel John Baker, decided to move his camp to Thomas Creek, where his nearly 200 men were attacked on May 17 by a slightly larger force of loyalist rangers and Indians. Baker ordered a retreat, directly into 100 British regulars moving to outflank his troops. The rebels fled into a swamp, losing three men killed and thirty-one captured. The next day the naval prong of the invasion force reached Amelia Island. Upon learning of Baker's defeat, the commander of the seaborne troops, Colonel Samuel Elbert, decided a further advance was too risky and canceled the invasion.[39]

With the American withdrawal, the initiative again passed to the British. Loyalist raiders, frequently accompanied by allied Indians, struck repeatedly against Georgia in the summer and autumn. In early 1778 they renewed their attacks, capturing Fort Barrington on the Altamaha River on March 13. The ease with which the incursions were carried out, and the Georgians' ineffective resistance, convinced Governor Tonyn that the British had sufficient strength in East Florida to conquer Georgia. In April he informed General Sir William Howe that "with this [St. Augustine] Garrison the Rangers and Indians, the province of Georgia may be taken in possession, which will give a fair opportunity to the Loyalists in South Carolina to show themselves." If the latter state's loyalists were as numerous as reported, Tonyn asserted, "I should apprehend that province would soon be compelled to subjection."[40]

Even while Tonyn was composing his letter, loyalists were providing further proof of their willingness to support the Crown. By late March about 400 loyalists from the North and South Carolina backcountry, all mounted, decided to escape to East Florida to avoid rebel persecution. As they moved across South Carolina, a panicked Governor Rawlins Lowndes wrote that "The Tories . . . have risen, and as if informed by the same spirit and moved by the same spring, have put themselves in motion at one and the same time throughout all parts of the state." As they marched they were joined by an additional 200 men, and on April 3 they crossed the Savannah River into Georgia. The South Carolina rebel militia managed to prevent additional loyalist parties from joining the main group, but in Georgia, Major General Howe failed to intercept the refugees. The loyalists gathered another 200 Georgians before arriving safely at St. Augustine to provide a valuable reinforcement to East Florida's garrison.[41]

The rebels responded to these events by undertaking a third invasion of East Florida. Once again Howe opposed the plan, although in the face of strong political pressure from the governments of the southern states he began organizing an invasion force. By mid-May the Americans reached Fort Tonyn on the St. Mary's River, which the British had evacuated and burned. Despite this success, Howe's army was plagued by desertion; many of the men who had volunteered to participate in the invasion were loyalists who planned to join the British as soon as they were close enough to do so. Skirmishing and harassment from parties of loyalist rangers further impeded the expedition. Even worse, the American commanders began arguing among themselves. Georgia governor John Houstoun and South Carolina militia brigadier general Andrew Williamson refused to take orders from Howe, while the officer commanding the naval squadron wanted to retreat and would not take orders from any officers of the land forces. Howe tried unsuccessfully to bring everyone together and formulate a plan, yet in the end the only point the contentious commanders could agree on was to retreat. On July 14 the Americans began their withdrawal. Major General Augustine Prevost, commander of the regular troops at St. Augustine, wrote dismissively of the rebel invasion that he had been "under very little apprehension of the enemy being able to effect any thing of consequence."[42]

The defeat of the rebel invasions of East Florida, Governor Tonyn's confidence that Georgia could be easily conquered based on the many successful raids carried out by loyalists, Indians, and regulars against that state, and the escape of so many loyalists to St. Augustine in 1778, together indicated that the prospects for large-scale British operations in the South were promising. Lord George Germain conceded in his March 1778 instructions to Clinton that because France had intervened on the Americans' side, "the War must be prosecuted upon a different Plan from That upon which it has hitherto been carried on." As the new commander-in-chief of the British army in America, Clinton was to focus his efforts during the summer campaign on raiding the New England coast and trying to force George Washington to fight a decisive battle. Regardless of whether these operations succeeded, Germain expected that they would be concluded by October and Clinton could then redirect his efforts southward. "It is the King's intention that an Attack should be made upon the Southern Colonies, with a View to the Conquest & Possession of Georgia & South Carolina," the minister explained. Once the rebels in Georgia had been defeated by British troops, loyalists could maintain control of the province while the British army moved against South Carolina.[43]

Germain expected Clinton to place his primary reliance upon the loyalists, although by this time he also expected Clinton and other British commanders to take advantage of whatever assistance Britain's Indian allies could provide. However, Germain remained reluctant to include the South's slaves in his plans, thereby leaving any decisions regarding their role to the army officers conducting the southern campaign.[44]

British officials were not the only ones who expected that a shift of their military efforts to the South was likely to be successful. American leaders in the southern states, civil and military alike, feared the consequences of a British invasion. Lieutenant Colonel John Laurens, an aide to George Washington and son of prominent South Carolina planter and politician Henry Laurens, commented on the probable outcome of a British offensive in South Carolina in his commonplace book. The British, he wrote, planned "to prosecute a vigorous offensive" in the South, and "as soon as an opening is given they will unquestionably proceed. . . . The feeble and mixed population of So Carolina—the number of disaffected—the great proportion of Slaves— the vicinity of warlike Savages almost devoted to the British interests render that Country less capable of its efforts for its defence than any other state." Laurens believed that once Clinton's forces had secured South Carolina, they would recruit the "numerous" loyalists in that state, who would soon be joined by "those of No Carolina—who will no longer be contained by the force of that Country. The dismemberment of two States. So great an acquisition of Territory to the Enemy—so considerable a Reinforcemt to their army—will enable them to continue their progress farther Northward— and it is not easy to limit their successes." Laurens's pessimistic assessment was echoed by those of South Carolina governor John Rutledge, Continental major general Benjamin Lincoln, and many other rebel officials.[45]

Clinton put the first phase of his plan into effect in November 1778, when he dispatched Lieutenant Colonel Archibald Campbell and some 3,000 troops from New York with orders to capture Savannah. Campbell reached Tybee Island on December 23, sent parties ashore to reconnoiter, and on December 29 brought his whole force ashore just south of Savannah. General Howe, who had resigned his command and was awaiting his replacement, General Lincoln, nevertheless took the field and posted his force of nearly 1,000 men on ground overlooking a rice swamp. If Campbell made a frontal attack, his troops would have to wade through the swamp and then climb to the plateau under heavy musket and artillery fire. Campbell climbed a tree to get a better view of the American lines, desperately seeking to avoid a costly frontal assault.[46]

Campbell's dilemma was resolved when a slave appeared with crucial information. The man, whose name has been recorded as either Quash or Quamino Dolly, told Campbell that "he could lead the Troops without Artillery through the Swamp upon the Enemy's Right." Campbell dispatched nearly 600 men to follow the slave, and they emerged from the swamp to catch the Americans completely by surprise. As the rebels' right flank crumbled, Campbell ordered a frontal assault. The Americans were routed, losing about 100 men killed and 450 captured, while British casualties totaled only 26 men. Campbell's troops soon reformed and marched into Savannah.[47]

In mid-January 1779 Campbell was reinforced by about 1,000 troops from St. Augustine under General Prevost, who had been ordered to march northward and support the force from New York. En route to Savannah, Prevost had captured Sunbury, Georgia's second-largest town, along with Fort Morris which protected it. Prevost left a small garrison at the post. The Georgia coast was now entirely in British hands.[48]

Having organized loyalist militia forces in Savannah and the inland communities as far as Ebenezer, Campbell wrote on January 19 that "I have got the Country in Arms against the Congress." Although he had been given a temporary commission as governor of the colony, Campbell urged the government to "hurry out a Proper Governour for this Province," believing that the restoration of British civil authority would win over those Georgians whose allegiance was wavering.[49] At the beginning of March, Germain ordered deposed royal governor Sir James Wright to return to Georgia, reassume his office, and make arrangements for the province's inhabitants to elect a legislature. This would provide an example to rebels in other colonies that the British did not intend "to govern America by Military Law; but, on the contrary, to allow them all the Benefits of a local Legislature, & their former Civil Constitution."[50]

Meanwhile, Campbell set out to complete the conquest of Georgia by seizing Augusta, the only significant town in the backcountry. He marched from Ebenezer with 900 men on January 24. The British occupied the town without resistance on January 31, and within a few days Campbell reported that 1,400 men "had joined us with their Arms; and took the Oath of Allegiance." To his dismay, however, Campbell found that it was too dangerous to keep his troops at Augusta. Rebel forces were gathering in strength on the South Carolina side of the Savannah River, and could easily interpose between his detachment and the main British army at Savannah. Furthermore, anticipated help from the Creek Indians had failed to materialize. The latter problem was the result of difficulties in communication. Stuart, who was based in Pensacola in British West Florida, had received orders to assemble the Creeks and bring them to Augusta, but by the time British agents journeyed to the scattered Creek towns and the warriors returned from their winter hunt, the delay was too great and Campbell evacuated Augusta on February 14.[51]

The British withdrawal brought harsh consequences for the loyalists who had supported Campbell. Some were hanged or simply executed, many had their houses burned, and others pleaded for clemency. Several told rebel officer John Dooly that they "were forced to Take the oath," and Dooly pointed out to his superiors that "there is a Good Many Good Men" who would join the Americans "if thay Can be pardond."[52] Most officers chose a moderate course and offered pardons to the loyalists, a course supported by exiled Georgia governor John Wereat despite the criticism of those who advocated harsher policies and claimed that he "coddled Tories."[53]

Several hundred Carolina loyalists on their way to join Campbell suffered a worse fate than did the loyalists of Augusta. James Boyd, a South Carolina refugee, had accompanied Campbell's expedition from New York with a colonel's commission from General Clinton issued on Boyd's promise to raise troops for the Crown. Boyd left Savannah shortly after its capture, traveling to the backcountry to recruit. After enlisting some 600 South Carolinians and nearly 200 men from North Carolina, Boyd marched to Augusta, pursued by rebel South Carolina militia under Andrew Pickens. Unaware that Campbell had left Augusta earlier in the day, Boyd halted along Kettle Creek on February 14 to rest his men. Pickens arrived and launched a surprise attack, scattering the loyalists. Boyd organized some of his men and resisted stoutly until he was mortally wounded and the loyalists remaining on the field retreated. Only 270 survivors reached the British lines outside of Savannah. Pickens captured and paroled most of Boyd's followers, declaring that the battle at Kettle Creek was "the severest check and chastisement the Tories ever received in Georgia or South Carolina."[54]

The British soon countered with a victory of their own. On January 29, North Carolina militia brigadier general John Ashe arrived near Augusta with about 1,100 men to reinforce the troops across the Savannah River from Campbell. When Campbell withdrew from Augusta, the new Continental commander in the South, Major General Benjamin Lincoln,

ordered Ashe to cross the river with his militia and the Georgia Continentals, some 1,300 men altogether, and follow the British. After crossing
Briar Creek, a tributary of the Savannah, the British burned the bridge.
Ashe brought up his troops and set up camp until the bridge could be
repaired. Campbell had instructions to return to Britain, but before leaving he proposed to Lieutenant Colonel James Mark Prevost, who had
assumed command of the detachment retreating from Augusta, that
troops be sent upstream on Briar Creek to outflank and attack the Americans. Prevost sent 500 men back toward Ashe's position on March 1 to
draw the rebels' attention, while about 900 British and provincial soldiers
carried out the flanking maneuver. These troops attacked the rebels on
March 3, routed the militia, and then overwhelmed the handful of Continentals. At a cost of only 16 casualties, the British captured 227 Americans and killed or wounded many more; Prevost estimated the rebel
dead on the battlefield at 150.[55]

The Battle of Briar Creek was followed by a lull in both sides' activity
as the rival commanders weighed future plans. In May, Virginia became
the scene of action for the first time in nearly three years when Clinton
sent a naval force under Admiral Sir George Collier carrying 1,800 troops
commanded by Brigadier General Edward Mathew to the Chesapeake
Bay. Collier and Mathew's objectives were to prevent Virginia troops
from reinforcing Washington's army and to destroy supplies intended for
the southern army, along with as many rebel ships as possible. The British
occupied Portsmouth on May 10 and used the town as a base for two
weeks, striking at American ships and supply depots in the area. They
seized or destroyed as many as 150 vessels, vast amounts of military supplies, and three thousand barrels of tobacco. Several plantations were also
burned. Opposition was so feeble that the British did not suffer a single
casualty. Collier was pleased to find many loyalists at Portsmouth and
suggested establishing a naval base there so that the navy might take advantage of its excellent port, but Mathew insisted on conforming to the
letter of his orders and the expedition returned to New York.[56]

Benjamin Lincoln had spent the weeks after Ashe's defeat at Briar
Creek building his army with the help of North Carolina governor
Richard Caswell and his South Carolina counterpart, John Rutledge. As
militia from both states arrived in Lincoln's camp at Black Swamp, South
Carolina, Lincoln's confidence grew. He decided to take action, writing

Rutledge that "I think we might act offensively with every rational hope of success." Lincoln planned to march up the Savannah River, cross into Georgia at Augusta, then push southward in an effort to press the British forces outside Savannah into the city. To secure South Carolina from any British incursions, Lincoln left Brigadier General William Moultrie and a detachment of troops at Black Swamp to guard the river crossings.[57]

Realizing that his force was too small to oppose Lincoln, especially if the Americans marched down the Savannah and united with Moultrie's men, General Augustine Prevost decided on a bold maneuver that he expected would upset Lincoln's plans. During the night of April 29, 2,000 British troops crossed the Savannah near Purysburg. The next morning they attacked Moultrie's 1,200 troops, nearly 1,000 of whom were militia. After a brief skirmish with a small force of Continentals, Prevost secured his position on the north bank of the river and Moultrie began to fall back. Moultrie wrote to inform Lincoln of the British move, but Lincoln dismissed Prevost's actions as a feint; he did, however, send 300 Continentals to reinforce Moultrie and asked Governor Rutledge to send Moultrie more militia. The American retreat increased in speed and disorder, with many of the militia leaving the detachment to protect their families. "The enemy carried everything before them with fire and sword," Moultrie observed.[58]

Moultrie and the remnants of his force reached Charleston on May 8, where he found "people frightened out of their wits." Three days later Prevost crossed the Ashley River to Charleston neck. As the British advanced, Polish count Casimir Pulaski, a brigadier general in the Continental Army, made a sortie from Charleston to attack Prevost's advance guard. Pulaski was repulsed with a loss of 14 killed, 42 captured, and an unknown number of wounded. The British then took up a position outside the line of defenses protecting the city.[59]

At the insistence of Governor Rutledge and the state's executive council, Moultrie was forced, against his own judgment, to enter into negotiations with Prevost regarding the possible surrender of the city. Prevost offered to pardon any inhabitant who would take the oath of allegiance to Britain; all others would become prisoners of war. Fearing that the city's defenders could not withstand an assault, state officials countered with an offer to declare South Carolina neutral for the remainder of the war if Charleston was spared, with the state's final status to be determined

As commander of the British force at St. Augustine, General Augustine Prevost (1723–1786), left, repelled three American attacks on East Florida before taking most of his force to Georgia, where he defeated a combined Franco-American attack during the siege of Savannah in 1779. Continental general William Moultrie (1730–1805), right, led South Carolina forces that withstood two British attempts to take Charleston, in 1776 and 1779. He was taken prisoner when Sir Henry Clinton's army captured Charleston in May 1780. (*Library of Congress*)

by negotiations at the conclusion of the war. Prevost rejected the proposal.[60] Many historians have argued that Prevost was foolish to reject the neutrality offer, although in actuality his decision was wise. He had no authority to discuss political matters, nor could he expect that General Lincoln and the southern Continental Army would accede to the agreement and withdraw from the state. Neither was it likely that committed South Carolina rebels outside of Charleston would accept the agreement and lay down their arms. Marching into Charleston upon accepting the state government's proposal, Prevost may well have found his situation completely reversed with his own force besieged by Lincoln's army.

Prevost, unwilling to risk being trapped on the Charleston Peninsula between the city's defenders and Lincoln's troops, withdrew during the night of May 12. Lincoln had belatedly realized that the British threat to Charleston was serious and was hastily marching toward the city, although he did not reach the Ashley River until May 24. Meanwhile, to avoid a confrontation with Lincoln's larger force, Prevost retreated leisurely along the coastal islands. In late May the British army moved from James Island to Johns Island, and established a post on the mainland north of the Stono River. The position was strongly fortified and connected to Johns Island by a bridge of boats; from their foothold on the mainland, the British could easily forage for supplies even though they were less than twenty miles from Charleston. Prevost kept the bulk of his force on Johns Island for nearly two weeks before deciding to withdraw all but a rear guard to Savannah. About 800 British and Hessian soldiers under Lieutenant Colonel John Maitland were left at Stono Ferry.[61]

Lincoln believed that the British post was vulnerable and decided to launch a frontal assault with 3,000 men while a smaller force under Moultrie crossed to Johns Island farther to the northeast to cut off the British. The Americans attacked on the morning of June 20, but after an hour of hard fighting were repulsed with a loss of some 300 men. Moultrie's supporting attack was never made. British casualties were less than half of those suffered by the rebels. After the battle the British resumed their retreat, with Maitland occupying Port Royal Island near Beaufort while Lincoln sought, yet could not find, an opportunity to strike another blow.[62]

Both sides remained relatively inactive during the intense heat of July and August. However, the quiet interlude came to an abrupt end on September 1, when a French fleet of thirty-one warships accompanied by transport vessels appeared off Savannah. America's ally had joined the fight in the Southern Theater. The French commander, Vice Admiral Jean-Baptiste Henri Hector Theodat, the Comte d'Estaing, promptly dispatched an officer to Charleston to arrange for cooperation with the American forces. The French general reached Charleston on September 4, and after consulting with rebel leaders, it was agreed that Lincoln with 1,000 Continentals and as many militiamen as he could assemble would join d'Estaing's troops outside Savannah a week later.[63]

Having been taken completely by surprise by the arrival of the French, Prevost hastened to construct defenses. British troops, civilian inhabitants, former slaves who had attached themselves to the army, and slaves from loyalists' nearby plantations labored together to dig trenches and build earthwork fortifications. Prevost benefited from the slow unloading of the 4,000 French troops and the lethargic progress of the American army, which did not reach the north side of the Savannah River until September 12, one day later than their planned rendezvous date with d'Estaing. The British general bought further time when, after d'Estaing summoned him to surrender on September 16, he asked for twenty-four

A veteran of the Saratoga campaign, General Benjamin Lincoln (1733–1810) took command of the Continental Army in the Southern Department in 1779. He experienced little success, suffering defeat at the 1779 siege of Savannah and being captured along with his army and the city of Charleston in 1780. (*National Park Service*)

hours to consider the demand and, in violation of military protocol, used the time to continue work on the defenses.[64]

On the same day that d'Estaing sent his surrender demand to Prevost, Lincoln joined the French with over 3,000 men, two-thirds of them militia. Prevost, too, received reinforcements. When he had learned of the French fleet's arrival, Prevost had sent orders to Maitland at Port Royal Island to march to the aid of the Savannah garrison. The British messengers were intercepted by the rebels, but Maitland, having obtained intelligence of Prevost's situation, took his 800 troops to Savannah on his own initiative. Unfortunately, upon reaching the river Maitland found his passage blocked by French warships. Marching upstream in search of a crossing, Maitland encountered several black fishermen who guided his troops through the swamps to a point where the British could cross the river unnoticed by the French navy. Four hundred men reached Savannah on September 16, bypassing the besieging forces and entering the town to the cheers of the defenders. The remaining half of Maitland's troops reached Savannah the next day. Although the French and Americans had witnessed the arrival of the first group, neither took any steps to prevent the rest of the British from reinforcing the Savannah garrison. Instead, each accused the other of negligence.[65]

Prevost was heavily outnumbered even after Maitland's arrival, so the general used every means possible to augment his forces. Prevost employed 350 loyalist militiamen in the defensive lines, along with 80 Creeks and Cherokees who had been in town when the French arrived. The general also armed about 200 former slaves and employed others to carry ammunition from the magazines to the front lines. Altogether, Prevost could field some 4,800 defenders against a combined Franco-American force of over 7,700 men.[66]

The French did not begin digging their siege approach trenches until the night of September 22. By October 3 they had come close enough to the town to begin their bombardment, which inflicted considerable damage to the town but much less harm to the defensive works, and caused very few casualties. Lincoln laconically remarked that the intense artillery fire failed to accomplish its "desired purpose . . . of compelling a surrender." After six days of blasting the defenders with cannon, d'Estaing and Lincoln decided that an assault was necessary if the town were to be captured quickly.[67]

The French and American attackers began moving into position during the night of October 8. Two French columns would attack the British garrison in the Spring Hill redoubt on the right of the defensive line, while two American columns struck the defensive lines to the left of the French, broke through, and rolled up the British defenses between their objective and the Savannah River. The plan might have succeeded if the assault had begun at the scheduled time of 4 a.m., but the approach march took longer than expected, the British heard the approaching troops and opened fire, making it difficult for them to form, and a frustrated d'Estaing began his attack before the other columns were ready, thus ensuring the assault would be made piecemeal. Despite the nearly two-hour delay and the loss of surprise, the French briefly broke through the British lines at one location, but were quickly repulsed. The Americans made little progress. D'Estaing and Lincoln broke off the attack, having suffered over 800 casualties, nearly three-fourths among the French. British losses totaled fifty-five killed and wounded.[68]

Lincoln hoped that the allies would attempt another assault, but d'Estaing, having suffered two wounds, refused. The comte was also unhappy with the military performance of his American allies, and prepared to leave Georgia. Lincoln's troops began their return march to South Carolina on October 18, and the next day the French began boarding their ships.[69] Prevost had held Savannah and won a significant victory; equally important, he had unwittingly demonstrated the potential of the southern strategy to succeed by uniting British troops, loyalists, Indians, and African Americans into an effective force that withstood a more powerful enemy. The lesson, however, appeared to go unnoticed by British officials in London and America.

In New York, Sir Henry Clinton had been tensely awaiting news of the outcome of the siege. Germain continued to urge him to expand the scope of operations in the South, writing on September 27 that "The feeble Resistance Major Genl. Prevost met with in his March and Retreat through so great a part of South Carolina is an indubitable proof of the Indisposition of the Inhabitants to support the Rebel Government." Clinton had intended to dispatch troops to attack South Carolina in October, but a rumored French threat to Jamaica caused him to postpone the expedition, and he delayed further upon learning that the French and Americans had besieged Savannah. If the enemy succeeded in capturing the city and Prevost's army, further plans for a southern campaign would have to be abandoned entirely. Now, the failed siege, from which Prevost's force had emerged virtually unscathed, allowed Clinton to launch the next phase of operations with Charleston its principal target.[70]

Clinton assembled ninety transports and a naval escort at New York, loaded them with over 8,700 men with artillery and other equipment, and sailed southward on December 26. The fleet's voyage was plagued by bad weather that sank a supply ship carrying heavy artillery and ammunition and injured most of the horses, forcing the animals to be thrown overboard. The ships did not begin to reassemble off Georgia's Tybee Island until early February 1780. After disembarking some of the troops at Savannah, the fleet returned northward to Simmons Island at the mouth of the North Edisto River, where the British began landing on February 11.[71]

The Americans were expecting a British attack on Charleston. Rather than meet Clinton's army south of the city, using the swamps and streams as obstacles to oppose the British advance, Lincoln chose to focus on strengthening the fortifications on Charleston neck. Clinton proceeded cautiously northward, was joined by the detachment that had marched overland from Savannah, and crossed the Ashley River on March 29. He commenced formal siege operations during the night of April 1, his troops digging a trench parallel to the American lines and constructing three redoubts only eight hundred yards from Lincoln's position. Meanwhile, the British warships under Admiral Marriot Arbuthnot had crossed the sandbar outside Charleston harbor, enabling them to threaten the city from the sea.[72]

Nevertheless, the Americans remained confident. Colonel Thomas Pinckney of the South Carolina Continentals described Charleston's defenders as "very well prepared to receive" the British. George Washington had taken steps to reinforce the threatened city, detaching the North Carolina and Virginia Continentals from his own army to join Lincoln; the last of these troops, Brigadier General William Woodford's 700 Virginians, arrived on April 7 to cheers and an artillery salute. As events soon proved, however, the defenders' optimism was without foundation.[73]

Arbuthnot's naval vessels successfully sailed past Fort Moultrie (the former Fort Sullivan) on April 8, easily accomplishing what Sir Peter Parker had failed to do four years earlier. Then, on April 14, Lieutenant Colonel Banastre Tarleton and the cavalry of his British Legion attacked one of the Continental cavalry regiments and its supporting militia guarding Charleston's communications with the South Carolina interior. Tarleton, whose cavalry's losses amounted to only two men wounded, surprised the Americans in camp near Biggin's Bridge, killing 15 men, wounding 18, and taking 63 prisoners along with 40 wagons loaded with supplies and nearly 100 badly needed cavalry horses. The success allowed a detachment under Lieutenant Colonel James Webster to cross the Cooper River to threaten American communication and supply lines north of Charleston. Four days after Tarleton's victory, over 2,500 British reinforcements arrived from New York, allowing Clinton to increase the force east of the Cooper. Clinton put his second-in-command, General Charles, Earl Cornwallis, in charge of operations in this area.[74]

The British meticulously continued pushing forward their siege lines despite efforts by the American artillery to delay their work. British cannon frequently bombarded Charleston, although Clinton hoped to minimize destruction as he expected to occupy the city soon. Other operations were equally successful. Tarleton struck the American cavalry again on May 5 at Lenud's Ferry, inflicting about one hundred casualties and capturing the same number of horses with a loss of only two men.

Few British officers were more feared or more hated than British lieutenant colonel Banastre Tarleton (1754–1833). His "legion" of cavalry and infantry repeatedly defeated American forces until he was finally beaten at Cowpens in January 1781. (*National Gallery*)

"This stroke," Cornwallis wrote with great accuracy, "will have totally demolished their cavalry." The next day, Fort Moultrie surrendered to the Royal Navy. Entirely cut off and with provisions running low, Lincoln surrendered Charleston and its garrison on May 12. Clinton reported the capture of over 5,600 prisoners. An additional 89 American troops had been killed during the siege and 138 wounded. The combined losses of the British army and navy were 99 killed and 217 wounded. It was the worst American defeat of the war.[75]

The effects of Clinton's victory appeared to promise hopes of further success. Clinton informed Germain on June 4 that "the inhabitants from every quarter repair to . . . this garrison to declare their allegiance to the King, and to offer their services, in arms, in support of his government." Some brought rebel leaders they had captured.[76] Over 2,000 people came to Charleston from across South Carolina in the weeks following Lincoln's surrender to take the oath to King George and volunteer their assistance. As British columns fanned out across the backcountry, occupying Ninety Six, Orangeburg, Camden, and Cheraw in South Carolina and Augusta, Georgia, thousands more announced their support for the Crown.[77]

To implement his plan to organize the loyalists into an effective militia, on May 22 Clinton appointed Major Patrick Ferguson of the 71st regiment to the post of inspector of militia in the South. Before Ferguson could begin work, however, he found himself thwarted by Lord Cornwallis. When Clinton returned to New York in early June, leaving 4,000 men with Cornwallis, who took command in the southern theater, the earl ordered Ferguson "to take no steps whatsoever in the militia business" until receiving further orders. Ferguson had become the victim of the dispute between Clinton and Cornwallis that had erupted in April, when Clinton received word from London that his request to resign his command, submitted the previous November, had been rejected. Cornwallis, who had expected to replace Clinton as commander-in-chief in America, was frustrated at this blow to his ambitions and became hostile toward Clinton; he also sowed dissent among the army's officers. Because Clinton had appointed Ferguson to the militia command, Cornwallis saw Ferguson as an ally of his rival, thus doing little to support Ferguson in carrying out his assignment.[78]

While Cornwallis caused unnecessary delays in organizing the loyalists, a series of events threatened to undermine British efforts to secure South Carolina and extend operations northward. On May 29, Lieutenant Colonel Tarleton's British Legion, augmented by a troop of regular cavalry, destroyed the last Continental unit in South Carolina. Colonel Abraham Buford's Virginia regiment had been en route to reinforce Charleston, but the city surrendered before he arrived. Cornwallis ordered Tarleton to destroy Buford's force or drive it from the state, and after a pursuit of 105 miles in 54 hours, Tarleton caught up with Buford at the Waxhaws, just below the North Carolina border. After Buford spurned a surrender demand, Tarleton attacked the larger American force and quickly annihilated it, killing 113 of Buford's 350 men, wounding 150, and capturing 53. British losses amounted to only 5 killed and 12 wounded. The Americans accused Tarleton of carrying out a systematic massacre of men who had surrendered or were attempting to, although there was no reliable evidence to substantiate such a claim. Nonetheless, it provided excellent propaganda for the rebels, who circulated the tale of the "Waxhaws Massacre" to encourage wavering supporters to continue the fight against the British.[79]

In North Carolina, loyalists encouraged by British success began to assemble in mid-June in expectation that the royal army would soon arrive in their state. Some 1,300 had gathered at Ramsour's Mill in Tryon

County on June 20, although one-fourth of them lacked arms. Rebel militia under General Griffith Rutherford, despite numbering only 400 men, attacked and routed the loyalists. Casualties were almost equal, about 70 killed and 100 wounded on each side, but North Carolina's loyalists were badly demoralized. The battle also caused Cornwallis to doubt the military value of the loyalists; he informed a subordinate that "the folly and imprudence of our friends are unpardonable."[80]

It was not until mid-June, just days before the Battle of Ramsour's Mill, that Cornwallis finally permitted Ferguson to begin his task of organizing and training the South Carolina loyalist militia. By June 27, Lieutenant Colonel Nisbet Balfour, a protégé of Cornwallis and no friend of Ferguson, was impressed enough with the latter's progress to report that he and Ferguson had organized 5,000 men into militia battalions at Ninety Six, Orangeburg, and adjacent districts. The commander at Camden, Lieutenant Colonel Francis, Lord Rawdon, had taken responsibility for organizing the militia in that region, and observed that the men were "not only well disposed, but very zealous."[81]

The British were not alone in seeking to mobilize militia in South Carolina; the Americans were doing the same, and had the advantage of utilizing a militia organization that had been in place since the beginning of the war as well as of Cornwallis's self-imposed delay in organizing the loyalists. When Captain Christian Huck with some cavalry of the British Legion and loyal militia was dispatched to recruit supporters of the Crown and suppress the rebels in present-day York County, local militia officers gathered some 500 rebels to oppose him. They attacked Huck and his 115 men on the morning of July 12, killing Huck and 35 of his troops and wounding or capturing several more. The engagement, known as "Huck's Defeat," inspired more rebels to take the field against the British.[82]

Many of these determined Americans flocked to the forces being organized by Thomas Sumter and Francis Marion, who would emerge as the most effective partisan leaders in South Carolina. On July 30, Sumter with 600 men attacked the British post at Rocky Mount in the north central part of the state. The 150 defenders, secure in three log buildings, repulsed the daylong assault, with light losses on each side. Sumter then gathered additional men and moved east to attack the British camp at Hanging Rock, which was not fortified. On the morning of August 6,

Sumter's 800 men surprised the 500 regulars and militia, putting most of the defenders to flight. Some of the British troops, however, managed to reform, while Sumter lost control of his men. Although he was eventually forced to withdraw with a loss of 12 killed and 41 wounded, Sumter had inflicted 200 casualties and his near-victory shocked the British. Indefatigable, Sumter then turned south toward Camden, but on the opposite bank of the Wateree River, where he captured Fort Carey guarding the ferry on August 15 and also seized supplies and reinforcements headed for Camden.[83]

Sumter's raid near Camden had been intended to support the operations of the reconstituted Continental Army in the South. In mid-April, George Washington had dispatched some of the best troops in his northern army to assist in the defense of Charleston. Seven regiments from Maryland and one from Delaware, numbering more than 2,100 men, were placed under the command of Major General Johann de Kalb, a former French officer with considerable combat experience in Europe. They had reached Petersburg, Virginia, when they learned of Charleston's surrender. After much discussion among the senior officers, it was decided to continue the march southward. The detachment arrived at Hillsborough, North Carolina, on June 22.[84]

De Kalb did not retain command for long. The Continental Congress, desperate to reverse American fortunes in the South, sought a general with a proven record of success to replace the captured Benjamin Lincoln. On June 13, the representatives appointed Major General Horatio Gates, the "Hero of Saratoga," to take command of the Southern Department. Gates was popular with Congress and generally well liked by his troops, but he was held in low regard by Washington, who believed that Gates had plotted to replace him as commander-in-chief of the Continental Army. Gates reached the army on July 25 and, although the army was short of supplies, decided to march immediately toward Camden. Along his route he met General Richard Caswell and added that officer's 1,500 North Carolina militiamen to his army.[85]

Lord Rawdon, commanding at Camden, learned of Gates's approach and ordered the troops at nearby outposts to unite in the town. Rawdon then marched north to delay Gates, falling back to Camden on August 12 while Gates encamped his army at Rugeley's Mill, thirteen miles north of the town. There Gates was reinforced by 800 Virginia militia under

Lieutenant Colonel Francis, Lord Rawdon (1754–1826), left, was one of the most effective British commanders in America. He served effectively under Lord Cornwallis before assuming an independent command, which he led to victory at the Battle of Hobkirk's Hill and the relief of besieged British forces at Ninety Six. Despite his extensive military experience, Lieutenant General Charles Lord Cornwallis (1738–1805), right, was unable to suppress the rebellion after assuming command of British forces in the South in 1780. His victories at Camden and Guilford Courthouse proved fruitless, and he eventually abandoned the effort to subdue the Carolinas. (*New York Public Library*)

General Edward Stevens. On August 13, having been informed by Rawdon that Gates was advancing, Cornwallis arrived from Charleston to take command of the British army.[86]

Coincidentally, both generals set their armies in motion at 10 p.m. on August 15. Cornwallis, having decided "to take the first good opportunity to attack the rebel army," intended to surprise the Americans in their camp at dawn. Gates's plan was more modest. He wished to occupy a strong defensive position behind Sanders Creek, about seven miles from Camden, from whence he could threaten the British garrison while Sumter and Marion cut the supply lines to the town. This, Gates expected, would either force the British to attack him in a prepared position, or cause them to evacuate Camden, in which case he could pursue them and seek an opportunity to attack.[87]

The vanguards of both armies met on the road north of Sanders Creek in the early morning hours, and after some skirmishing the two generals prepared for battle. The field was narrowed by swamps that prevented either force from attempting to outflank the other. Gates posted one brigade of Continentals on his right, between the road and the western swamp, and his militia on the left from the road to the eastern swamp. The second Continental brigade was placed in the center as a reserve. Altogether, Gates had over 4,000 men. Cornwallis, with 2,200 troops, deployed his British regulars on his right, the provincial troops (loyalist regulars) on his left, and held one regiment of British troops and Tarleton's cavalry in reserve.[88]

At daybreak, Gates ordered his militia to attack the British right, while the Continentals made a supporting attack west of the road and the reserve brigade advanced to occupy the militia's former position. Cornwallis simultaneously ordered his right to attack the militia while his left advanced in support. As the militia and British regulars surged toward each other, the sight of solid lines of redcoats charging with leveled bayonets struck panic in the militiamen. All but one regiment of North Carolinians fled, most of the men never firing a shot. The British right then engaged the Continental reserve brigade, while the provincials and the Continentals grappled to the west. Bitter combat followed for more than half an hour. Cornwallis committed his infantry reserve, but could not break the deadlock. Finally, he noticed a gap between the Continental brigades and ordered Tarleton's cavalry to charge through the opening. This maneuver broke the American line, and a disorderly retreat ensued. Gates was long gone from the field by this time. He and other officers had attempted to rally the militia but were caught up in the torrent of running men and swept away to the north. The American army had been destroyed. In the confusion that followed no accurate casualty figures were compiled, though the British reported capturing 700 men and hundreds more were killed or wounded. Cornwallis counted only 324 casualties among his own troops.[89]

Cornwallis followed up his victory by ordering Tarleton to find and attack Sumter. The hard-driving cavalry commander caught up with the unsuspecting partisan officer at Fishing Creek on August 18, launched an immediate assault, and routed the Americans. Sumter managed to escape, but he left behind 150 men killed and wounded and over 300 prisoners. Tarleton also released the British troops Sumter had captured three days earlier and recovered all of the supplies as well.[90]

In the aftermath of their defeat at Camden, the Americans managed to win a few small victories: partisans defeated a detachment of provin-

Major Patrick Ferguson (1744–1780), a Scottish officer, served as inspector of loyalist militia in South Carolina. His troops were surrounded at Kings Mountain in October 1780 by American militia, and Ferguson was killed while trying to break through the enemy lines. (*New York Public Library*)

cials at Musgrove's Mill on August 17, and Francis Marion's men harassed and dispersed loyalist militia in the Pee Dee River area in late August and September. These successes were too insignificant to prevent Cornwallis from advancing into North Carolina. The British occupied Charlotte on September 26, but the earl found himself in a difficult position, with rebel partisans hovering nearby, harassing outposts and foraging parties. With his communications virtually cut off, Cornwallis was unaware that the British position in the South was under serious threat.[91]

On September 14, 600 rebels under Georgian colonel Elijah Clarke attacked the British post at Augusta. Lieutenant Colonel Thomas Brown's provincials, assisted by several hundred Creek and Cherokee Indians, withstood their assailants until September 17, when a relief force of provincial troops under Lieutenant Colonel John Harris Cruger, commandant at Ninety Six, approached. Clarke retreated northward, where Patrick Ferguson with 100 provincials and about 1,000 militia had advanced to cover Cornwallis's left flank. Upon hearing of Clarke's retreat, Ferguson moved farther west in an unsuccessful attempt to intercept the rebels. Ferguson's maneuvers appeared to threaten the settlers living west of the Appalachians, and hundreds of these "Overmountain Men" marched east to attack the loyalists. Ferguson retreated to Kings Mountain, twenty-five miles west of Charlotte, and appealed to Cornwallis for assistance.[92]

For reasons that remain obscure, Cornwallis sent no aid, and on October 7 Ferguson was surrounded by the Overmountain Men, who had been joined by rebel militia from the western Carolinas. Although the two forces were roughly equal in size, the loyalists were exposed on the bare, relatively flat hilltop while their attackers found plenty of cover on the forested slopes of Kings Mountain. Ferguson led several bayonet charges that scattered the rebels, but eventually they secured a foothold atop the hill. Ferguson was killed leading a charge, and his surviving men surrendered. The victory boosted American morale while simultaneously dispiriting the loyalists. When news of the disaster reached other loyalist militiamen, many deserted. Cruger suspected that loyalists in the vicinity of Ninety Six secretly decided "to submit as soon as the Rebels" arrived in that district. Realizing that Ferguson's defeat had upset his plans to invade North Carolina, Cornwallis abandoned Charlotte and encamped his army at Winnsboro, South Carolina, where it could cover the region between Camden and Ninety Six.[93]

Cornwallis and most of his officers lost all confidence in the loyalist militia. "The idea of militia, being of consequence, or use, as a military force—I own I have now totally given up," Balfour informed Cornwallis. With the partisans continuing their harassment of the British as well as the loyalists still embodied in the militia, Cornwallis dispatched Tarleton to strike at Marion. Before anything could be achieved, the earl recalled Tarleton and sent him to counter Sumter, only to have his cavalry commander suffer a severe check at Blackstock's Plantation on November 20. Cornwallis, meanwhile, had taken steps to increase his regular force. In mid-September Clinton had dispatched 2,500 men under General Alexander Leslie to make a diversionary raid in the Chesapeake Bay. Realizing that he needed reinforcements, Cornwallis ordered Leslie to bring his troops to South Carolina, telling the general that he needed his men since he could not rely on the "dastardly and pusillanimous" loyalists.[94]

When Cornwallis resumed his campaign, he would be facing a new American commander. Gates had been discredited by his defeat at Camden; even worse, he had been humiliated when it was learned he had left the field, then gone to Charlotte to reorganize the army, and finding no substantial force there, had ridden to Hillsborough, North Carolina, to

Upon taking command of the Continental Army in the South in December 1780, General Nathanael Greene (1742–1786), left, conducted a bold and effective campaign against the British. Although he never won a battle, he wore down the British forces until they were forced to withdraw to the coast. General Daniel Morgan (1736–1802), right, emerged from retirement to assume command of a detachment of Nathanael Greene's army. Morgan's brilliant tactics at the Battle of Cowpens resulted in the near annihilation of a British force and helped change the course of the southern campaign. (*Library of Congress*)

seek aid from the state legislature. He had accomplished this 180-mile journey in just over three days. Although his actions may have been justified by the circumstances, Gates's behavior gave the appearance of cowardice. Congress removed him from command and now asked Washington to name a replacement. The general chose one of his most trusted subordinates, Major General Nathanael Greene, a Rhode Islander and former Quaker who had served capably if unspectacularly since the beginning of the war. Greene arrived at Charlotte on December 2 and assumed command of the southern Continental Army. Greene found his force to be weak; however, it had received one important addition. Upon being given command in the South, Gates had prevailed upon Congress to promote his Saratoga comrade, Daniel Morgan, to brigadier general and call him out of his self-imposed retirement. Morgan had not reached the army until after its defeat at Camden, but he would prove himself to be extremely valuable in the upcoming campaign.[95]

Greene's army had grown to a strength of 2,500 men, of whom less than 1,000 were Continentals. He decided that he could not remain at Charlotte, as there were not enough provisions available in the area to feed his troops. He therefore took a risk and divided his army, taking most of his men to Cheraw, South Carolina, and sending the remainder under Morgan to the northwestern part of the state. Greene hoped that this move might induce Lord Cornwallis to divide his own army, providing an opportunity for the Americans to defeat the British in detail.[96]

Morgan set out from Charlotte on December 21 with 320 Maryland and Delaware Continentals, Lieutenant Colonel William Washington's reconstituted regiment of 100 cavalry, and 200 Virginia riflemen. This "Flying Army," as it was called, was to collect militia in the region west of the Catawba River, and Morgan was to act "either offensively or defensively as your own prudence and discretion may direct," Greene wrote. "The object," Greene explained, "is to give protection to that part of the country and spirit up the people, to annoy the enemy in that quarter; collect the provisions and forage out of the way of the enemy."

Cornwallis responded exactly as Greene had hoped. Leslie had arrived in Charleston on December 14, and in accordance with his instructions from the earl he left 1,000 men in that city and marched inland with 1,500. While waiting for Leslie to join him, Cornwallis sent Tarleton with 1,100 men to prevent Morgan from attacking Ninety Six and, if possible, bring the Flying Army to battle. Cornwallis would wait until Leslie arrived and then march northwest to interpose the main British army between Morgan and Greene. Tarleton began his march on January 2, 1781.[97]

Morgan learned of Tarleton's approach on January 14. The American general ordered a retreat, hoping to cross Broad River at Island Ford on January 16, but muddy roads slowed his march. Morgan therefore decided to prepare for battle. He chose a position on slowly rising ground where the field was constricted by a ravine to the west and a creek to the east. When Tarleton arrived, he would have only one tactical option: a frontal attack. American prospects improved as large numbers of militia, including several hundred under Colonel Andrew Pickens, continually arrived at Morgan's position, known locally as the Cowpens. These reinforcements brought his total strength to between 1,800 and 2,400 men. To avoid the disaster that had befallen Gates when the militia fled at Camden, Morgan formed his army in three lines. A screen of militia sharpshooters was in front, with the militia's main body in a second line farther back, and the Continentals on the highest ground at the northwestern end of the field. Morgan instructed the militiamen to fire two or three volleys at the British and then fall back behind the Continentals.[98]

Tarleton reached the Cowpens early in the morning of January 17, studied the American position, and questioned his loyalist guides about the terrain. He quickly deployed his troops for battle, but the area was so confined that he had to keep his cavalry and the battalion of the 71st Regiment in reserve. As soon as his men had formed, Tarleton ordered a charge. The American militia lines fired as instructed, then fell back behind the Continentals. The British infantry, although exhausted from hard marching and having suffered substantial casualties from the militia's fire, engaged the Continentals. The opposing lines exchanged musket fire, while Tarleton, seeing that the field in that area was wide enough to allow him to commit his infantry reserve, ordered the 71st Regiment forward "to threaten the enemy's right flank" and drive the rebels from the field.[99]

Lieutenant Colonel John Eager Howard of Maryland, commanding the Continentals, saw the British moving to strike his flank. Realizing that such a move would overwhelm the Continentals, he ordered his rightmost company to pull back and re-form at a right angle to the main line. "Whether my orders were not well understood or whether it proceeded from any other cause, in attempting this movement some disorder ensued in this company," Howard wrote. The troops "fell back" and "the rest of the line expecting a retreat was ordered, faced about and retreated." Morgan, enraged at what he interpreted as the flight of the Continentals, rode up and demanded an explanation for the withdrawal. Howard coolly explained and pointed out that his troops were still "in perfect order" while the British, believing the battle won, had broken ranks to pursue. Calmed, Morgan told Howard to fall back another hundred yards and face about. The Continentals did so and delivered a withering volley into the oncoming British. Howard ordered a bayonet charge which, he said, "threw them [the British] into confusion . . . and an unaccountable panic extended itself along the whole line. . . . A general flight ensued." Tarleton tried to restore the situation by ordering his cavalry reserve to charge, but instead the mounted troops wheeled and raced from the field. Tarleton found himself, along with a handful of British officers, in close combat with William Washington and some of his cavalry. The British commander managed to break off the action and escape, leaving behind 110 men killed and 700 prisoners, 200 of them wounded. American losses were less than 150 men.[100]

Cornwallis had not yet left camp despite his promise to cooperate with Tarleton because Leslie's troops, delayed by rain and sodden roads, did not arrive until the morning of the battle. When he heard the news later in the day, the furious earl determined to pursue Morgan, defeat him, and recover the prisoners. Cornwallis marched on January 19, thus allowing Morgan, who had retreated immediately after the battle, a two-day head start. The British marched to Ramsour's Mill in North Carolina, arriving on January 25 to find that Morgan was twenty miles ahead on the opposite side of the Catawba River. Cornwallis decided to speed his march by destroying most of his wagons and baggage, which took two days. Another day was lost to heavy rains, so that the British did not resume their pursuit until January 28.[101]

The events that followed became known as "the Race to the Dan" River. Greene brought his force from Cheraw to link up with Morgan's troops at Salisbury, North Carolina. Although illness forced Morgan to leave the army, Greene directed a rapid yet orderly withdrawal, fighting rearguard actions to delay the British, while Cornwallis was constantly thwarted by rain-swollen rivers and a lack of boats, Greene having removed all of them to the opposite shore whenever his army made a crossing. On February 14, Greene crossed the Dan River to safety in Virginia, where he rested his men from their exertions. Cornwallis had lost his gamble, noting that "heavy rains, bad roads, and the passage of many deep creeks, and bridges destroyed by the enemy's light troops, rendered all our exertions vain."[102]

Cornwallis fell back to Hillsborough, hoping to recruit loyalists to increase his ranks, which had been much depleted by casualties, illness, and desertion during his furious march. Loyalists came to his camp, but showed little interest in volunteering after viewing the exhausted and bedraggled redcoats. One North Carolinian, Dr. John Pyle, did raise a force of 400 mounted loyalists and was on his way to join Cornwallis on February 25 when he encountered Lieutenant Colonel Henry Lee's legion of infantry and cavalry, along with Andrew Pickens's militia, near the Haw River. Lee had been sent to reinforce the southern army in late 1780, and Greene had sent his legion and Pickens's men back into North

Carolina on February 19. Because Lee's troops wore green uniform coats similar to those worn by the soldiers of Tarleton's British Legion, Pyle mistook Lee for Tarleton. Lee took advantage of the error, pretended he was Tarleton, and when the loyalists were riding past the rebel line the Americans attacked them, killing at least ninety of Pyle's followers, wounding many more, and dispersing the rest. Pickens expressed satisfaction with the outcome of the engagement, which came to be known as "Pyle's Massacre." "This Affair . . . has been of infinite Service," the militia commander informed Greene. "It has knocked up Toryism altogether in this part" of North Carolina.[103]

Greene had brought the rest of his army back to North Carolina on February 22, reinforcements of Virginia Continentals and militia from that state having increased his strength to some 4,600 men. Cornwallis could muster only 2,000 troops, but he was eager for a fight, convinced that his regulars could defeat the rebels in a pitched battle. The two armies maneuvered for several days before Greene occupied a strong position at Guilford Courthouse on March 14. Replicating the tactics that Morgan had employed so successfully at Cowpens, the American general deployed two lines of militia backed by a third line of Continentals as Cornwallis approached the next day. The earl promptly formed his men for battle and launched a frontal assault.[104]

The British fought their way through the two lines of militia. The second line, composed of Virginians, was positioned in woods and the Americans were dislodged only after bitter fighting. Cornwallis observed that "the excessive thickness of the woods rendered our bayonets of little use, and enabled the broken enemy to make frequent stands, with an irregular fire, which occasioned some loss, and to several of the corps great delay." Thus the British regiments emerged into open ground in piecemeal fashion to confront the final American line of Continentals. Cornwallis's soldiers attacked nonetheless, were checked on the American right, but on the opposite flank, the 2nd Guards Battalion routed the inexperienced 2nd Maryland Continentals before engaging the veteran 1st Maryland. The regiment's commander, Colonel John Gunby, was pinned under his wounded horse; John Eager Howard assumed command and, as at Cowpens, ordered a bayonet charge. The Marylanders broke the elite of the British army. However, finding themselves isolated on the field with other British regiments emerging from the woods,

Howard ordered a withdrawal. Greene, unwilling to risk the loss of his army if he continued fighting, decided to break off the action.[105]

Cornwallis held the field, yet the ground had been won at an unacceptable cost. More than one-quarter of his army had been lost, 532 irreplaceable casualties. The Americans counted over 1,200 casualties, some 1,000 of them categorized as missing, and many of these were militia who had fled uninjured and might return to fight again. Cornwallis decided to fall back to Wilmington, where the British had established a base in January. There he could rest his troops and procure supplies while pondering his next move.[106]

Greene followed Cornwallis at a distance, reaching the Deep River on March 26. Two days later he ended the pursuit in favor of a plan he had been considering for some time. He explained his intentions to George Washington on March 29. "If the Enemy falls down towards Wilmington . . . it will be impossible for us to injure them. In this critical and distressing situation I am determined to carry the War immediately into South Carolina." Greene explained that if Cornwallis did not do the same, the British could be driven from "their posts in that State. . . . If they leave their posts to fall they must lose more there than they can gain" in North Carolina. "All things considered," Greene concluded, "I think the movement is warranted by the soundest reasons both political and military." Greene's decision to strike at South Carolina, in conjunction with Cornwallis's later decision to ignore the American move, would eventually determine the outcome of the southern campaign.[107]

The British commander had a different idea for his army's future operations. Despite positive orders from Clinton to hold South Carolina, the earl's attention was attracted to Virginia. Clinton had sent an expedition to the Chesapeake Bay in late December 1780 to make a diversion to assist Cornwallis, followed by a second force that brought British strength in Virginia to 5,500 men. Cornwallis decided that if he marched to Virginia and combined his force with the troops already there, he could conquer that state and isolate Greene's army. He informed Clinton of his intentions on April 10, writing that "Until Virginia is in a manner subdued, our hold of the Carolinas must be difficult, if not precarious. The Rivers in Virginia are advantageous to an invading army; but North Carolina is of all the provinces in America the most difficult to attack." Cornwallis began his northward march on April 25, leaving the British in South Carolina to fend for themselves. He would not find the decisive victory he sought in Virginia.[108]

By the time Cornwallis departed Wilmington, Greene had reached Camden, South Carolina, where Lord Rawdon exercised field command of the British forces in that state. Greene occupied a strong position on Hobkirk's Hill, just north of the fortified town, astride the same road where the British and American armies had met the previous August, though much closer to Camden. Rawdon, outnumbered by Greene's 1,500 Continentals, noted that "I did not think the disparity of numbers was such as should justify bare defense." After gathering reinforcements and "arming our musicians, our drummers, and in short everything that could carry a firelock, I mustered above nine hundred men," Rawdon wrote. On the morning of April 25 he led them on a concealed march through the forest. Emerging from the trees, Rawdon's vanguard struck the unsuspecting troops on Greene's left flank.[109]

Greene reacted quickly, forming his troops and then, finding that "the Enemy were . . . advancing only with a small front," ordered a counterattack while Rawdon's men were still strung out in columns in the woods. Greene also ordered William Washington with his cavalry to circle around the British and attack their infantry from the rear. The American advance temporarily drove back the British, but Rawdon continued to extend his line as his units reached the field. Part of the 1st Maryland, immediately east of the road, was thrown into confusion, causing Colonel Gunby to order the whole regiment to fall back. The 2nd Maryland, farther east, was left isolated under heavy British pressure, while the 1st Virginia on Greene's right became disorganized, thus leaving the 2nd Virginia isolated as that regiment pushed down the hillside. Washington, instead of following orders, found a makeshift aid station in the British rear and began paroling wounded soldiers and their attendants rather than attacking Rawdon's infantry. Taking advantage of the confusion, Rawdon pressed his attack. Greene reluctantly ordered a retreat.[110]

The American defeat at Hobkirk's Hill nearly ended Greene's gamble to invade South Carolina. He had lost over 260 men, only a few more casualties than Rawdon's force had suffered, but Greene's prospects appeared gloomy. His campaign, however, was redeemed by the successes of Henry Lee and Francis Marion, whose combined force had severed the supply line between Charleston and Camden while Rawdon was focused on Greene's army. The American commander had detached Lee and his legion to collaborate with Marion, the two forces uniting on April 14. Lee and Marion moved the next day against Fort Watson on the Santee River, forcing the garrison to surrender on April 23. With his supply line cut, Rawdon had no choice but to evacuate Camden during the night of May 9.[111]

The Continental Army entered Camden the next morning, shortly after the last British troops had departed. While Greene pursued Rawdon, British posts across South Carolina fell to the Americans: Orangeburg to Thomas Sumter on May 11, Fort Motte to Lee and Marion on May 12, and Fort Granby to Lee on May 15. Greene decided that he could not bring Rawdon to battle, opting instead to march into the backcountry to strike the isolated post at Ninety Six while sending Lee to join Andrew Pickens and the militia in besieging Augusta, Georgia.[112]

Augusta held out for two weeks. On May 20, while Pickens gathered militia outside the town, Lee attacked the nearby British post of Fort Galphin on the South Carolina side of the Savannah River, seizing a quantity of badly needed arms and other supplies. The legion then joined the militia at Augusta, where Lieutenant Colonel Thomas Brown with a few hundred provincials and loyalist militia staunchly defended the fortified town. Brown used every means he could conceive to resist the siege, raiding the approach trenches frequently to delay the Americans and even digging and detonating a tunnel under the siege lines, which turned out to have been too short to reach the American positions. His efforts failed. Outnumbered, with rebels firing rifles and artillery into his fortifications from a log tower they had built, Brown surrendered on June 5.[113]

Greene did not fare as well at Ninety Six. He reached the post on May 22 at the head of just over 1,000 men; no militia had joined him to offset the casualties his army had suffered at Hobkirk's Hill or replace sick soldiers. Greene found the town "much better fortified and [the] garrison much stronger in regular troops than was expected." Lieutenant Colonel John Harris Cruger, commanding the defenders of the palisaded town and adjacent earthwork, the Star Fort, so called because of its shape, mustered 350 provincials and 200 local loyalist militiamen. Greene decided to take the post by siege, focusing his efforts on the Star Fort.[114]

While the Americans inched forward toward the British lines, a messenger sent by Cruger reached Rawdon, who was in Charleston, on June

3 to report the threat to Ninety Six. By a stroke of good fortune, three regiments of British regulars had debarked in town that same day. Rawdon, although in ill health, decided to organize an expedition to relieve Cruger. It took several days to prepare the troops and gather supplies, so that Rawdon was unable to begin his march until June 11. He commanded a powerful force of nearly 2,000 men. Two days later, Sumter informed Greene that the British were hurrying to the aid of Ninety Six's defenders. The American general ordered Sumter and other militia officers to delay Rawdon's advance, but they proved unable to do so. Sumter incorrectly predicted which route Rawdon would use, took position to block it, and then found that Rawdon had moved via another road.[115]

Unwilling to abandon his effort to take Ninety Six, Greene decided to storm the defenses before Rawdon arrived. He had been reinforced by Lee's legion and Pickens's militia from Augusta, which encouraged him to make the risky assault. On June 18, Lee's legion and the Delaware Continentals attacked and captured a small fort west of the town, but a larger assault on the Star Fort was repulsed with considerable loss. Greene, knowing Rawdon was nearby, retreated across the Saluda River. Rawdon hoped to trap and destroy Greene's army in the backcountry, so after reaching Ninety Six on June 21, he marched another forty miles in pursuit of the Americans. Finally, he conceded that "our troops were by that time so overcome with fatigue that I was obliged to halt." He took his force back to Ninety Six, where he and Cruger decided that they could not maintain a post so far from Charleston. Rawdon ordered that Ninety Six be evacuated. The British army returned to Charleston, accompanied by hundreds of loyalist refugees.[116]

Greene followed the retreating British, concluded he could not bring them to battle, and took his army to the High Hills of Santee to rest during the summer heat. He also worked to gather reinforcements as he planned his next campaign. When the Continental Army fought again, Greene would no longer have to face his nemesis, Lord Rawdon. That capable officer returned to England to recover his health. His replacement as commander of the British field army in South Carolina, Lieutenant Colonel Alexander Stewart, had arrived with the reinforcements in early June and had never served in America. He was held in low regard by many of his fellow officers.[117]

Stewart took post at Orangeburg in July. At the end of the month he marched northward to McCord's Ferry on the Congaree River, only twenty miles from Greene's camp although on the opposite side of the Santee River. Henry Lee, who was scouting the British force, began urging Greene to attack Stewart while the latter was so far from support. Greene at first rejected the proposals, insisting his army was too small. By August 14, however, he had decided to make the move and began calling upon the militia to join him.[118]

Greene reached the Congaree River on August 30, but by that time Stewart had fallen back to Eutaw Springs on the Santee River. Greene followed, reaching Burdell's Tavern, seven miles from the British camp, on the evening of September 7. Stewart, completely unaware of Greene's presence, had less than 1,700 men fit for duty. Greene had two regiments of Maryland Continentals, two others from Virginia, and three from North Carolina, along with Lee's legion, William Washington's cavalry, and two companies of Delaware Continentals. In addition to the regulars, he had been reinforced by South Carolina state troops, Marion's and Pickens's South Carolina militia, and militia from North Carolina. His force totaled, at a minimum, nearly 2,800 men.[119]

On the morning of September 8 Stewart sent 310 men detached from various regiments to gather sweet potatoes on nearby plantations to feed his troops. Soon after they left camp, two American deserters arrived and informed Stewart of Greene's location. Stewart sent a party of cavalry and light infantry to verify the report; the troops stumbled into the head of the American column and were driven off. The firing attracted the British foragers to the road, where most were immediately captured. When Stewart's cavalry commander, Major John Coffin, returned and told him the rebels were approaching, the British commander immediately deployed for battle.[120]

Greene formed his troops in two lines, with the militia in the front, the Continentals in the second line, Lee's legion guarding the right flank, and Washington's cavalry and the Delaware companies in reserve. On the left flank, the South Carolina state troops held their ground against "a galling fire" from a British battalion posted in the ravine along Eutaw Creek, their front screened by thick brush. Greene opened the attack with the militia, who "fought with a degree of spirit and firmness that reflects the highest honor upon this class of Soldiers," Greene declared

Nathanael Greene attacked the British army on September 8, 1781, and in four hours of heavy fighting nearly drove that force from the field. British troops defending a brick house checked the American advance, but British casualties were so high that they abandoned their efforts to hold the interior of South Carolina. (*New York Public Library*)

later. When the North Carolina militia gave way, Greene sent the North Carolina Continentals to take their place in line. These troops, however, eventually wavered and fell back under the heavy British fire. Believing that their enemy was on the verge of defeat, the British troops charged without orders, only to receive a severe check as Greene committed his Maryland and Virginia Continentals in a counterattack.[121]

Victory seemed within Greene's grasp, but as the Continentals pursued the fleeing British, some took refuge in a brick house and could not be dislodged. The battalion in the creek bed fell back, part of it taking position behind a palisade that extended from the brick house to the creek, the rest remaining in the creek bed where they continued to deliver flanking fire into the American lines. Greene tried to batter the brick building with his artillery but failed, even after the gunners moved their cannon so close to the building that they were shot down by the defenders, who made a sortie and rolled the abandoned guns next to the house. With Stewart reforming his troops and Greene's options running out, the American general ordered Washington to dislodge the British from the creek bed while Lee attacked Coffin's cavalry on the British left and outflanked Stewart's infantry. Both attacks failed. A frustrated Greene ordered his army to retreat to Burdell's Tavern.[122]

Once again, Greene had suffered a tactical defeat; he reported about 550 casualties. British losses, however, were even higher. Stewart lost almost 850 men, nearly half of them prisoners. The British army had been decimated. On the evening of September 9, Stewart began retreating toward Charleston.[123]

For all practical purposes, the Battle of Eutaw Springs marked the end of the British southern campaign, although its epitaph would not be written until October 19, when Cornwallis surrendered at Yorktown. Both sides conducted raids and harassing actions after the battle, but the outcome had been sealed. The British remained confined to the environs of Wilmington, Charleston, and Savannah until they evacuated those cities. Wilmington was abandoned in November 1781, Savannah evacuated in July 1782, and Charleston in December. What had begun as a promising operation ended in defeat and disaster.

Much of the blame for the British failure rests squarely on Lord Cornwallis. He unnecessarily delayed Patrick Ferguson's efforts to organize the loyalist militia, quickly lost confidence in the loyalists, and by the end of 1780 had virtually ended efforts to mobilize them. He made only feeble, reluctant efforts to seek support from the Indians, and he ignored a potentially valuable resource in the thousands of slaves who had flocked to the British army. While many were employed in the commissary, quartermaster, hospital, and other departments, no effort was made to arm them. Doing so could have easily doubled or trebled the size of the British army in the South, adding men who would fight with desperate courage to avoid reenslavement. Thus Cornwallis abandoned or ignored the three pillars of the southern strategy, instead attempting to subdue the southern states with British regulars and veteran provincial troops in pitched battle, a costly and ultimately unsuccessful approach.

Cornwallis made several other errors: he failed to coordinate the movements of the main army with its detachments, contributing to the costly defeats at Kings Mountain and Cowpens. He ignored his commander's orders to make the defense of South Carolina his first priority, setting off first on a fruitless pursuit of the American army across North Carolina and later, with even worse consequences, deciding to shift operations into Virginia. It was not a stellar display of military leadership, as the results clearly demonstrated.

However, British failures were not solely the result of British decisions and actions. The Americans also exerted great influence on the campaign's outcome. When affairs appeared at their worst, Americans still continued to take the field under partisan leaders like Sumter, Marion, and Pickens, harass the loyalist militia and keep it from acting effectively, and strike at British posts and units when opportunities arose. Horatio Gates failed at Camden, but the lessons of his defeat regarding the best use of militia were applied with success at Cowpens and Guilford Courthouse. Nathanael Greene never won a battle, yet he won the campaign by remaining persistent in the face of defeat, collaborating with the partisans, and waging what essentially became a war of attrition that depleted the British forces and ultimately rendered them unable to control the territory they had conquered in 1780. Had Cornwallis possessed Greene's military adaptability, capacity to cooperate with local militia leaders even when they proved troublesome, and adeptness in coordinating the efforts of his army with supporting forces and detachments to maximize their combined effectiveness, the contest in the Southern Theater may have had a different outcome.

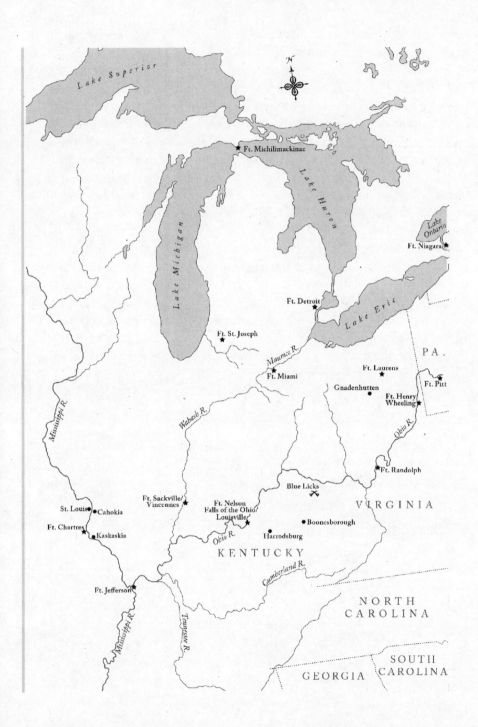

THE

WESTERN THEATER

The Theater of Fear

Mark Edward Lender

I t is no easy thing to describe the Western Theater of the War for Independence. What was the West? The farthest backcountries of the Carolinas, Virginia, and Pennsylvania—or even Georgia? Trans-Appalachia out to the Mississippi, and the old Northwest and Southwest? The West was all of these places in the minds of colonial Americans, and these vast regions would all figure in the Revolution. But as a military theater the boundaries of the West were porous, as various groups, military and civilian, traversed the region going and coming from the East, the Northwest, Canada, Spanish territory to the southwest, and even beyond the Mississippi. In fact, one of the last engagements of the war occurred in modern Arkansas. The West was the largest theater of the war. It was also the most complex: The region gave full play to the almost kaleidoscopic elements of the conflict: the patriot-tory civil war, imperial rivalries, the colonial rebellion against the empire, internecine struggles among Native American tribes and factions of tribes, the freelance schemes of private settlers and adventurers, and, most significant, the clash between Indians and expansionist land-hungry Americans.

This latter factor lent an atmosphere of desperate violence to the theater. Whites saw western lands as the key to economic prosperity in a successful new nation, with Indian antagonists as racially inferior savages incapable of "civilization." Looking east, Indians saw white expansion as an existential threat to their independence, and thus to their cultural and even physical survival. These rival visions of the future allowed for little compromise. Those locked in such a struggle often found scant use for compassion or mercy; the West was a place where violence was frequent and ferocious, with few distinctions between combatants and noncombatants. While the Revolution spawned instances of unrestrained brutality everywhere, in no other theater did terror and atrocity emerge as the norm. Indeed, this chapter argues that the West would see the War for Independence at its most brutal—the West was the theater of fear.

As the War for Independence ignited, the West—for present purposes all of the regions mentioned above—was not completely *terra incognita*. While accurate cartography began only in 1778,[1] by 1763 a century of Indian wars, imperial conflicts, trading ventures, and settlement attempts (usually illegal) had seen thousands of Europeans cross the Appalachians. After the Seven Years' War scattered French and Spanish trading posts remained in the Ohio and Mississippi River valleys, with British traders and Indian agents (often one and the same) pressing into the interior as well. Colonial governments and speculative land companies sent exploratory and surveying parties—including a young George Washington—into the Ohio Valley and beyond. Spain and Britain, who had inherited enormous western territories from the defeated French, were well aware of the commercial potential of East-West trade links via the Ohio and Mississippi rivers.

Among most colonists, however, land hunger drove interest in the West. On the eve of the Revolution that hunger was never stronger, while at the same time British efforts to control white western expansion were crumbling. The Proclamation of 1763, which Britain had hoped would restrict white emigration and prevent Anglo-Indian conflicts, and which had caused widespread colonial resentment, had never stopped the westward movement. Bowing to colonial protests, the British negotiated treaties with the Cherokees and the Iroquois that moved settlement boundaries west and white settlers surged into western Virginia, Kentucky, and through the North Carolina backcountry into modern Tennessee.

The treaties opening the immigration floodgates, however, were fraught with controversy. Among the Cherokees, heavily defeated by colonial forces in the Anglo-Cherokee War of 1758–61, factions disagreed with the Treaties of Hard Labor (1768) and Lochaber (1770) that pushed the tribe west of the Alleghenies. Angry Cherokees sporadically harassed settlers on the Virginia and Carolina frontiers. The Treaty of Fort Stanwix (also 1768) was equally problematic. At Stanwix, the Iroquois ceded claims to lands south of the Ohio—that is, to most of Kentucky—claims never accepted by the region's Shawnees.[2] Shawnee resistance to white encroachments culminated in Lord Dunmore's War in 1774, when Virginia forces under royal governor John Murray, fourth Earl of Dunmore, defeated the Shawnees and allied Mingos. But to anyone who looked, it was clear Indian resentments remained and that many tribes or factions of tribes were willing to act on those resentments.

Yet low-level hostilities, while deadly to individuals or small parties, failed to deter settlers. The Kentucky region saw a steady stream of American emigrants. Daniel Boone had explored part of Kentucky by the late 1760s, and in 1771 he helped plant the first white settlement in modern Tennessee at Watauga (now Elizabethton). In 1775, a month before Lexington and Concord, Boone, working for the Transylvania Land Company, blazed the Wilderness Road through the Cumberland Gap from Tennessee into Kentucky. He established Boone's Station (which became Boonesborough), a permanent Kentucky settlement, to which he moved his family in September 1775. Another pioneer, James Harrod, founded Harrodstown (now Harrodsburg, Kentucky) in 1774, while a year later

Overleaf: The 1778 "new map" of the western portions of Virginia, Pennsylvania, Maryland, and North Carolina that extends to the Mississippi and included such places as Kaskaskia, and Cahokia. One of the earliest fairly accurate maps of Trans-Appalachia, the "New Map" gives a sense of the vastness of the Western Theater, the lack of roads, and the great distances separating established Indian and white villages and fortified posts. (*Library of Congress*)

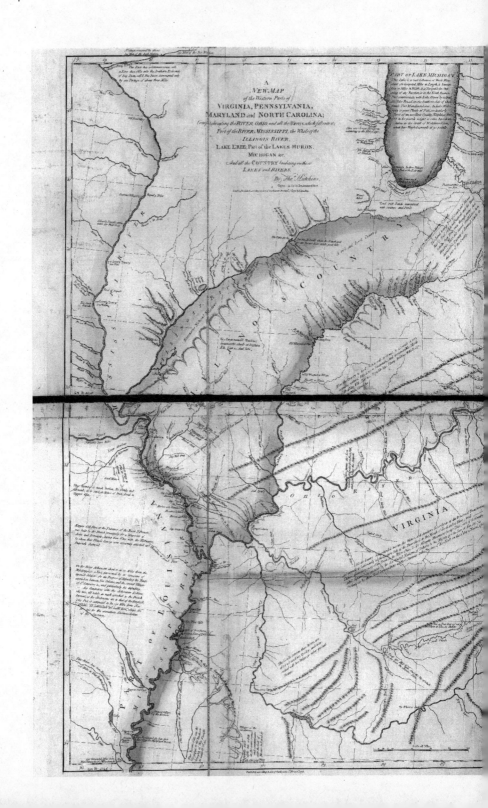

In 1775 a party under Daniel Boone's leadership began construction of "Fort Boone," which evolved into the permanent fortified town of Boonesborough. Timber cleared to build the stockade also left a good field for defensive fire, and the town survived repeated Native American raids. (*New York Public Library*)

another party laid out a large camp they called Lexington, in honor of the recently famous Massachusetts town.[3] Boone, Harrod, and the Lexington settlers were in fact private adventurers out to make fortunes in real estate. Their settlements, and most others that followed in the mid-1770s, consisted of a dozen or fewer cabins with a stockade or blockhouse, and all were illegal in that residents held no formally recognized land titles. Nevertheless they formed extra-legal militias to defend themselves, and even to attack local Indians. Indeed, the white immigration process can be described as quasi-military—a process of "clearing and holding." While there was no general Indian war, by 1775 sporadic tribal resistance forced early colonists to abandon some of their Kentucky outposts—Lexington, for example, would not be permanently settled until 1779. But the trend was clear: Land hunger was driving Anglo-Americans west despite any dangers or dubious land claims.

As angry as many Indians were at white encroachments, the coming of the Revolution did not immediately trigger a frontier war. Given their unsuccessful military history with the British and colonial Americans, the tribes initially reacted cautiously to the rebellion. Senior Indian leaders, especially among the numerous Cherokees and Shawnees, were especially wary; they grudgingly conceded the necessity of trading land for peace with the whites. Moreover, they urged neutrality in the dispute between Britain and its American colonies, worried that an alliance with the wrong side could endanger trade with whites who supplied vital access to gunpowder, munitions, and manufactured goods. Farther south the powerful Creeks agreed. They saw no reason to get involved in the rebellion and maneuvered for advantageous trading relationships with anyone willing to deal. Why rush to war on behalf of either side in a struggle among whites?

Voices of moderation, however, did not go unchallenged. Indeed, divided councils among the tribes were the norm as younger Native Americans chafed at the quiescence of their seniors in the face of white land-grabbing. They saw the situation in stark terms: White westward expansion was a virtual invasion and an existential threat to their independence and ways of life, if not their physical survival. This generational divide signaled a disintegration of tribal unity, of which there was no better example than the Cherokee experience. In March 1775, a month before Lexington and Concord, at what historians have called the Treaty of Sycamore Shoals (in modern Tennessee), Cherokee chiefs met with North Carolinian Richard Henderson, who represented the Transylvania Land Company—another group of private adventurers with no legal right to deal with the Indians. The senior chiefs, including the respected Attakullakulla (Little Carpenter), who had tasted defeat in the Anglo-Cherokee War, sold over 20 million acres of Cherokee territory in Tennessee and Kentucky for about £10,000 in trade goods. The transaction sparked outrage among competing land companies and colonial governments, which refused to recognize the sale. But white reaction was nothing compared to the fury of younger Cherokees. Their spokesman was Dragging Canoe—the son of Little Carpenter. The chasm between younger and older Cherokees could not have been more graphic. Dragging Canoe's reaction to the proposed treaty (as recorded by British Indian agent Alexander Cameron) merits quoting in full:

> Whole Indian Nations have melted away like snowballs in the sun before the white man's advance. They leave scarcely a name of our people except those wrongly recorded by their destroyers. Where are the Delawares? They have been reduced to a mere shadow of their former greatness. We had hoped that the white men would not be willing to travel beyond the mountains. Now

that hope is gone. They have passed the mountains, and have settled upon Tsalagi [Cherokee] land. They wish to have that usurpation sanctioned by treaty. When that is gained, the same encroaching spirit will lead them upon other land of the Tsalagi. New cessions will be asked. Finally the whole country, which the Tsalagi and their fathers have so long occupied, will be demanded, and the remnant of the Ani Yvwiya, The Real People, once so great and formidable, will be compelled to seek refuge in some distant wilderness. There they will be permitted to stay only a short while, until they again behold the advancing banners of the same greedy host. Not being able to point out any further retreat for the miserable Tsalagi, the extinction of the whole race will be proclaimed. Should we not therefore run all risks, and incur all consequences, rather than to submit to further loss of our country? Such treaties may be alright for men who are too old to hunt or fight. As for me, I have my young warriors about me. We will hold our land.[4]

Dragging Canoe was no rogue lone wolf. While Little Carpenter and other older chiefs had had enough of fighting, Dragging Canoe's defiance resonated with many other Cherokees; in fact his reasoning eventually struck a chord with thousands of Native Americans who saw no other alternative to dispossession but to fight. Representatives of several northern tribes later endorsed the militancy of the younger Cherokees: "Better to die like men," a British Indian agent recorded them as saying, "than to diminish away by inches."[5] And as to fighting, Dragging Canoe would be heard from soon enough.

Shortly after Sycamore Shoals, events to the north took an equally unsettling turn. When word of Lexington and Concord reached colonial settlements in Kentucky, residents reacted quickly. The independence movement offered an opportunity to link illegal land claims to the Revolution; led by attorney John Gabriel Jones and militia officer George Rogers Clark, the Kentucky settlements eventually persuaded Virginia to grant Kentucky county status and to legitimize regional land claims. Again, many Indians objected. In November 1775 Cornstalk, a Shawnee chief who had fought Virginians in Lord Dunmore's War, minced no words in a message to the Continental Congress: "Our lands are covered by the white people," he wrote, "& we are jealous that you still intend to make larger strides. We never sold you our Lands which you now possess on the Ohio [River] . . . & which you are settling without ever asking our leave or obtaining our consent." Cornstalk asked Congress to understand Indian distress and to halt illegal land seizures.[6] Congress gave no such answer. Cornstalk wanted no more fighting, but he could not control the passions of a younger generation. As historian Ethan Schmidt has noted, the continuing stream of white settlement from Virginia, Pennsylvania, and the Carolinas "created a generational divide among Ohio Valley Indians quite similar to that among the Cherokees."[7]

A number of tribes or factions of tribes clung to neutrality, including many Cherokees, Creeks, and the Delawares. But for most Indians neutrality gave way with the realization that standing aloof from the eastern struggle offered no protection from continued American westward migration. It appeared that rebel victory would lead only to a tsunami of white settlement; the only real alternatives were—as Dragging Canoe had insisted—Indian retreats to the point of total dispossession or to defend Indian lands through force of arms. War, as we know, would lead to Indian alliances with the British; but it is important to note that Native Americans made these alliances for their own reasons and in their own interests, not out of any particular regard for King George. Indian resistance to Anglo-American expansion would have flared with or without the patriot independence movement.

Low-intensity clashes between settlers and Indians had never fully stopped in the Ohio Valley even before the Revolution, but major hostilities began in earnest between the Cherokees and the Carolinas and Virginia. This was the Cherokee War of 1776, and in fact it was a continuation of the Anglo-Indian war that preceded it—as were virtually all of the Indian wars of the Revolution. In July violence flared as Dragging Canoe led militant Cherokees onto the warpath in the western Carolinas. It was a campaign of small-scale guerilla raids against isolated farms and settlements, a pattern typical of frontier warfare. The attacks spread terror along the South and North Carolina frontiers, killed some 60 South Carolinians, and devastated nearly fifty miles of the North Carolina frontier. Dragging Canoe had acted unilaterally, and the British were less than enthusiastic at the news. London, unsure of Native American loyalties (many of them, after all, previously had fought alongside the French) and equally unsure of the consequences of an Indian war, had not decided to actively enlist Indian allies in the imperial war effort. In fact, the Cherokee assaults were indiscriminate, striking whites of all political persuasions, and British Indian agents feared the violence would drive neutral or even loyalist-leaning colonials into the rebel camp seeking protection. The British probably were right, and the rebel governments marshaled a response that confirmed royalist fears.

With Continental troops unavailable, retaliation fell to Virginia and the Carolinas. With planning assistance from Continental major general Charles Lee, some 6,000 state troops moved against *all* Cherokees, even those who had stood aloof from Dragging Canoe. Patriot tactics also were typical of the period and resembled a form of a medieval "Chevaunche"—a large-scale plundering of enemy territory to demoralize an opponent, strip them of food and supplies, kill anyone who showed any resistance, and leave the enemy too disorganized to continue the fight. It worked. One North Carolina officer bluntly explained the outcome: they "marched to the Cherokee nation to suppress the Indians; burnt their town, killed and destroyed as many of the Indians as we could get hold of; remained in the nation as long as we could get provisions, and was compelled to return back."[8] By September patriot forces had devastated dozens of Cherokee settlements in the western Carolinas and modern Tennessee, and by November most Cherokees were finished. They signed treaties relinquishing some 5 million acres of homelands, including virtually all that remained in South Carolina. Only Dragging Canoe held out. The young chief led his followers south to found new towns on the Chickamauga Creek near modern Chattanooga, Tennessee. Henceforth they were the Chickamauga Indians, and they became the scourge of the southwestern frontier.

Shawnee neutrality died as well. By early 1777 Cornstalk and other senior chiefs informed patriots they could no longer restrain younger Shawnee warriors. The Americans were hardly surprised, as raiding bands had been taking scalps for months. Patriots also knew most Shawnees had allied with the British. The architect of the new arrangement was Quebec superintendent of Indian affairs and lieutenant governor Henry Hamilton. Appointed in 1775, Hamilton, a former soldier, proved good at his job. Stationed at Fort Detroit with only a small garrison—a de-

An able administrator and military leader based in Detroit, Henry Hamilton's (1734–1796) effective encouragement of and support for Indian offensive operations in Trans-Appalachia enraged patriot authorities. Captured at Vincennes in February 1779, Hamilton was held in close confinement in Virginia until paroled in 1780. He returned to London after his formal exchange in 1781. (*New York Public Library*)

tachment of the 8th Foot, some Canadian militia, and a few artillery-men—he achieved a working rapport with the regional tribes, including those in the Ohio River Valley. The lieutenant governor was aware of growing hostilities to the south, but his early instructions forbade en-couraging Indian attacks. This changed in 1777. British efforts to crush the rebellion had failed, and with Indian resistance to white encroach-ments stiffening anyway, London finally decided to court Native Amer-icans as combatants. Hamilton was to encourage and assist Indian forays against rebel settlements in Kentucky and western Pennsylvania, and to that end he offered ceremonial war belts to Indian leaders with promises of material aid, including the support of loyalist militia and British offi-cers. Tribes including the Wyandots, some previously neutral Delawares, and to Cornstalk's distress, the majority of Shawnees, jumped at Hamil-ton's offer. Although Hamilton later denied it, patriots widely believed he offered bounties for white prisoners and scalps (American rebels called him the "Hair-buyer"). While he sincerely regretted the loss of civilian lives, Hamilton understood that the Indian campaign would inevitably cause noncombatant deaths.[9] Supported by Detroit, war parties prepared to wrest control of Trans-Appalachia from the Americans.

Learning of Hamilton's initiative, Americans planned a preemptive strike into the Ohio Valley. In October rumors of the expedition prompted Cornstalk and a small party, including his son, Elinipsico, to travel to the Virginia outpost at Fort Randolph (modern Point Pleasant, West Virginia) to discuss the deteriorating situation. The rebels cancelled the operation after recruiting efforts failed; but at Fort Randolph the militia commander, Captain Matthew Arbuckle, Sr., detained the Shawnee delegation. Unsure of what to do with Cornstalk, he requested instructions from Continental brigadier general Edward Hand, commanding the Continental garrison at Fort Pitt. Before Hand could respond, local militiamen, enraged at the death of a comrade in a skirmish, murdered the Indians in cold blood. The killers escaped punishment when witnesses refused to testify against them. Hand realized Cornstalk's death meant all-out war with the Shawnees; and in Virginia Governor Patrick Henry reached the same conclusion. Cornstalk's murder appalled him, but the governor was impelled to warn frontier communities to look to their defenses.[10]

The popular narrative of the War for Independence has frequently slighted the significance and success of the Indian campaign in the West. Once the Indians decided on war, no frontier settlement was safe; and that included the residents of western North and South Carolina, Georgia, Virginia, Maryland, New York, and Pennsylvania. Indeed, patriots were unprepared for a major frontier war, especially one with imperial support. This support was more than material. The West hosted a network of British agents and traders, many of whom had lived for years among various tribes; some had taken Indian consorts and adopted tribal culture. They served as intermediaries between the Native Americans and royal officials and often advocated effectively for Indian interests. Almost to a man they declared for the Crown and did their best to align the tribes with the royal cause; and as "embedded" personnel among the Indians they played active roles in military operations as advisors and direct combatants. They gave the British considerable reach across the entire West. Along the Mississippi, John Colbert was a zealous loyalist and campaigned with the Chickasaws; Alexander McKee and the Girty brothers—Simon, James, and George, raised among the Indians—were active in the Ohio Valley. Farther south Alexander Cameron advised Dragging Canoe; and among the Creeks, the mixed-blood Alexander

McGillivray was a prominent chief.[11] There were others, and their names became anathema to patriot Americans.

Initial rebel defenses centered on three main forts: Pitt (modern Pittsburgh), a Continental post, Patrick Henry (now Wheeling, West Virginia), and Randolph. Virginia had constructed Fort Henry for frontier defense during Lord Dunmore's War in 1774; similar concerns saw the colony establish Fort Randolph in 1776 on the site of an outpost abandoned after Dunmore's War. There were smaller posts as well, and over time rebels would build additional stockades, many of them private affairs such as "John Holliday's Fort," also in western Virginia, and "Martin's Station" in Kentucky (more on these later). Indian raiders, however, easily slipped past the forts, and individual farms and travelers were vulnerable. The Ohio Valley militias were little match for the Indian offensive as Shawnees under Blackfish and Blue Jacket killed and captured Americans, drove off livestock, destroyed crops, burned cabins, and sent captives and scalps to Detroit.

Nor were the forts immune to assault. Twice, in 1777 and 1782, militia suffered casualties holding Fort Henry against parties of Mingos, Wyandots, Shawnees, and Delawares. Indians unsuccessfully besieged Fort Randolph in 1778, but patriots saw fit to abandon the isolated post the following year. The Indians burned it to the ground.[12] Boonesborough also came under sporadic attack but held out, although white casualties mounted. There were innumerable small skirmishes outside these fortified positions, which at times were little more than prisons for those sheltering inside. By the end of 1777 the only settlements left in Kentucky were Boonesborough and the smaller posts of Harrod's Town (or Harrod's Fort) and Fort Logan (modern Stanford). In 1784 John Filson, Kentucky's first historian, development "booster," and master of understatement, put it mildly when he wrote that the Indians "have continued ever . . . troublesome neighbors to the new settlers."[13]

Things were no better for patriots farther south. Operating from their new towns in southeastern Tennessee, and supplied by John McDonald, British assistant superintendent of Indian affairs in the South, Dragging Canoe's Chickamaugas repeatedly ambushed whites on the rivers of Kentucky and Tennessee. They killed the grandparents of frontiersman and future congressman David ("Davey") Crockett. Accompanied by British agents, a large party of Chickamaugas and Muscogee (Upper Creeks) hit the backcountries of Georgia and South Carolina.[14] To this point in the war, the Indians held the initiative, and they were winning.

Ultimately most of the western tribes, or at least factions of them, were drawn into the conflict. The numerous Creeks never committed their full support to the British, but war parties occasionally sallied against the Americans; the majority—to the unease of both the British and Americans—chose to conserve their strength to deal with whichever side emerged victorious. Like the Creeks, the Choctaws generally favored the British but participated only sparingly in the fighting. They scouted the Mississippi River for the British and over 1779 and 1780 helped the British defend West Florida. On the other hand, some Choctaws fought for the Spanish. The less numerous Chickasaws stood firmly with Britain, patrolling the Mississippi and joining in the fight against American incursions into the Illinois country. Only the small tribe of Catawbas in South Carolina (traditional enemies of the Cherokees) sided with the patriots, for which they suffered at the hands of the British and the other Indians.[15] Even if all the tribes did not commit wholeheartedly to the imperial war effort, from 1777 onward western frontier settlements were subject to virtually constant threats. From the rebel perspective it seemed as though they were facing a massive and coordinated Native American onslaught, an onslaught actively assisted by British matériel and often with white loyalists as allied combatants.

Rebel responses to the Indian offensive were problematic. While patriot leaders were aware of the situation in the West, the Continental Army could do little. Hard-pressed in the East, American regulars would be a rarity anywhere in Trans-Appalachia. Indeed, Continental resources were so scarce that Congress failed to organize a formal Western Department until 1777. Headquartered at Fort Pitt at the confluence of the Monongahela and Allegheny rivers (the site of the old French Fort Duquesne), the department was responsible for defending the frontiers of Pennsylvania, Virginia, and Maryland. Assigned forces at any given time consisted only of two understrength Continental regiments (the 8th Pennsylvania and 9th Virginia), a small contingent of Maryland riflemen, occasional independent companies, and attached artillery and medical personnel. Department commanders were brigadier generals Edward

Hand (1777–1778) and Lachlan McIntosh (May 1778–March 1779) and colonels Daniel Brodhead (March 1779–May 1781) and John Gibson (May–September 1781). After September 1781, Brigadier General William Irvine commanded at Fort Pitt for the rest of the war.[16] These men were capable and diligent officers, but of all the Revolutionary theaters, their regular forces remained the smallest. Departmental muster rolls never counted more than 953 troops, including sick and others unfit or unavailable for duty; those actually "Present Fit for Duty & On Duty" numbered only some 660 at their peak in early 1779. Thereafter departmental strength declined steadily, and by May 1780 the count was 462, and only a paltry 389 in December 1780.[17]

Whatever the troop strength at Fort Pitt, departmental commanders faced a difficult assignment. As historian Brady Crytzer has pointed out, Fort Pitt's commandants seldom got on with the local populace. This was true even in the aftermath of the Seven Years' War, when Colonel Henry Bouquet described "Pittsburgh as 'a colony sprung from Hell,'" and during the Revolution "not much had changed in that regard." As late as 1781 Irvine disparaged Fort Pitt as "nothing but a heap of ruins," a post unworthy of "an officer of his rank."[18] Throughout the war there was significant loyalist sentiment around Pittsburgh, and settlers of all political persuasions resented military authority in any case. Recruiting local militia or volunteers to supplement the thin Continental garrison was never easy; thus the regional outposts for which Fort Pitt was responsible never were effectively manned. Along with several smaller outposts, these included Forts Henry, Randolph, Crawford, in present day Burrell Township, Pennsylvania, and McIntosh, overlooking the Ohio River in modern Beaver, Pennsylvania.[19] Transportation was always a challenge. The region had many navigable rivers, but most inland travel depended on Indian trails and rude tracks between fortified positions. Thus communications with the East were slow and irregular, and supplying Fort Pitt was daunting. Despite garrison hopes, local settlers were not always keen on parting with produce, especially without immediate cash payment.[20] At one point, Colonel Brodhead resorted to impressing local crops and forage to supply his troops—to the outrage of regional settlers. Brodhead also used funds intended for recruiting to supply existing soldiers, for which he was court-martialed (but exonerated). The situation never improved. Upon taking up his command at Fort Pitt, General

Irvine was astonished at the condition of the garrison: "when I arrived no man would believe from their appearance that they were Soldiers, nay it would be difficult to determine whether they were *White Men.*" No Continental department ever was abundantly supplied or financed, but the Western Department was an especially hard-scrabble operation.[21]

However, if the Western Department was never a major command, it was hardly inactive. Its various commandants remained on the lookout for opportunities to strike at the Indians—those "Rascals," according to Brodhead—and they never lost sight of British-held Detroit. With so few Continentals, however, Hand and his successors had to rely on militia for any sizable effort, and many of the militia proved truculent and ill disposed toward the authority of regular officers (occasionally they even stole Continental stores).[22] Thus early rebel offensives in the region came to little; indeed, the first was an abject failure. In February 1778 General Hand led 500 militia from Fort Pitt, striking toward British-supported Mingo (Seneca) towns on the Cuyahoga River in the Ohio country. To Hand's despair, foul weather forced a trek back to Fort Pitt. Worse, the militia proved undisciplined, caught no warriors, and on their return march murdered a number of neutral Delawares, including three women. Thus the expedition was mocked as the "squaw campaign," an effort that only further incensed the Indians.[23] Hand succeeded only in proving that patriot forces in the West were too few and of insufficient quality to conduct operations far beyond Fort Pitt—and that the fort itself was too far removed from the Ohio country to adequately support major operations there. The situation called for forts farther west and for regular troops.

Later in the year Brigadier Lachlan McIntosh, Hand's replacement, did little better, although he tried to extend the frontier and he did make the attempt with Continental regulars. McIntosh's goal was ambitious: he hoped to push all the way to Detroit and knock out British support for Native American operations. As an initial step, the general established Fort McIntosh (humbly named for himself) about 30 miles down the Ohio; he intended the post as an advanced staging area. He then sent some Continentals and militia westward, and they got as far as modern Bolivar, Ohio, where they built Fort Laurens (named for Henry Laurens, president of the Congress). Laurens was about 106 miles from Pittsburgh, but the rebels advanced no farther. McIntosh intended the fort as yet another staging base for a later advance, but it proved to be a virtual prison camp for its garrison. Sallying from Detroit in February 1779, Captain Henry Bird of the 8th Foot besieged Fort Laurens with a force of redcoats and Indians. The American troops, under Colonel John Gibson, held but were reduced to eating their own moccasins. Bird eventually gave up the siege, but Colonel Brodhead, who had succeeded McIntosh, ordered the fort abandoned in the summer.[24]

Fort Laurens was a fruitless venture—just further proof that Trans-Appalachian expeditions of any size faced exceedingly problematic logistics. Supplies were difficult to transport and almost impossible to replenish in the interior. Moreover, the sparsely settled frontier above the Ohio offered few recruiting prospects, so manpower was essentially limited to those who marched with the original force, meaning there was no chance to occupy and secure an area. Fort Laurens was the farthest west any Continental Army detachment moved during the war—for all the good it did. Troops from Fort Pitt, regulars and militia, eventually would play a more important role in the war, but their time had not quite arrived. For the time being—at least through the first half of 1779—patriots in the West, their offensives frustrated or ineffectual, lay mostly on the defensive.

As the fighting in the West spread, its ferocity became notable—in fact its brutality was central to the western experience. The war in the West continued a pattern of conflict dating from the first Anglo-Indian wars of the seventeenth century. These conflicts, as the accounts of John Grinier, Peter Silver, and Patrick Griffen have explained, were ghastly affairs, imbued with a deep-seated racial hatred on the part of whites—a hatred often reinforced by religious convictions that Indians were savages literally in league with the devil—and a sense of existential struggle on the part of Native Americans.[25] The absence of regular armies also contributed to the brutality. The ad hoc militias and their Indian opponents knew or cared little about Enlightenment notions of *jus in bello*—the rules of so-called civilized warfare that sought to limit the excesses of military behavior. There were exceptions: Indians would sometimes take prisoners, especially children, to adopt into their tribes to replace losses; and there were occasions when British or Spanish officers accompanying

Indian operations would protect prisoners. In general, however, both sides made war on combatants and noncombatants alike.[26] Indeed, Native Americans were less concerned with the few American soldiers in the West than they were with the influx of land-hungry farmers. Farmers spelled the end of Indian homelands and hunting grounds, so of course the tribes saw civilian settlers as legitimate targets.

There was another dimension to the growing Indian war that patriots found especially disturbing. While racial hatreds of Native Americans were in full play among frontier whites, ideological concerns also stoked their fears. The full nature of republicanism is beyond our ken here, but the zeitgeist is crucial: whatever else it was, republicanism was an ideology of *fear*. It dwelt on fears of conspiracies against liberty, of plots by tyrants to "enslave" the citizenry, of machinations by a corrupt metropole to subvert the virtue of property-owning and liberty-loving free men in America. Those who believed in British conspiracies had no trouble believing in plots among others, and there seemed ample evidence that Indians were scheming grand alliances against whites. Colonists could look to the recent past at Pontiac's "rebellion" to justify their trepidation, and in the North the Iroquois Confederacy was a standing example of Indian political and military potential. Historian Robert M. Owens has written that such fears were "white nightmares," and western events during the Revolution seemed to give them substance.[27] The illegal settlers on the Henderson purchase (which they called Transylvania) caused near hysteria when they circulated a specious letter supposedly proving a Cherokee-British alliance—and its impact was all they could ask for. In Congress, Virginia delegate Thomas Jefferson wanted the Cherokees driven beyond the Mississippi.[28] With or without such deception, however, realities were serious enough. Not only did Dragging Canoe remain on the warpath after 1776, but he sent emissaries to the Creeks and tribes in the Ohio Valley proposing a united front against the whites. The Shawnees were cooperating with the Delawares, Wyandots, and other tribes in their attacks in Kentucky, and with Hamilton and various British agents offering Indians imperial support, many patriots envisioned a vast conspiracy at work in the West. These developments, coupled with the ferocity and effectiveness of the Native American offensive, were more than enough to confirm patriot suspicions of a plot (or plots) against them. The West was indeed the theater of fear.

Frantic western settlers appealed desperately to patriot authorities for help. Congress and the states conceded the perils facing the West and other frontier areas, and they even identified what they considered the enemy's strategic center. Take Fort Detroit, they reasoned, and cut off the flow of British supplies, and the striking power of the western tribes would crumble. Both Hand and McIntosh, however ineffectually, had moved west with attempts on Detroit in view. In fact, McIntosh launched his disappointing venture after Congress had formally urged an operation against the British stronghold. Other senior patriots maintained the focus on Detroit. Major General Philip Schuyler believed taking the British fort was the key to peace on the frontiers of Pennsylvania, New York, New Jersey, and North Carolina. Washington agreed. "I have ever been of the opinion," he later wrote to Jefferson, "that the reduction of the post of Detroit would be the only certain means of giving peace and security to the whole Western Frontier."[29] But there was little help to send. In addition to the violence in Trans-Appalachia, frontier communities in central Pennsylvania and northern New York had endured devastating Iroquois raids. Washington, struggling just to hold the Continental Army together and to maintain operations against the British in the North and East, could spare no additional regulars for what he considered a peripheral theater. Sober estimates of the troops necessary to take Detroit and garrison smaller outposts ran to 3,000 men, including 1,200 Continentals, and the Continental Army was rarely strong enough to detach such a force.[30] With blunt realism Washington concluded that settlers on the frontiers or in other isolated locations would have to protect themselves. Such was the hard calculus of war. True, in 1779 he did send Sullivan's expedition into Iroquois country (we will return to this episode); but other than the sorry experience at Fort Laurens and occasional raids mounted from the garrison at Fort Pitt, the Continental Army did not venture deeply into Trans-Appalachia. American regulars fought their battles in the East and South, leaving the West largely to look to itself.

Largely—but not entirely. If the Continental Army was unavailable, Virginia marshaled a state effort to defend Kentucky, then a Virginia county. The impetus came from Kentucky leaders, and these prominently included George Rogers Clark. After privately dispatching spies into the Illinois country—roughly present day Illinois and Indiana—he concluded the best way to defend the frontier below the Ohio River was to knock out the British support structure above the Ohio that sustained much of the Indian campaign. That meant taking the Illinois settlements planted by the French before the Seven Years' War that remained as trading centers and forward British staging and supply bases. Targets would include the posts of Kaskaskia, Cahokia (both in modern day Illinois), Vincennes (Indiana), and smaller villages along the way. Clark's intelligence also indicated the loyalties of the region's French *habitants* to the British were ambivalent, and that the towns were virtually undefended. In December 1777, after considerable persuasion, Clark sold an initially skeptical Virginia governor Patrick Henry on his plan. With the decision to proceed, however, Henry cloaked the mission in secrecy, limiting details to a small circle of senior legislators. Commissioned a lieutenant colonel, Clark was to raise an "Illinois Regiment" of 350 men, take Kaskaskia, and then pursue other opportunities he thought promising. Thus began the best-known American military operation of the Western Theater.

Clark's expedition was not without its doubters. As historian Consul W. Butterfield has observed, many Kentuckians preferred to defend south of the Ohio rather than moving north; other Virginians considered Kentucky too sparsely populated to merit a major operation, while still others thought the military situation had deteriorated to the point that prudence indicated abandoning most of Kentucky until after the war.[31] In fact, the operation never proved popular enough to recruit over 200 men. In any case, the expedition sallied on May 12, 1778, taking boats down the Monongahela River to the Ohio and reaching the Falls of the Ohio on May 27. Clark established an island base camp in the middle of the rapids, safe from attacks from either shore.

The island encampment produced a largely unsung development that Native Americans, if they had thought about it, might have found more alarming than Clark's small expeditionary force. Twenty families had accompanied Clark, demonstrating that Anglo-American emigration would continue despite the Indian war. They planted corn on the island—thus "Corn Island"—and the following year moved to the south shore of the Ohio to found what became Louisville, named in honor of Louis XVI and the Franco-American alliance. Like other settlers, those transplanted from Corn Island, as well as new arrivals, built blockhouses and defensive stockades. Louisville was a strategic point. The Falls of the

Ohio constituted the only barrier to navigation between Fort Pitt and
New Orleans; and the nascent town soon prospered as a portage point
around the falls for trade moving north and south, including covert
Spanish aid to the patriots. Control of the Ohio, many Americans hoped,
would foster commercial links with the Mississippi Valley and the port
of New Orleans. As early as summer 1776, Virginia already had sent a
mission downriver from Fort Pitt to New Orleans to explore military
and commercial contacts with the Spanish.[32] For the moment that was
a longer-term issue, but in the short term the new town promised an
outlet for Kentucky produce, thus encouraging even more white settlers—a Native American nightmare. In the West, fear worked both
ways.

Clark moved downriver and into Illinois in July. He encountered no
opposition as he took Kaskaskia and smaller outposts all the way to the
banks of the Mississippi at Cahokia. Backtracking, Clark then moved
on Fort Sackville at Vincennes. The local militia, mostly French *habitants*, surrendered without firing a shot, and several hundred Ohio Valley
French swore allegiance to Virginia and Congress, encouraged by news
of the recent Franco-American alliance. Clark's intelligence of the previous year had been correct: Former French subjects felt little empathy for
George III. Neither did some Indians who, impressed with Clark, declared for the Americans.

In Detroit, news of Clark's success appalled Lieutenant Governor
Hamilton—and for good reason. The loss of a few small outposts was
the least of his worries; of much greater concern was the British ability
to hold Native Americans for the imperial cause. Hamilton knew that
most Indians were fighting for reasons of their own, and that their support for Britain was an ancillary consideration—a way to multiply their
force against American expansion. Tribes repeatedly made clear their expectation of material aid, gifts, and promises of direct military support
in return for their service. Failing that, Indians made it equally clear that
they could withdraw from cooperation with the Crown, fight on their
own, or even do business with the rebels or (in the Southwest) the Spanish, who were edging closer to war with Great Britain. When Clark
marched unopposed to the Mississippi, it left many Indians questioning
events, and tribes as distant as the Odawa (Ottawa) from Michilimackinac
(in what is today upper Michigan) sent delegations to meet with the cu-

rious Virginian. Clark consulted with Ojibwas, Odawas, Potawatomis, Fox, Mississaugas, Winnebagos, Sauks, and other tribes, most of whom had been openly hostile or cool toward the patriot cause. Most remained so after speaking with Clark, but they demanded more from the British in gifts and supplies in return for their continued loyalty.[33] And why not? If a small American force could traverse the West with impunity, tribes could reasonably ask what good were British promises of protection and alliance. For that matter, now that France was in the war, why should French *habitants*, some of whom hoped for a French return to Trans-Appalachia, not go over to the rebels? Hamilton *had* to act.

He did so, and his campaign was as noteworthy as Clark's. The lieutenant governor assembled a force of some 30 regulars of the 8th Foot, 145 Canadian militia, and 60 Native Americans, mostly Odawas. The expedition left Detroit on October 7, 1778, heading toward Vincennes, some 300 miles away.[34] Hamilton gathered volunteers on the way, including some Indians who had just pledged loyalty to Clark; he also threatened dire consequences to any French *habitants* who went over to the rebels. He reached Vincennes on December 17 with over 500 men. Confronted with this force, the Canadian militia at Fort Sackville— Hamilton called it a "miserable picketted work called a fort"—that had gone over to Clark promptly switched sides again. Local civilians did likewise; western loyalties were nothing if not malleable.[35] Remaining in Vincennes, Hamilton thought he had done enough for the time being; he decided to winter in the village and retake the other Illinois outposts in the spring. Now Clark faced the task of reversing the fortunes of war.

Clark was in Kaskaskia in late January 1779 when he learned of Hamilton's counterstroke. He quickly gathered some 170 men, and in a truly epic march—a trek in many respects comparable to Benedict Arnold's march on Quebec of 1775—in three weeks he slogged 180 miles through freezing weather and across swollen rivers to reach Vincennes. On the evening of February 23, Clark easily took the town and opened fire on the fort; inside Sackville the surprised Hamilton refused an initial surrender demand and a subsequent truce offer. Confronted with the lieutenant governor's intransigence, Clark decided on a grisly warning to the besieged garrison. The colonel had four captured Indians tomahawked in cold blood in front of the fort. Clark made no apology for the murders, seeing them as payback for white casualties, and espe-

An early proponent of colonial westward expansion, under Virginia's auspices, George Rogers Clark (1752–1818) campaigned against the Indians almost continuously between 1778 and 1783. He was the most capable rebel military leader in the West, but despite tactical successes he never landed a knock-out blow against his Anglo-Indian enemies. (*Library of Congess*)

cially since they led Hamilton to concede the hopelessness of his position. He surrendered on February 25, and Clark had him sent to Virginia where he was imprisoned, much of the time in irons, until exchanged in 1781.

Hamilton's surrender sent shock waves across the West. The chief problem for the British lay with the northern tribes—the Odawas, Ojibwas, and others from the Great Lakes region. Unlike the Native Americans in the southeast and Ohio Valley, they were not facing the immediate brunt of American immigration; thus, while allied with the British and sending warriors into the fray, they felt less compulsion to be active combatants on any terms but their own. They had "renegotiated" their loyalty to the British cause after Clark's initial invasion, and after the second fall of Vincennes—with the loss of a lieutenant governor and his detachment of regulars—the Great Lakes Indians expressed reservations about the royal cause. Their alarm increased exponentially in the summer and autumn with the American decision to carry the war into Iroquois country, seemingly a clear sign that patriots might take the war in the West with greater seriousness.

The invasion came after lengthy frontier pleas for Continental help against the Indians. With the eastern war relatively quiescent—the British in New York were mounting no major operations—Washington felt he could spare the men and resources for a major strike against the Iroquois, who had kept the New York and Pennsylvania frontiers in turmoil. In June 1779 the commander-in-chief sent Major General John Sullivan with some 3,200 troops into western New York with orders to devastate Indian lands and make it impossible for the Iroquois to sustain themselves economically and socially—and to knock them out of the war for at least a season. In the campaign's only pitched battle, Sullivan defeated the Iroquois and their Tory allies at Newtown (near modern-day Elmira). Thereafter, like the operations against the Cherokees almost three years earlier, the expedition was an infantry "chevaunche." Patriot troops pursued a scorched-earth campaign, burning out Indian towns, destroying crops, and driving the Iroquois toward Fort Niagara. There many Indians starved and froze to death over the winter; it was war against almost the entire Iroquois population, not just the warriors. The Indians were furious in their suffering.[36]

As Sullivan campaigned, the Western Department came alive: Brodhead launched an offensive of his own. The western commander had itched to strike at the Senecas (members of the Iroquois Confederacy, also called Mingos) of northwestern Pennsylvania and southwestern New York. In April 1779 the colonel was positively breathing fire: "I will soon strike a Blow," he promised one of his officers, "that will convince the Villains of there errors. The woods will soon swarm with men, and I have every thing on the way for making my route with the Sloughter of Victims. Mingoes," he predicted, "will die first and then our enemies at Detroit and [Fort] Niagara. The scene will be closed with the remaining Rascals that may be found in arms against us."[37] It was brave talk, but Brodhead lacked the "swarms" of men necessary for a major operation, and a skeptical Washington told him to hold off, citing a lack of resources.

In the summer, however, the colonel got his chance. In July the commander-in-chief approved a movement by Brodhead, thinking it would provide a diversion in favor of Sullivan's larger expedition. Thus on August 11 the colonel left Fort Pitt with a mixed force of some 600 Continentals (9th Virginia, 8th Pennsylvania, and Maryland riflemen), militia, and allied Delaware Indians; they moved up the Allegheny, heading toward the Seneca towns to the north. Aside from a minutes-long skirmish at Thompson's Island on August 18 or 19, Brodhead met little resistance. Many Seneca warriors had marched east to oppose Sullivan, and Brodhead's men found only deserted villages, which they burned and pillaged with a free hand. After a typical sweep of Indian territory the expedition returned to Fort Pitt on September 14, having destroyed the villages of Buckaloons, Conewago, Yoghroonwago, and Mahusquechikoken and seizing ample stores of corn, livestock, and other plunder.[38] Washington was well satisfied and heartily congratulated Brodhead in general orders: "The activity, perseverance, and firmness which marked the conduct of Colonel Brodhead and that of all of the officers and men of every description in this expedition, do them great honor, and their services entitle them to the thanks, and to this testimonial of the General's Acknowledgment."[39] Brodhead's operation was the only example the war would see of the Western Department moving in support of an operation from the East.

Viewed from Detroit, the far northwest, and the Ohio country, the activities of Sullivan and Brodhead were alarming. How far would the Americans go? Would they move west in overwhelming force? Under the circumstances it was all the British could do to maintain the allegiance of the Great Lakes tribes. Credit for maintaining working ties with the northern Indians went to Arent De Peyster, an American-born British regular who had replaced Hamilton in Detroit. His tact and persuasion convinced most Indians, some of whom were in communication with the Americans, that their best chance for an independent future lay in an Anglo-Indian alliance. What would happen to the tribes later, he asked, if they had to face victorious Americans alone? Fears among the Odawas and Ojibwas also calmed when it became clear that neither Sullivan nor Brodhead were moving farther west. But the new Detroit commandant knew never to take the tribes for granted, and he repeatedly wrote Governor Sir Frederick Haldimand at Quebec City, pleading for additional funds to keep the Indians supplied with gifts—that is, to keep buying Native American loyalty.[40] De Peyster also wanted troop reinforcements in case some of the Indians actually turned on the British, and in the event Clark marched against Detroit. Haldimand had no troops to send and grumbled at the mounting expenses, but he sent the money. He had to. If he hadn't, he was fairly certain the Spanish would have.

Haldimand was right: In 1779 Spain declared war on Great Britain and became an overt player in the western conflict. Not that the Spanish had been bystanders earlier in the war. Spain was no friend to rebels or republics, but it was happy to discomfort its former enemy; and since 1776 the Spanish had sent covert financial and material aid to the Americans. Much of this aid, both before and after Spain entered the war, wound its way up the Mississippi to the Ohio and on to Fort Pitt, a lengthy and difficult upstream journey. It could also be dangerous. Indeed, in October 1779 on the shores of the Ohio near modern Dayton, Kentucky, a large Indian party with loyalist support ambushed camping American boatmen coming back from New Orleans; a few rebels got away but some 70 were wiped out.[41] The Spanish, while still technically at peace with Britain, also had given cover to American traders who plied the Mississippi under the Spanish flag. Spain even sheltered combatants. In 1778 the congressional Commerce Committee sanctioned a mission against British outposts on the lower Mississippi River. In January navy captain James Willing (brother of Thomas Willing, the business partner of Continental superintendent of finance Robert Morris) led 29 men down the Ohio; reaching the Mississippi, they raided the Natchez region in a fashion that would have embarrassed common banditti. They pillaged with a free hand, burned out plantations, kidnapped 650 slaves, and then found refuge in Spanish Louisiana.[42] In nearby West Florida the British were livid; they eventually reestablished control of their posts, but tension ran high between the rival imperial powers.

Thus by early 1780 the British war effort in the West faced multiple challenges. The Spanish were threatening along the gulf coast; Clark was still in the field and, as the British knew, looking for a way to move against Detroit; and Native Americans were exasperated by continuing American immigration and the seeming British inability to react effectively. The imperial cause was at something of a crossroads. At best the western war was a stalemate, which over time could work only in favor of the Americans and the Spanish. At Detroit the Shawnees and other Northwestern tribes saw the situation as critical, and now they demanded

Successor to Lieutenant Governor Henry Hamilton at Detroit, Arent Schuyler De Peyster (1736–1822) labored diligently to maintain Anglo-Indian alliances against the rebel Americans, repeatedly (and accurately) warning the Indians of the consequences of an American victory. (*New York Public Library*)

more than logistical support; they wanted the direct support of British regulars. They told De Peyster the British had to commit troops to turn the tide—either that or the Indians would be "under the disagreeable necessity of falling back . . . or else quit the ground & go to the Southward."[43] De Peyster commanded only a limited number of regulars, but again fearful of wavering Indian commitments to the war, he nevertheless agreed to organize an expedition in support of a renewed Native American offensive.

In fact, De Peyster was doing exactly what the government back in London thought necessary. Alarmed at the wider scope of the conflict— it was now a world war—and at the lack of a decision in North America, Lord North's ministers concluded a serious western initiative was in order. The plan was threefold. Ideally an operation mounted from Fort Michilimackinac by Lieutenant Governor Patrick Sinclair would sweep the Americans and Spanish out of the Illinois country, taking St. Louis, Cahokia, Kaskaskia, and Vincennes. Movements from West Florida would counter the Spanish in the Mississippi Valley, including the capture of New Orleans. Finally, forces out of Detroit would take the Falls of the Ohio (where Clark had erected Fort Nelson) and Fort Pitt, thus regaining the initiative in Kentucky.[44] Details, however, were left to local commanders and, as in the Burgoyne fiasco of 1777, the various British operations received minimal coordination. Indeed, poor planning, lack of resources, tactical differences between the British and Native Americans, and enemy action frustrated the grand design (and it is charitable to call it that).

Spanish operations proved fatal to two elements of the plan. In West Florida, Brigadier General John Campbell was to advance on the Mississippi—but Campbell's offensive never took place. Instead, with open war, the Spanish moved first. Under Louisiana governor Bernardo de Gálvez they quickly swept the British out of the lower Mississippi and then turned east. In 1780 they took Mobile, and the following year, on May 10, 1781, Campbell surrendered at Pensacola. The Spanish also frustrated Sinclair's expedition from Michilimackinac. In May 1780 they successfully defended St. Louis against an attack by tory-led Indians (composed mostly of Sioux, Fox, Sac, Chippewas, Menominees, and Winnebagos), while directly across the Mississippi Clark beat off a simultaneous assault on Cahokia. These defeats ended British efforts to control the Mississippi Valley, and in December the Spanish went north on the offensive. They dispatched Captain Don Eugenio Pouré with sixty Spaniards and an Indian contingent to raid Fort St. Joseph near the southern tip of Lake Michigan. They took the post by surprise in February 1781, grandly claiming the fort and surrounding territory for Spain, although they withdrew after a stay of several hours.[45] Nevertheless, the raid clearly was an expression of Spanish interest in the West—and of how the Western Theater had become part of the wider world war raging among Europe's imperial powers.

The only British initiative to produce any success was De Peyster's, and even it failed to prove decisive. At Detroit the lieutenant governor tasked Captain Henry Bird—the nemesis of the patriot outpost at Fort Laurens—with command of an expedition of 150 British regulars, tory militia, approximately 1,000 Indians, and two cannons (a 3- and a 6-pounder).[46] Bird marched on May 25, 1780, with the intention of moving to the Falls of the Ohio. Other than Fort Pitt, if any one western target could be described as strategically important, it was the falls and the nascent town of Louisville. Posted there, an Anglo-Indian force could cut river navigation that brought new settlers and supplies into the region from the East, block Spanish aid moving up the Ohio from the West,

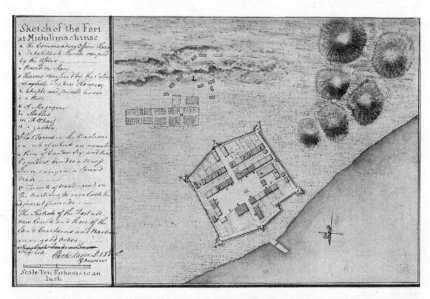

Sketch of the Fort at Michilimackinac, 1766, by Lt. Perkins Magra. At the head of Lake Michigan, Michilimackinac was the headquarters of Lieutenant Governor Patrick Sinclair, who supported the various Great Lakes tribes in attacks against American settlers and militia. The map is oriented with north to the bottom. (*Library of Congress*)

and launch destructive raids into the Kentucky interior. Alexander McKee, long-time British Indian agent and Bird's second-in-command, felt sure the seizure of the falls "would have been a fatal stroke to the enemies settlements" in Kentucky. In Quebec, Haldimand thought taking the falls was essential to British success.[47] Patriots fully appreciated the strategic importance of the location—its loss would have undone most of Clark's work—and in 1778 Clark had ordered construction of a defensive post, Fort-on-Shore, to guard it. (The post was subsequently enlarged and renamed Fort Nelson, in honor of Virginia governor Thomas Nelson, Jr.—another reminder that the chief effort in the West was Virginian, not Continental.) The falls was a logical target.

Yet Bird never made the attempt. Despite his pleas, he was unable to convince the Native American contingent of the wisdom of the move. They feared that Clark, then near the junction of the Ohio and Mississippi rivers, would march against them. The fear was groundless. Clark would have faced moving against the current coming up the Ohio and could not have stopped Bird from reaching the falls. In any case, Clark had only some 200 men, far fewer than Bird's command. But such was Clark's reputation that the Indians were adamant; they preferred not to fight him and instead insisted on an expedition up the Licking River, an Ohio tributary, to attack the small Kentucky outposts at Ruddell's (also Ruddle's) Station and Martin's Station. Bird had no choice but to agree.

These settler posts stood no chance against the Anglo-Indian advance. At Ruddell's the whites initially refused to surrender, and a shot from the 3-pounder merely chipped a log on the blockhouse. When Bird brought up the 6-pounder, however, the rebels gave in with the understanding that their lives would be spared. After the surrender, however, Bird was unable to restrain the Indians, who killed about 20 Americans before plundering and taking the rest prisoner. Bird was disgusted, but he was able to maintain order when Martin's Station surrendered shortly thereafter. In early August the expedition returned to Detroit with some 300 prisoners. It was a difficult march, and the Indians killed prisoners unable to keep up (mercy killings from the Indian perspective).[48] Following tradition the Indians also kept some white children to adopt into their tribes. At Detroit questioning of the prisoners revealed that many were not committed patriots. Some had gone west in search of cheap lands and to escape the war in the East, and a number even agreed to serve in Tory militia in exchange for British protection.

While Bird's expedition produced no decisive military results, it did restore some Native American faith in the British. Five years into the war, Bird had demonstrated how vulnerable the Kentucky settlements remained; some alarmed Kentuckians pulled up stakes and headed back East. Bird also left Clark thoroughly frustrated. Arriving at the falls later in August, the Virginian briefly tried to block the main routes to Virginia in an effort to stem the reverse tide. Clark even tried to halt land sales, insisting Americans should serve in an attack on Detroit before settling.[49] He had no luck. The best he was able to do was mount an ineffectual raid against several Shawnee towns—another "chevaunche" that burned villages, killed few warriors, and produced nothing of strategic value. While the British were defeated (or facing defeat) along the Mississippi or in Florida, elsewhere the Anglo-Indian effort had regained the initiative in the Northwest.

Events later in 1780 underscored this fact. In perhaps the most curious episode in the Western Theater, a former French officer, Agustin de

La Balme, entered the Illinois country and raised the French standard. He had volunteered his services to the Continental Army and had served briefly as inspector of cavalry; but he resigned in 1777 and went west under circumstances never fully explained.[50] In any case, lacking any and all official authority, de La Balme launched a freelance operation. Beginning at Kaskaskia he rallied several hundred French Canadians, who may have believed his arrival signaled a French return to Trans-Appalachia. The alacrity with which they joined de La Balme certainly reflected no loyalty to George III. Marching under the French flag, de La Balme headed for Detroit, evidently seeking to replicate Clark's success against Vincennes; he hoped Canadians at Fort Detroit would rise to join him. It was not to be. Over several days in early November, Miami Indians under Little Turtle virtually wiped out de La Balme's party at the village of Kekionga and on the Eel River in Indiana (modern Whitley County). It was a resounding Indian victory, and it made Little Turtle's reputation as a war chief—and like Dragging Canoe, he would be heard from again.[51] For the present, except for Vincennes, Cahokia, and Kaskaskia, de La Balme's defeat left the vast balance of the Illinois country in Native American hands.

Clark, however, remained committed to an offensive against Detroit. He recognized that knocking out De Peyster's stronghold was the surest way to cripple Indian offensive capabilities. In this he had Governor Thomas Jefferson's full support. The governor had hoped raising two battalions of state troops and erecting a line of fortifications would "form a complete Western defence" on the Virginia frontier; but the state neither raised the required manpower nor established effective outposts. Under the circumstances he joined Clark in yet another call for an expedition against Detroit. Again Washington agreed in principle but once more pointed out the inability of the Continental Army to do much. The commander-in-chief ordered Colonel Brodhead to furnish Clark with necessary supplies and artillery; if possible Brodhead also was to reinforce Clark with Continentals from Fort Pitt—but Clark had to recruit the bulk of the manpower. To Jefferson's disappointment (not to mention Clark's), in mid-February 1781 Brodhead concluded he could not spare the men for Detroit; in fact, he received orders to dispatch men to Richmond to counter Benedict Arnold's incursion into Virginia (besides, as we will see, Brodhead had plans of his own which precluded sending troops to Clark).[52] Credit Clark with persistence, however. In June he asked again about assistance from Fort Pitt, and once more the commander-in-chief noted the impossibility. Even if Fort Pitt was to detach Continentals, Washington concluded, the force would be too small to take Detroit.[53] The lack of Continental assistance may not have mattered, however, as Clark was never able to enlist enough volunteers to make an offensive feasible. And moving against Detroit with a minimal force was a fool's errand—de La Balme had proved as much. De Peyster was safe.

With Detroit secure, the Indian offensive continued with neither side wasting compassion on opponents. In April 1781 Brodhead sallied from Pittsburgh with 150 Continentals, linked up with 134 militia at Fort Henry, and then marched on the Delaware villages in Ohio. Since 1778 most Delawares had tried to remain neutral or sided with the Americans; some Delaware leaders actually had proposed the formation of a Delaware state with representation in Congress. But Anglo-American pressure on Indian lands, which Brodhead initially had tried to stop, had splintered Delaware loyalties. Most were gravitating toward the British; thus Brodhead's mission was something of a preemptive strike. His men pillaged the Moravian hamlet of Lichtenau, then attacked the settlement of Coshocton. Accounts differ on exactly what happened in the village, but clearly an outrage took place. Rebels torched Coshocton, slaughtered livestock, and then murdered fifteen captured warriors in cold blood.[54] Coshocton reflected white hatred of the Indians, but the murders did nothing to alter the regional military balance. If a few Delawares adhered to the American alliance, Brodhead's expedition succeeded only in driving most of the tribe firmly into the anti-patriot camp, and the war in the Ohio Valley tribes only intensified.

This war-to-the-knife had its equals in the other theaters of the War for Independence—the Mohawk Valley of New York State and the bitter civil war in the South being obvious examples—but the frequency and ferocity of the violence in the Western Theater was unmatched. Moreover, as the war wound to its climax in the East, British-backed Native Americans maintained the upper hand in much of the West. Shawnees and allied tribes, determined to defend the Ohio Valley, or to at least keep settlers south of the river, hit almost constantly at settlements in

Illustration from Thomas Baldwin's narrative of the attack on his farm in Kentucky, 1781. The attack on the Baldwin farm was typical of Native American raids against white home-steads—and an object lesson in the perils of settling any distance from fortified settlements. *Narrative of the Massacre, by the Savages, of the Wife and Children of Thomas Baldwin, Who, since the Melancholy Period of the Destruction of His Unfortunate Family, Has Dwelt Entirely Alone, Secluded from Human Society, in the Extreme Western Part of the State of Kentucky*, New York, 1835. (*Library of Congress*)

Kentucky, northeastern Tennessee, and southwestern Virginia. They even helped foil Clark's plans for a descent on Detroit. In August 1781 at Laughery Creek, near present-day Aurora, Indiana, Indians and loyalists under the Mohawk Joseph Brant (who fortuitously happened to be west consulting with De Peyster) decimated a contingent of Pennsylvania militia under Archibald Lochry on their way to join Clark's hoped-for mission. Clark could never replace the lost Pennsylvanians.

Farther west, the Chickasaws proved equally capable. They shook off Spanish and American peace overtures and hit Spanish and American parties along the Mississippi, Ohio, and Tennessee rivers; in June 1781 they forced patriots to abandon Fort Jefferson, which Clark had planted just below the junction of the Ohio and Mississippi. As late as April 1783 James Colbert, the long-time British agent among the Chickasaws, led a band of tories and Indians across the Mississippi in an ill-fated raid on the Spanish at Fort Carlos (modern Gillett), Arkansas.[55] Thus, while not always successful militarily, various tribes nevertheless held the initiative in the defense of the Mississippi and Ohio valleys and Northwest through 1783 and beyond.

While the Shawnees and others campaigned, southward the Chickamaugas marshaled their greatest effort of the war. During the summer of 1781 Dragging Canoe raided settlements along the Cumberland River in Tennessee, forcing whites to evacuate all but three regional outposts until 1785. Although attacked, Fort Nashborough, forerunner of modern Nashville, was one of the hold-outs. Twice, in 1781 and 1782, Cherokees, sometimes with Creek and loyalists allies, also struck into northeastern Georgia and western South Carolina, devastating much of Wilkes County and raiding settlements along the Oconee River. Cries for vengeance rang throughout the Carolina backcountry, keeping the cycle of violence in full swing.

Indeed, the attacks provoked strong patriot responses. In Georgia, Andrew Pickens and other militia leaders led South Carolina and Georgia troops against Indian towns, burning and taking prisoners—a replay of the events of 1776. In Tennessee, Colonel John Sevier moved against other Cherokee bands, including those following Dragging Canoe. Sevier was a hardened veteran. In October 1780 he had led Overmountain Men against British major Patrick Ferguson and his tories at Kings Mountain, and then came home to lead a sweep of Cherokee towns. He did the same in 1781 and 1782. These were "search and destroy" missions—the "chevaunches" we have seen repeatedly— that destroyed towns crops and spread hardship among the Cherokees. They also spread further resentment. While many Cherokees sued for peace, many others, as in 1776, joined Dragging Canoe. Under the young war chief, they again built new towns in remote areas of Tennessee and Georgia and fought on. Dragging Canoe continued diplomatic efforts with other tribes. In November 1782 he met with a delegation of Great Lakes tribes seeking help for operations in Kentucky, the Illinois country, and even for an assault on Fort Pitt (that never took place). The chief's brother, Turtle-at-Home, then led seventy Chickamaugas north to fight alongside the Shawnees.

Throughout the mayhem neither side could land anything approaching a knockout blow. There is no point in cataloguing the litany of raids and counterraids that beleaguered the West. It is enough to note they kept Trans-Appalachia in a perpetual state of anxiety, if not terror. Among

MASSACRE OF THE CHRISTIAN INDIANS.

The Gnadenhutten Massacre, March 1782. The incident was one of the most disgraceful atrocities committed by either side in the Western Theater. After capturing the undefended Moravian village of Gnadenhutten, rebel militia voted to slaughter the pacifist Christian Lenape Indians, including women and children. The actual murders took place indoors. (*New York Public Library*)

whites it was a brave—foolish is a better word—individual or family that traveled alone or beyond a defended village or outpost. And, as the fates of Gowen's Fort and Ruddell's Station proved, even defended positions were not always safe. But within the bloody cycle of war neither side could hold ground. Patriot and Native American raids, as the operations of Dragging Canoe, Brodhead, Clark, and Sevier demonstrated, were followed by withdrawals. Both sides pillaged and burned, killed enemies and took prisoners (whose fate could be worse than death), without doing anything decisive. For the most part the comings and goings of war parties and opposing militias settled little or nothing. All the while, as historian Ethan Schmidt has noted, "incidents of bloodshed and atrocity became the norm throughout the west"; and if Indians and whites feared the norm, they were also inured to it.[56]

Some incidents, however, still had the power to shock even hardened combatants. In an example of hideous cruelty, on November 3, 1781, only weeks after Cornwallis had capitulated at Yorktown, patriot defenders of Gowen's Fort in western South Carolina (near modern Landrum) surrendered to a party of Dragging Canoe's Chickamaugas and loyalists under Captain William ("Bloody Bill") Bates. Bates had promised quarter, but when the patriots grounded arms Bates ordered the massacre of men, women, and children. At least 10 Americans died on the spot while others were captured and later tortured to death. A lucky few escaped to spread the news to a terrified and infuriated countryside.[57] Atrocity followed atrocity. In early March 1782 Pennsylvania militia under Colonel David Williamson slaughtered 96 pacifist Lenape Indians, including 29 women and 39 children, at Gnadenhutten, a Moravian mission on the Muskingum River in Ohio. It was an act of pure savagery that appalled even some (but by no means all) patriots. As historian Rob Harper put it, patriots who were appalled "looked the other way," cowed by a political context of Indian hatred and not wanting to risk the obloquy that might result from demanding justice for the murdered Lenape.[58] Outrage hardly described Native American reactions, and there was retribution. Three months later Indians overwhelmed 480 Virginia militia near modern Sandusky, Ohio. They captured Colonel William Crawford, a friend of Washington's, and in retaliation for Gnadenhutten they tortured and burned him at the stake.[59] The news stunned the commander-in-chief. "I am particularly affected with the disastrous fate of Colo. Crawford," he wrote grimly that "no other than the extremest Tortures which could be inflicted by Savages could, I think, have been expected, by those who were unhappy eno' to fall into their Hands; especially under the present Exasperation of their Minds for the treatment given their Moravian friends [at Gnadenhutten]. For this reason, no person should at this Time, suffer himself to fall alive into the hands of the Indians."[60] Here indeed was fear at its deepest. And, of course, the cycle of violent retribution continued as Clark once more (November 1782) swept through Ohio Valley Indian towns—yet another chevaunche with little military effect.[61]

Crawford was not alone in defeat. Aside from maintaining the normal raids, in March 1782 Wyandots won the so-called Battle of the Clouds (or Estill's Defeat) in eastern Kentucky, killing most of the small militia of Estill's Station, not far from Boonesborough. On August 19 Wyandots and tories ambushed an ineptly led militia force, killing and capturing over 80 rebels in the Battle of Blue Licks, Kentucky, the last major engagement west of the Appalachians. Daniel Boone barely escaped, while a shot through the neck killed his son, Israel.[62] If any further evidence was needed, Blue Licks amply demonstrated the continuing Indian-

British ability to strike hard in the West, even as the war wound down in the East.

By 1783 the military situation in the Western Theater had become a "stalemate."[63] The Indians still held the tactical initiative; Crawford, de La Balme, and Blue Licks amply demonstrated that the tribes could defeat even relatively large hostile forces caught in the open. Patriot forays by Clark, Sevier, Pickens, and even the egregious Williamson could overrun defenseless Indian towns, but to little effect. As long as warrior casualties remained low—and Indian raiding tactics usually prevented the losses inherent in stand-up battles—the tribes and loyalist allies could regroup and continue the fight with British supplies and logistical support. Well after Yorktown, Clark still feared an attack from Detroit and even considered the destruction of the Kentucky settlements possible; settlers "have been obliged to keep close in Forts," he reported to Irvine, and the Indians were "so numerous" that Clark could not muster the manpower to fight them.[64] In short, as the war ended in the East, patriots could march into the Trans-Appalachian countryside but they could never hold or secure it. The Ohio and Mississippi valleys and the Northwest and Southwest remained largely "Indian Country," and the American victory at Yorktown never meant peace in the West.

Yet even while losing individual battles, whites were gradually winning the long war. Since Indian dominance of the countryside made American efforts to settle on widely separated individual farms virtually suicidal, circumstances compelled settlers to live near fortified posts, most of which gradually offered effective defenses against all but the largest (or luckiest) enemy operations. As new emigrants arrived in Tennessee and Kentucky, they lived, in effect, in military colonies; and if smaller forts remained vulnerable, larger towns proved able to withstand Native American threats.

Booneborough's stockade held off and then discouraged repeated attacks; and at the Falls of the Ohio, Louisville, buttressed by newly built Fort Nelson's large stockade and full moat, was impervious to assault. Lexington expanded quickly and was able to defend itself after 1779, and nearby Bryan's Station proved too hard a nut for Native American raids to crack. The expanding white frontier was thus a region of fortified points, often in supporting distance, each with its own militia. That is, the colonists had continued and perfected their de facto "clear and hold" policy. In Detroit, De Peyster had identified the pattern but was unable to counter it.[65] Thus, if the tribes largely controlled the countryside, except at limited times and under limited circumstances (as in the aftermath of Bird's expedition), they were never able to drive the whites out or to prevent continuing emigration. Indeed, from a few outposts in 1777, Kentucky's population had increased to some 8,000 settlers by 1782, and then soared to 50,000 by 1787, and 73,677 by 1790. In Tennessee the beleaguered settlements of the 1780s grew to 35,691 residents in 1790, and to over 105,000 in 1800.[66] Such demography, backed by arms, was the making of an eventual Native American defeat.

The emphasis, however, is properly on "eventual," for in the short run Yorktown and the Treaty of Paris meant little west of the Appalachians. The treaty had conceded Trans-Appalachia, including the Northwest and territories out to the Mississippi, to the new republic. Despite the claims of some historians to the contrary,[67] the military situation in the West, and Clark's exploits in particular, had little (probably nothing) to do with the territorial settlement. Rather, Britain gave up the West for diplomatic and economic reasons; there were no patriot troops above the Ohio River and the Americans had not secured the area militarily. The peace agreement left the Indians perplexed; it included no mention of the Native Americans. Indeed, the British had never consulted them before signing the treaty, and most tribes justly felt betrayed by the Crown. The peace ended overt British support to the tribes. Yet the Anglo-Indian connection was never fully severed. Citing American treaty violations, the British refused to evacuate Detroit and other Northwest forts; and while they stopped overtly supporting the tribes, clandestine aid continued to flow in the form of trade: weapons and supplies for furs.[68]

In many respects the war in the West had been a war unto itself. Military operations in Trans-Appalachia often (in fact, usually) had little bearing on events in the East; the conflicts on the western frontiers hardly influenced the British decision to seek peace after Yorktown. With or without the British, many Native Americans remained at war. Little Turtle and Blue Jacket (who had fought at Blue Licks) refused to recognize American sovereignty; and Dragging Canoe never gave up; he even sought support from the Spanish (with Britain out of the war, Spain

hardly wanted a new republic on their colonial borders). The Chickamauga chief continued to seek Indian allies against the whites, and one
of his young warriors, Tecumseh, would later succeed in assembling one
of the most powerful Indian confederacies ever to confront American
expansion. The Chickamaugas continued hostilities into the 1790s, and
in the Ohio Valley the Indian wars never really stopped. The Shawnees
and Miamis (under Little Turtle) were actively resisting white encroach-
ments as early as 1784, and what became known as the Northwest Indian
War dragged on for another decade. By then white pressure was building
on the Creeks in Georgia and in what would become Alabama, and ferocious warfare erupted in the early 1800s. From the Native American
perspective, the War for Independence was merely another chapter in
the continuing war for the independence of their homelands and ways
of life. Yorktown and the Treaty of Paris brought peace to much of the
new republic, but not to the territories it claimed in the West. The West
remained an active seat of war and of fear. It would take Fallen Timbers
and the Treaty of Greenville to end the Northwest fighting, and bloody
campaigns and later treaties to end it in the old Southwest. No matter
what the time line, however, the Revolution led inexorably to Native
American defeat east of the Mississippi River—no matter which side the
tribes had supported. Arent De Peyster had been right when he told the
tribes they could not stand alone against land-hungry Americans.

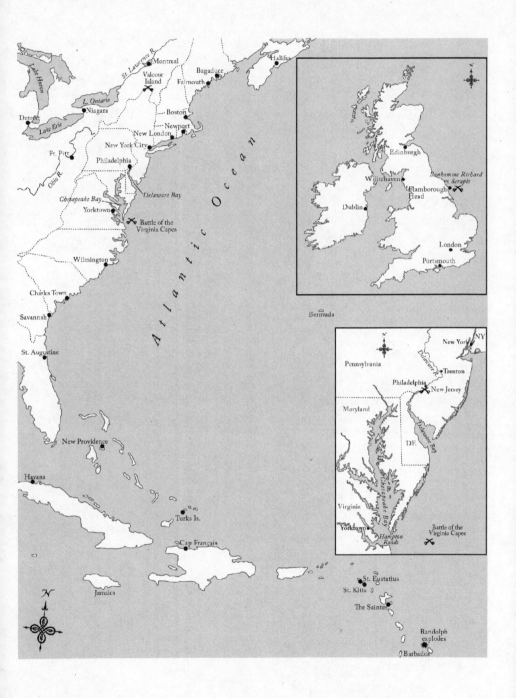

THE
NAVAL THEATER

The War on Open and Inland Waters

Charles P. Neimeyer

Less than two months after the "shot heard round the world" was fired at Lexington, Massachusetts, Congress quickly moved to establish a "continental" army. Northern representatives such as John Adams believed that in order for the Revolution to be successful, the southern colonies must find common cause in the plight of their New England brethren. Hence Adams argued in favor of appointing the widely admired Virginia militia colonel George Washington as the new commander-in-chief of the army. Possessing a personal gravitas that few other candidates for the job exhibited, Washington saw his appointment rapidly and unanimously ratified by the entire Continental Congress— a singular event for this famously contentious body.

As Adams was to quickly discover, however, the establishment of a complementary Continental navy proved to be much more controversial. Unlike the formation of the army, all thirteen colonies had flourishing pre-war maritime establishments. Any new congressional innovation in this particular realm was sure to be met with suspicion. Indeed, the loudest calls for a Continental navy came from the smallest state, Rhode Island, whose delegates urged "for building at the Continental expence a fleet of sufficient force for the protection of these colonies, and for employing them in such manner and places as will most effectually annoy our enemies, and contribute to the common defence of these colonies . . . until peace, liberty and safety are restored and secured to these Colonies upon an equitable and permanent basis."[1] Nevertheless, congressional pushback was not long in coming. Pro-navy advocate John Adams lamented that "the opposition [in Congress] was very loud and vehement."[2]

Congressional delegates south of New England, with the notable exception of merchant Christopher Gadsden of South Carolina, immediately arose against the Rhode Island proposition. Samuel Chase of Maryland was a major opponent. He called the notion of a Continental navy the "maddest idea in the World, to think of building an American Fleet. . . . We should mortgage the whole Continent." Edward Rutledge of South Carolina went even further, describing the creation of a navy as "the most wild, visionary, mad project that had ever been imagined" and compared the action to "an infant taking a mad bull by the horns." He further predicted that a navy would "ruin the character, and corrupt the morals of all our Seamen [making] them selfish, piratical, mercenary, [and] wholly bent on plunder."[3]

Many in Congress believed that each state should look to its own navy as the principal means of resistance against the more capable Royal Navy. Others saw trying to compete with the Royal Navy as hopeless and argued that commerce raiding by privateers and letters of marque vessels would prove much more cost effective in the long run. During the course of the American Revolution, Congress commissioned approximately 2,000 privateers/letters of marque. In fact, all these ideas were simultaneously attempted by Congress and the states to limited degrees of success. Moreover, Congress never got consensus on appointing a maritime equivalent of George Washington. The United States Navy did not appoint its first rear admiral, David G. Farragut, until the outbreak of the American Civil War. Consequently, for most of the Revolutionary War, the administration of Continental maritime affairs fell to the Marine Committee in Congress.

There were more problems. Besides the expense inherent in maintaining even a small navy, American shipyards had little to no experience building men-of-war larger than a privateer sloop or light frigate. Further, the Royal Navy considered Yankee-built ships of that time period to be of poor quality. Saddled with a weak industrial base, the colonies had only "3 iron foundries capable of casting cannon for warships." Finally, the colonial seafaring manpower pool had little to no experience with combat at sea. "Only three of the American navy's original twenty-six captains had any prior experience in the British navy."[4]

With Congress still entangled in debate over establishing a navy, George Washington decided the time was right to organize a local maritime force of his own. He did so by renting Marblehead native Colonel John Glover's schooner *Hannah* for "ONE Dollar pr. Ton pr. Month." The *Hannah* was quickly outfitted with "four 6-pounder guns" and flew the "Appeal to Heaven" flag. After initially getting chased back into port by more powerful British men-of-war, the *Hannah* was able to capture the *Unity*, a merchantman bound for Boston. However, there was a problem with this prize. The *Unity* had been the former property of a New Hampshire congressman, John Langdon, and had only been recently captured by the Royal Navy. Washington ordered the ship returned to its original owner.[5]

During the fall of 1775, Washington expanded his local navy by several more ships. One of his most successful appointments was that of Captain John Manley, who was ultimately given command of the armed schooner *Lee*. On November 27, 1775, the *Lee* caught up with the British ordnance ship *Nancy*, "a brigantine of 250 tons." Easily taking the vessel, Manley had captured a treasure trove of military stores desperately needed by Washington's army, then in camp at Cambridge, Massachusetts. *Nancy*'s cargo hold contained hundreds of muskets, ammunition, barrels of precious gunpowder, and pieces of ordnance including a massive 13-inch brass mortar that excited much commentary among the sailors. On its barrel was inscribed the initials G.R. (for Georgius Rex—King of Great Britain). Someone had crudely scratched out the initial "R" and replaced it with a "W" (for Washington). Even Abigail Adams took notice of it and wrote her husband John in Philadelphia that "it is a most grand mortar, I assure you."[6] Unfortunately during a March 3, 1776, bombardment of Boston designed to draw enemy attention away from Henry Knox's efforts to place artillery on Dorchester Heights, the barrel split after only its third discharge and could no longer be fired.[7]

While Washington's tiny rented navy did what it could around Boston, it was Royal Navy attacks against American coastal towns and cities that proved to be the strongest catalyst for congressional action in forming a truly Continental navy. The Royal Navy suddenly seemed inclined to expand its aggressive naval activity beyond New England. For example, in response to the removal of cannon from a battery in lower Manhattan, the HMS *Asia*, a 64-gun ship of the line, fired on the town "for over three hours." Its captain stated to the citizens that if such action took place again, "the Mischiefs that may arise must lie at their Doors, and not mine."[8] To the south in the Chesapeake Bay, Lord Dunmore, the deposed royal governor of Virginia, took station with the 20-gun HMS *Fowey* and raided tidewater plantations at will. What really got the attention of the plantation owners was Dunmore's declaration to liberate slaves and use them as soldiers against their former masters. These incidents and more served to turn congressional navy opponents into advocates now that the threat had arrived at their own doorsteps.

More immediate news also helped the naval cause. One of the last ships to depart Philadelphia before hostilities fully commenced in 1775 was the packet *Black Prince*. Commanded by John Barry (who later provided invaluable service to the American navy), the *Black Prince* sent word that two large Royal Navy transports had departed the British Isles loaded with reinforcements for the garrison of Canada. This news allowed Congress to reopen the debate on the efficacy of creating a Continental navy, and it did not take long for key members of the pro-navy faction to wear down the objections of the anti-navy contingent, especially in the South. To add fuel to the fire, Commander-in-Chief Washington had written to John Hancock that he had intelligence that "a Fleet consisting of a 64 & 20 Gun Ship, 2 Sloops of 18 Guns, 2 Transports with 600 Men were to sail from Boston as of yesterday—that they took on Board two Mortars, four Howitzers, and other Artillery calculated for the Bombardment of a Town." Washington believed that "the Ministry [was] determined to push the War to the utmost."[9] For the moment, Congress felt some urgency to act.

On October 13, 1775, on the very day that Captain James Wallace on the HMS *Rose* threatened to bombard the port town of Newport,

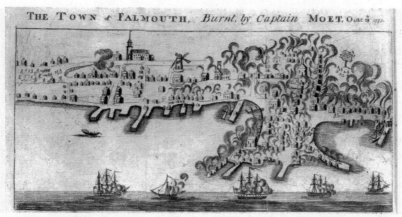

British naval commander captain Henry Mowat bombarded the town of Falmouth, Massachusetts, on October 18, 1775, just five days after the Continental Congress resolved to create a Continental navy. Mowat later played an instrumental role in the 1779 American defeat at Penobscot Bay. (*Library of Congress*)

Rhode Island, and one week prior to an immensely destructive Royal Navy raid on Falmouth, Massachusetts (modern-day Portland, Maine), Congress officially established a Continental navy and resolved:

> That a swift sailing vessel, to carry ten carriage guns, and a proportionate number of swivels, with eighty men be fitted with all possible dispatch, for a cruise of three months. . . . That a Committee of three be appointed to prepare an estimate for expence, and lay the same before Congress, and to contract with proper persons to fit out the vessel. . . . That another vessel be fitted out for the same purposes [and] a committee [be] appointed to bring in regulations for [a] navy.[10]

In one fell swoop, Congress brought a navy into being to be procured at Continental expense and made it clear at the same time that it would be administered and controlled by its own naval committee. The delegates next moved to appoint its first three members, while legal expert John Adams got to work writing up new required naval regulations. The seafaring-minded Silas Deane of Connecticut was appointed. He was soon joined by John Langdon, delegate from New Hampshire and previous owner of the disputed prize *Unity*, and pro-navy southerner Christopher Gadsden of South Carolina.

In Congress, the demand for newly outfitted Continental navy vessels picked up steam. The naval committee (later known as the Marine Committee in 1776) formally added on John Adams of Massachusetts, Stephen Hopkins of Rhode Island, Richard Henry Lee of Virginia, and Joseph Hewes of North Carolina. By late October, the congressional mandate for warships doubled to four. Hopkins was very influential and often held late-night committee meetings in taverns near the Philadelphia waterfront. John Adams later remarked that his time on the Marine Committee was among the most convivial he could ever remember.

> Governor Hopkins of Rhode Island, above seventy Years of Age kept us all alive. Upon Business his Experience and judgment were very Useful. But when the Business of the Evening was over, he kept Us in Conversation till Eleven and sometimes twelve O Clock. His Custom was to drink nothing all day nor till Eight O Clock, in the Evening, and then his Beveredge was Jamaica Spirit and Water. It gave him Wit, Humour, Anecdotes, Science and Learning. He had read Greek, Roman and British History: and was familiar with English Poetry particularly Pope, Tompson [Thompson] and Milton. And the flow of his Soul made all his reading our own, and seemed to bring to recollection in all of Us all We had ever read. I could neither eat nor drink in those days. The other Gentlemen were very temperate. Hopkins never drank to excess, but all he drank was immediately not only converted into Wit, Sense, Knowledge and good humour, but inspired Us all with similar Qualities.[11]

Congress purchased the *Black Prince* from the Philadelphia firm of Willing and Morris and renamed the vessel *Alfred*. Budding revolutionary shipwright Joshua Humphreys was paid 360 pounds to turn this vessel into what became a 30-gun warship. In similar fashion and armament, a second merchant vessel was purchased and boldly renamed *Columbus*. Two smaller Philadelphia-based vessels were also procured and turned respectively into the 14-gun *Andrew Doria* and the 14-gun *Cabot*.

While these ships were fitting out, the committee thought it prudent to recommend that Congress raise two battalions of Continental marines for service with the new navy. On November 10, 1775, the creation of the Continental marines won easy approval. George Washington, however, was none too happy about it. He believed that raising marines would affect his ability to remedy his chronic Continental Army man-power shortage. As a result the marines were only able to recruit about five companies of men. Their mission was to provide marine detach-ments for the new Continental navy ships being procured by Congress.

A small 12-gun sloop of war originally from the Rhode Island state navy and known as the *Katy* was renamed *Providence*. Congress added this vessel to the growing Continental squadron. Congress also later en-hanced the squadron with three Maryland-built sloops: the *Wasp* (8 guns), the *Fly* (8 guns), and the *Hornet* (10 guns). Amazingly, Congress resolved to build 13 new frigates mounting between 24 to 32 guns each. The committee members naively assumed these ships could be ready in just four months.[12] In reality it would be a few years before the new frigates were able to go to sea.

The committee discovered that purchasing ships was easier than find-ing the proper mariners to man them. One of the problems of this early Continental navy effort was that the committee had a tendency to award leadership positions to their relatives and friends. For example, Stephen Hopkins's younger brother Esek was named "First Captain" and given overall command of the growing squadron. The captaincy of the *Alfred* went to Silas Deane's brother-in-law Dudley Saltonstall. Rhode Island favorite son Abraham Whipple gave up the command of the *Providence* in favor of the larger 28-gun *Columbus*. Whipple was also married to a niece of the Hopkins brothers. One of the smaller vessels, the 14-gun *Cabot,* went to Esek Hopkins's son John. In sum, New Englanders, al-ready well known to the committee and also having familial connections, gained nearly all of the commands. Even the lone Pennsylvanian, Nicholas Biddle, "likely owed his appointment" to connections, when in a nod to his prominent Philadelphia-based family, he was offered com-mand of the 14-gun *Andrew Doria*.[13]

So bothersome were the depredations of Lord Dunmore in Virginia that as 1776 dawned, Congress gave instructions to Esek Hopkins to immediately prepare his squadron for action, and he was told in no un-certain terms to head directly for the Chesapeake Bay. His orders stated that "if by such intelligence [the British] are not superior to your own you are to immediately enter said bay, search out and attack, take or de-stroy all the Naval Forces of our Enemies that you may find there. If you are so fortunate to execute this business successfully in Virginia you are to proceed immediately to the Southward and make yourself Master of such forces as the Enemy may have both in North and South Carolina. . . . Having completed your business in the Carolina's you are without delay to proceed to the Northward directly to Rhode Island, and attack, take and destroy all the Enemies Naval force that you find there."[14]

These were fairly bold and explicit instructions. Christopher Gadsden even sent out an elegant new flag to the squadron commander. It featured a coiled rattlesnake on a yellow field with the words "Don't Tread on Me" emblazoned below the figure. Nevertheless, despite his orders and inspirational commander's flag, weather delays caused Hopkins to make very slow progress getting into the open sea.

Meanwhile, George Washington still confronted the British army penned up inside Boston. By the beginning of 1776, he had been able to procure four schooners. As his sole remaining schooner captain, Washington made the energetic John Manley his "Commodore" in charge of all of his remaining vessels. Manley's *Hancock* put to sea in late January and was soon able to capture the British merchantman *Happy Return*. Manley quickly took another prize called the *Norfolk*. His good luck required him to detach a considerable part of his crew to sail his prizes into nearby Plymouth, Massachusetts, thus leaving *Hancock* with only sixteen men onboard. It was at this moment that the powerful 8-gun British tender *General Gage* showed up. The *General Gage* was escorting two smaller merchant vessels. Despite the odds, Manley decided to square off against the British ship and fight it out so that his prizes might make their escape. Firing at each other "for a half an hour" both ships dueled to an inconclusive draw, but Manley's prizes made it safely into Plymouth.[15]

The situation changed on March 17, 1776, when the British abandoned their occupation of Boston once and for all. In response, Manley formed his surviving schooners into a "wolf pack" where their larger numbers might enable them to pick off Royal Navy stragglers. However, in a counter-counter-measure to Manley's new tactical innovation, the British threw in larger men-of-war such as the 32-gun frigate HMS *Niger* to act as escorts. Once this countermeasure took place, there was very little Manley's tiny schooner squadron could do to impede the evacuation fleet.[16] In truth, after the British departure there was little further need for George Washington's rented navy.

Esek Hopkins (1718–1802) was the first appointed commodore of the newly established Continental navy. An accomplished merchant captain and privateer from Rhode Island, Hopkins led the first American naval squadron to land forces on a foreign shore during a raid on New Providence, Bahamas, on March 3, 1776. (*New York Public Library*)

While the British were preparing to evacuate Boston, Esek Hopkins decided to ignore his congressional instructions; instead, he sailed his squadron to the Bahamas. Arriving on March 1, 1776, Hopkins anchored his vessels off Grand Abaco Island. On the way down, the small sloops *Hornet* and *Fly* had gotten separated from the rest of the group due to an at-sea collision with one another. While waiting for these vessels to reappear (the damaged *Hornet* never did), the Americans captured two small British sloops trying to escape from New Providence. The prisoners informed Hopkins that most of the military stores ashore had already been evacuated by the British, but the forts guarding the harbor were only lightly manned by local militia.

Hopkins's original plan was to land his marines and bluejackets using the newly captured sloops and sail right into the harbor with the aim of taking the two forts, Nassau and Montagu, by surprise at dawn the following day. However, Hopkins blundered and allowed the militia in Fort Nassau to see the sails of the rest of his squadron. They sounded an alert and Hopkins was forced to ultimately recall the sloops and the marines. Instead, on the afternoon of March 3, Hopkins decided to land his marines and sailors on a beach near Fort Montagu. By 2 p.m. the marines and sailors, directly supported by the sloops *Providence* and *Wasp*, conducted the first amphibious landing on foreign soil in the history of the United States (although technically the colonies had not yet declared their independence). The local militia defending Fort Montagu quickly surrendered without too much resistance.[17]

Continental marine captain Samuel Nicholas's men were able to seize seventeen cannon that had been spiked by the militia. Unfortunately, they found very few barrels of precious gunpowder. Because the landing party of sailors and marines were totally fatigued after two full days of nonstop activity, Hopkins decided to wait until the morning of March 4 to march on Fort Nassau and capture the rest of the town. At daybreak, Nicholas had his marines up and moving toward the fort, which surrendered without resistance. Now that the harbor was safe to enter, the *Alfred* made its way in. Even though they missed out on securing much gunpowder, the spoils of shot and shell and other military stores were more than the little squadron could possibly take with them. Even with the late arrival of the sloop of war *Fly* on March 11 and having his ships exchange their stone ballast for cannonballs, Hopkins was still forced to make a contractual arrangement to carry away the rest of the haul.[18]

While Hopkins was busy at New Providence, the *Edward*, tender to the frigate HMS *Liverpool*, chased an American merchantman known as the *Wild Duck* into Philadelphia. The *Wild Duck* had visited St. Eustatius in the West Indies and arrived, after a narrow escape from the *Edward*, loaded with two thousand pounds of precious gunpowder and other military stores. Congress was so impressed with the sailing qualities of the *Wild Duck* that the delegates proposed to buy it and send it over to Wharton's shipyard for conversion into a fighting vessel. Renamed the *Lexington*, the ship was offered to the former commander of the *Black Prince*, John Barry. *Lexington* carried sixteen 4-pounder guns and numerous swivels. By American standards, it was a fairly powerful ship. During the spring of 1776, with several British vessels known to be threatening Delaware Bay, the Pennsylvania Committee of Safety sent its tiny state flotilla of row galleys out into the bay to engage this rising threat. As a further security to the river, engineers had sunk sharply pointed chevaux-de-fries in the river channel just below the water's surface. Designed to puncture the hull of any unsuspecting ship, these water obstacles were both feared and effective.

Born in County Wexford, Ireland, and later immigrating to America, John Barry (1745–1803) is widely considered as the father of the Continental navy. Appointed a captain by Congress, Barry commanded a number of Continental navy vessels during the American Revolution, including the 28-gun frigate *Effingham* which was later destroyed at Burlington, New Jersey. (*Private Collection*)

John Barry decided it was also time to take the *Lexington* out into the bay to confront what he believed would be vessels no larger than a sloop. Instead what he got was the 44-gun frigate HMS *Roebuck*. Commanded by Captain Andrew Snape Hamond, the *Roebuck* was under orders to level any floating or shore batteries and render useless any river obstructions that the ship might encounter on the way upriver toward Philadelphia. Nonetheless, Barry used *Lexington*'s shallow draft to advantage, and he was able to skirt past the *Roebuck* by keeping close to shore.

Once it was clear that Esek Hopkins was not going to provide relief to the Chesapeake region, Barry headed directly toward Hampton Roads. It was not long before he spotted the *Edward*, commanded by Lieutenant Richard Boger—the same ship that had originally chased the former *Wild Duck* into Philadelphia. Even though *Edward* carried only six 4-pounders to *Lexington*'s sixteen guns, Barry's sailors were going to experience their first real fight. *Lexington* fired the first broadside, but its rounds did little initial damage. *Edward* returned fire to better effect, but Boger realized he was outgunned and made a run for it. A lucky *Lexington* shot hulled the *Edward* at the stern near the waterline, and a huge amount of seawater came cascading into the vessel. Soon the battle was all over. John Barry and the *Lexington* had won the Continental navy's first engagement at sea against a British armed combatant.[19]

For the next seventeen months, the nascent Pennsylvania state navy proved its worth in keeping British ships out of Philadelphia. In company with the Continental navy ship *Reprisal* under Captain Lambert Wickes and the Pennsylvania navy vessel *Montgomery* commanded by Thomas Read, a larger number of state-owned row galleys stood off a determined attempt by two British frigates, HMS *Roebuck* and *Liverpool*, to clear the river of obstructions. By this time Barry had returned to Philadelphia and was enthusiastically welcomed home by one and all. Due to his success at sea, Barry was given command of the newly built 28-gun Continental ship *Effingham*, "one of four new frigates being built in Philadelphia."[20] Unfortunately, the *Effingham* was far from ready.

Despite John Barry's initial success, a confrontation with the 20-gun HMS *Glasgow* nearly did in the early Continental navy. Leaders in Congress could not understand the failure of Esek Hopkins to destroy this single vessel, given the firepower of his entire squadron. Coming upon *Glasgow* just off Block Island during the night of April 6, 1776, Hopkins maneuvered his ships close enough in the darkness so that a sailor aboard *Cabot* was able to throw a hand grenade from his fighting top onto the British ship's main deck. Causing little harm, the grenade fully alerted *Glasgow*'s commanding officer, Captain Tyringham Howe, of his imminent danger. Howe eventually fired two full broadsides directly into *Cabot*, killing the sailing master and wounding its captain, John B. Hopkins. The nearby *Andrew Doria* maneuvered wildly to avoid colliding with the staggering *Cabot*. The flagship *Alfred* moved up, but a lucky shot from *Glasgow* temporarily took out *Alfred*'s steering gear. Consequently, *Glasgow* was able to rake the American vessels from stem to stern as *Alfred* briefly wallowed on the waves. Throughout the running fight, both larger American vessels, *Columbus* and *Alfred*, kept getting in each other's way. Inexplicably, the sloop *Providence* stayed well out of range. At this point, the *Glasgow* made a run to link up with James Wallace's squadron, known to be near the mouth of Narragansett Bay. Once the *Glasgow* got near the bay, Esek Hopkins called off the chase. Hopkins and his entire squadron put into New London, Connecticut.

Captain Nicholas Biddle of the *Andrew Doria*, for one, was completely disgusted by the entire affair. Writing to his brother James he stated:

If it was thought the Conquest would be easy there was no Courage shewn in the Attack. . . . There was no order in the Matter. Away we all went Helter Skelter one flying here and another there to cut [off] the Retreat of a fellow who did not fear us. I kept close to the Admiral [Esek Hopkins] that I might the sooner Receive his Orders. But he had none to give. And the *Cabot* Running off Obliged Me in order to Clear her to go a little out of my way. And before I could Regain My ground the *Alfred* had sheered off. Had I behaved as [John Burroughs] Hopkins did, had I run on without Orders and brought on the Action in the Night I think I should have lost my Commission before now.[21]

It was not long before serious recriminations began. Rumors over the *Glasgow* fiasco swirled through the town of New London. Abraham Whipple of the *Columbus* faced accusations of cowardice and malfeasance. Whipple demanded a court-martial to clear his name. The court found Whipple not guilty of cowardice but believed he had made some errors in judgment during the *Glasgow* gunfight. Two days later, Whipple himself sat on another court to consider the behavior of Captain John Hazard of the *Providence*. This time the court found Hazard guilty of egregious conduct and he was cashiered from the service. *Alfred's* senior lieutenant, John Paul Jones, was given command of *Providence*. Elisha Hinman was given command of the *Cabot* while the wounded John B. Hopkins recuperated. In fact, from 1776 to 1780, "at least seven Continental captains were hauled before a court-martial. Only one of those, John Manley, was acquitted." Five of the seven were ultimately dismissed from the service.[22]

In one case of luck for the Americans during the spring of 1776, Nicholas Biddle's *Andrew Doria* captured two transport vessels carrying Scottish reinforcements for the British army in New York. However, not long after manning the transport *Oxford*, the prisoners were able to overwhelm Biddle's prize crew. The *Oxford* sailed due west to Hampton Roads only to be retaken again by the *Liberty* and the *Patriot* of the Virginia state navy. The Highlanders were marched off to a prisoner-of-war camp near Richmond.[23] The other transport, the *Crawford*, was eventually retaken by the British frigate HMS *Cerberus* before it made port. In a final odd twist, as the transport neared its destination of New York City, the *Crawford*, off Fire Island, was captured for a third time by the

Continental sloop *Schuyler* commanded by Lieutenant Charles Pond. The Scottish soldiers, who had elected to stay onboard the *Crawford*, became prisoners anyway.[24]

On June 20, 1776, congressional discontent with Esek Hopkins became manifest. Congress ordered Hopkins, Dudley Saltonstall, and Abraham Whipple to Philadelphia to answer for their conduct both during the New Providence raid and the *Glasgow* affair. In truth, Congress was angry that Hopkins had not complied with its instructions to deliver some of the captured New Providence cannon to the Pennsylvania Committee of Safety. Writing to a friend in New London from Providence, Rhode Island, Hopkins noted that "I now have the Gentlemen here from the Committee of Safety of Philadelphia but I expect they will not be able to get more Cannon here than I expected they would at New London. What will be the event of their not Succeeding I can't at present tell. I am well Convinced that sending them away will be of very ill Consequences to the Continent, and their not going will have no other bad Effect but on me who had better Suffer than the Community."[25]

However, delegates from the southern states were the most upset. They believed Hopkins had not complied with his original instruction to go to the Chesapeake Bay and later the Carolinas. By going on his Bahamas raid Hopkins had left them in the lurch against the likes of Lord Dunmore. Congress voted to censure Hopkins but at this point did not immediately relieve him of command. It might have been better for him if they had. While the acerbic John Adams chalked up the censure decision to anti-New England sentiment, the action caused Hopkins's own officers to lose confidence in him, and Congress eventually removed him from command altogether in early 1778.

There was some good news for the Continental navy in 1777: the thirteen new frigates were nearly complete. Congress had decided that "five were to carry thirty-two guns, five, twenty-eight, and three, twenty-four."[26] In a political move, these vessels had been built in seven separate shipyards up and down the Atlantic seaboard. Congress also reordered the naval officer list and appointed captains to these new commands. Once again, political connection seemed to overshadow demonstrated fitness for command. For example, James Nicholson of Maryland was placed at the top of the list because Marine Committee member Richard Henry Lee sponsored him. Nicholson had only served in his state navy and never before commanded a Continental vessel at sea. Conversely, the proven, highly capable John Paul Jones ranked eighteenth on the list. The higher one's name appeared on the list, the more likely that individual would get one of the new frigates. In fact, James Nicholson virtually demanded one because of his good fortune being placed at the top of the list. Nevertheless, not a single one of the new frigates was still in service by 1781. Ultimately, the Royal Navy captured more than half (seven of thirteen) of these vessels. One of those taken was John Manley's *Hancock*. This ship was reflagged as the HMS *Iris*.[27]

The Continental navy was to suffer even more indignities. In March 1777, the *Cabot* was captured by the HMS *Milford*. Later that fall, the capable Lambert Wickes, on the *Reprisal*, was lost at sea off Newfoundland. Only the ship's cook survived to tell the tale. Furthermore, the long awaited debut of James Nicholson went awry when his new frigate *Virginia* ran aground at the mouth of the Chesapeake Bay as he was trying to break out into the open sea. His ship was captured by a British boarding party as he ignominiously fled the scene in his captain's gig.

Many of the Continental navy's original ships were also lost during this timeframe. The *Columbus* was captured off Point Judith, Rhode Island. Even the old *Alfred* eventually fell prey to the Royal Navy. In 1778, in the middle of a lopsided fight against the 64-gun HMS *Yarmouth*, the new frigate *Randolph*, commanded by Nicholas Biddle, spectacularly blew up with the loss of over 300 hands, including Biddle, when a spark touched off its powder magazine. The 32-gun *Raleigh* was also captured by the British that same year.

Before the loss of all these fine ships, Congress contemplated commissioning at least three ships of the line designed to carry 74 guns each. Where they were going to get the ordnance and sailors for even a single "74" one can only guess. Most likely, Congress hoped the French might provide at least the hardware and ordnance. Only the 74-gun *America* would be completed just before the war officially ended, and Congress immediately sold it to the French. During the course of the American Revolution, while the Royal Navy possessed dozens of ships of at least 64 guns, the most substantial Continental navy vessel was never larger than a 32-gun frigate.

To make matters worse for the Americans, by September 1777 an entire fleet led by Lord Richard "Black Dick" Howe entered Delaware Bay.

His ships were supporting the army of his brother, William Howe, then marching on the American national capital of Philadelphia after having soundly beaten George Washington's Continental Army on September 11 at Brandywine Creek. Lord Howe's fleet guaranteed that no American warship was going to make it past him. Of the four new frigates under construction in Philadelphia, including *Effingham*, *Washington*, and *Delaware*, only the *Randolph* under Nicholas Biddle made it to sea before Howe's ships completely shut down the Delaware River. The other three were stuck at their moorings in Philadelphia.

After Brandywine, Philadelphia was doomed and so were the trapped American frigates. The British marched in and occupied the city on September 26, 1777. Despite this setback, Washington believed he could deny the British the use of the city port facilities, making the British occupation of Philadelphia largely moot. With his river obstructions still mostly in place, Washington decided to occupy Fort Mifflin, sometimes called the Mud Fort due to its location on a large mudflat in the Delaware River, and Fort Mercer on the New Jersey shore. This might be enough to keep the British from being resupplied from the sea. John Barry and Thomas Read took the new frigates *Effingham* and *Washington* to a safer location at Burlington, New Jersey. Charles Alexander, captain of the frigate *Delaware*, attempted along with some Pennsylvania state row galleys to attack British shore batteries being set up near the Philadelphia docks. Instead, he accidentally ran the *Delaware* aground and was forced to surrender.[28]

However, on the bright side for the Americans, due to the channelizing effect of the chevaux-de-fries obstructions still in the Delaware River, the British 64-gun *Augusta* and 18-gun sloop *Merlin* also ran aground on the treacherous river shoals. The *Roebuck* attempted to tow *Augusta* off but failed. The Americans responded with fire ships but lit them too early to have any effect on the grounded vessels. Instead, it was the state navy row galleys along with artillery fire from Fort Mifflin that proved decisive. The fire also forced the *Roebuck* to drop down the river, and they held off another frigate, HMS *Isis*, from entering the fray. The *Augusta* eventually caught fire and blew up with the loss of about 60 men including the ship's chaplain. It was the single largest vessel lost by the British during the entire war. Captain Hamond from the *Roebuck* burned the *Merlin* to keep it from falling into American hands.[29] For the Pennsylvania navy, October 23, 1777, was one of its finest days of the war. Furthermore, just a few days later, the Americans salvaged, among other supplies, many of the cannon in the wrecked *Augusta* and *Merlin*.

By November 1777, the Royal Navy and shore-based artillery fire had made Fort Mifflin a living hell, and it was eventually abandoned by the Americans once all their artillery had been disabled. Fort Mercer, however, had fought off a determined Hessian assault, but the loss of Fort Mifflin meant that the British could resupply their troops in Philadelphia directly from the sea. At the suggestion of George Washington and against the wishes of John Barry, the *Effingham* and *Washington* were scuttled on the New Jersey riverbank. While a few Pennsylvania state row galleys were able to slip past the British shore batteries, the Americans were forced to burn much of the state navy, including the Continental vessels *Andrew Doria*, *Hornet*, *Wasp*, *Racehorse*, and *Fly*—a sad end for many of the first ships of the Continental navy.[30]

During 1778, the Americans finally secured an open alliance with France. This new relationship temporarily allowed the Continental navy to bring the war at sea to British home waters. Nevertheless, one by one the new Continental frigates were either destroyed before getting into action or taken in combat by the Royal Navy. However, now able to openly use French ports, a few enterprising American commanders took advantage of this situation. American commissioners in France such as Benjamin Franklin kept a supply of congressionally pre-signed "blank commissions" on hand. Franklin did not hesitate to hand these out to individuals he deemed of sufficient energy to carry out the war in European waters on behalf of America. Further, the Franco-American alliance legally allowed American navy captains to outfit and home port vessels in France. One such commission recipient was Irish-born Gustavus Conyngham.[31]

Conyngham was originally given command of the Continental navy ship *Surprize*, and with this vessel he proceeded to take a few prizes in the English Channel. This was prior to the formal Franco-American alliance of 1778. Thus the use of any French port by the Americans for military purposes was strictly forbidden by international law. In order to appease the loudly complaining British ambassador, the French threw Conyngham and his crew in jail and his prizes were returned to their British owners. Released a month later, Conyngham was soon able to get another vessel, a cutter named *Revenge*. Conyngham was told to proceed directly to America but was given discretion to take prizes if attacked or if he was in need of provisions.[32]

Conyngham's own crew convinced him that taking prizes was what really motivated them, not an unprofitable trip across the Atlantic to America; so Conyngham took a circuitous route around the entire British Isles taking a few prizes along the way. In early 1778, he proceeded to the coast of Spain where he captured more vessels. Conyngham became *persona non grata* with the Spanish court when he allowed his prize-hungry crew to take a neutral Swedish brig. This final straw required Conyngham's *Revenge* to leave immediately for American waters at long last. Unfortunately for him, the *Revenge* was later captured by the 20-gun HMS *Galatea* off the Delaware capes. Due to his nefarious reputation, Conyngham was clapped in irons and sent to a naval prison in Great Britain. Although released and recaptured a second time, Conyngham escaped prison in 1781 but was not given another command before the war ended.[33]

One of the most successful French-supported American naval captains was John Paul Jones. In 1778, while in command of the Continental sloop *Ranger*, Jones famously raided the British port of Whitehaven and followed this attack by capturing the 20-gun HMS *Drake* after a vicious hour-and-five-minute battle. He also took several merchant prizes along the way.

Jones returned to France largely unnoticed. His reward was to be given command of the converted merchantman *Bon Homme Richard*. However, this vessel was not ready to go to sea and Jones remained stuck in Brest, France. After months of exasperating delay, the *Bon Homme Richard* was finally ready for combat. The American-built frigate *Alliance* would accompany Jones on his next foray against the British home islands. This vessel had been brought back to France by the Marquis de Lafayette. Lafayette contemplated working with Jones and conducting a spectacular amphibious raid on a large British city such as Liverpool. Unfortunately for both Jones and Lafayette, the *Alliance* was commanded by the unstable Pierre Landais, a French naval adventurer who had unwisely been given a Continental navy commission by Congress.

While the French were giving serious thought to mounting a large-scale amphibious landing in southern England, sickness swept through

Born in Scotland and later immigrating to America, John Paul Jones (1747–1792) is probably the most renowned of the Continental navy commanders of the American Revolution and shares the title of father of the Continental navy with John Barry. John Paul Jones most famously commanded the converted French merchantman *Bon Homme Richard* against the HMS *Serapis*. (*Library of Congress*)

the fleet and caused the senior French admiral D'Orvilliers to cancel the operation. Soon afterward, Jones took *Bon Homme Richard*, *Alliance*, and the French frigate *Pallas* on a cruise around the British Isles. On September 23, 1779, Jones engaged the new British frigate HMS *Serapis* off Flamborough Head, England. The *Pallas* engaged a smaller British ship, the *Countess of Scarborough*, while Jones and *Serapis*, commanded by Captain Richard Pearson, faced off and exchanged broadsides in a fiery engagement. Maneuvering for advantage, Jones realized that the faster, more powerful *Serapis* would likely win this kind of fight, so he sought to get the *Bon Homme Richard* as close to *Serapis* as possible and take the vessel in a boarding action. While this occurred the *Alliance* stood well off and Landais failed to properly engage in the fight. At times Landais seemed to actively seek out *Bon Homme Richard* as his target instead of *Serapis*. Jones had little time to think of this due to several of his 18-pounder guns bursting upon discharge. Jones was now clearly outgunned. Things seemed to be going against him when thanks to better seamanship on his part, Jones was able to get both vessels lashed together—so close that the opposing gun muzzles were nearly touching.

Like two prize fighters in a clinch, Jones fought it out with the British at point-blank range. Nearing nighttime, Jones made preparations to board *Serapis*. Jones's marines in the fighting tops picked off sailors from *Serapis* trying to cut the grappling hook lines that held the ships locked in a deadly embrace. Jones fought to keep the ships together while Pearson struggled to break free so that he could use his superior firepower to his advantage. The carnage on both decks was horrible. Jones's marines and top men were able to kill or wound most of Pearson's weather deck sailors, since he had embarked a larger than normal complement of marines. These men were predominately volunteers from the Irish Regiment Walsh then in service for the king of France. Their presence proved decisive. The suppressive fire by Jones's marines enabled a sailor named William Hamilton to walk out on a yardarm and drop grenade after grenade onto the British vessel's deck and down open hatches. Unfortunately for Jones, his own ship was sinking rapidly because of the damage meted out by *Serapis*'s main gun battery. His only hope was for Pearson to strike his colors before *Bon Homme Richard* went under.[34]

A grim Pearson fervently hoped that Jones would surrender first. Meanwhile, Jones personally directed the shots of his three remaining 9-pounder guns. Someone on *Bon Homme Richard* "called out for quarter." It was certainly not Jones. Pearson responded, "Do you ask for quarter?" to which Jones allegedly replied, "I have not yet begun to fight." Finally, after considerable pounding by Jones, the mainmast of the *Serapis* fell as Pearson tore his colors down. After three and a half hours of nearly non-stop fighting *Serapis* finally surrendered. The *Countess of Scarborough* was also taken by *Pallas* during the engagement. Nonetheless, the severely damaged *Bon Homme Richard* was doomed, forcing Jones to transfer his flag and those crewmen still left alive to *Serapis*. "Jones estimated his loss at 150 killed and wounded out of a total of 322"—an incredible casualty rate for a single ship-to-ship fight.[35]

The upshot of the *Bon Homme Richard/Serapis* duel was significant. Soon after word of Jones's victory made its way to England, the Admiralty devoted a considerable amount of energy and resources to catch him before he could return to France. They neglected to blockade the Dutch coast, however, and this was exactly where Jones put in with the damaged *Serapis*. Jones's single victory was a tremendous psychological boost for the American navy, which had known mostly defeat in 1778 and 1779. To the average Briton, so frightening was "the pirate" John Paul Jones that the *London Morning Post* wrote soon after the battle that

The *Bonhomme Richard* commanded by John Paul Jones defeated the British frigate HMS *Serapis* off Flamborough Head, England, on September 23, 1779. It was during this battle that Jones was alleged to have shouted at his opponent, "I have not yet begun to fight." (*New York Public Library*)

"Paul Jones resembles a Jack o' Lantern, to mislead our marines and terrify our coasts, he is no sooner seen than lost."[36]

With the notable exception of Jones's single victory over *Serapis*, the year 1779 cannot be viewed as anything other than an unmitigated disaster for the Continental navy and marines. The worst naval debacle of the entire war for the Americans took place at Penobscot Bay. Three years after their forced departure from Boston, the British created a small fort at the town commonly called Bagaduce (modern-day Castine, Maine). Located near the tip of a rocky peninsula that dominated the mouth of the Penobscot River, this enclave was a place of refuge established by the British for New England loyalists. The Royal Navy provided three sloops to support the fort: the 20-gun *North*, the 18-gun *Nautilus*, and the 18-gun *Albany*. These vessels were commanded by the capable Captain Henry Mowat—the same man who had leveled the town of Falmouth in 1775. Brigadier General Francis McLean was the senior ground force commander for the British. He had with him elements of the Halifax garrison, the 74th Foot (Argyle Highlanders), and the 82nd Foot (the

Hamilton Regiment). In all, including attachments, McLean had about 700 men ashore.[37]

For this 1779 expedition, the Continental navy provided three vessels: the sloop *Providence*, the new frigate *Warren*, and a recently captured brig *Diligent*. Even some state navies pitched in. Among other vessels, Massachusetts sent the aptly named 16-gun *Tyrannicide*, the 10-gun *Hazard*, and the 16-gun *Active*. New Hampshire provided the 22-gun state frigate *Hampden*. Accompanying the combat ships were at least twenty-one transports, armed privateers, and other supply vessels. Dudley Saltonstall, commander of the *Warren*, was named acting commodore of this ersatz fleet. Brigadier General Solomon Lovell of Massachusetts was in charge of the ground forces. Even the famous Paul Revere, now a lieutenant colonel of artillery in the Massachusetts militia, played a role. While Lovell raised about 900 recruits for the venture, many were ill-suited for the rigors of a combat campaign on the rugged Maine coast.[38]

The attack on the fort and ships at Bagaduce was intended to be a joint operation, but it was never totally clear who was in charge. The Board of War had ordered Saltonstall "to take every measure and use your utmost Endevours to Captivate, kill or destroy the Enemies whole Force both by Sea and Land and the more effectively to answer that purpose, you are to Consult measures and preserve the greatest harmony with the Commander of the Land Forces, that the navy and army may Cooperate and assist each other."[39]

Since McLean's land fortifications were far from finished, a more aggressive campaign might have proven decisive for the Americans. McLean later admitted he intended to surrender after firing a few rounds at the Americans once they began their assault. However, in late July 1779, the cautious Saltonstall began the action at long range against Mowat's outgunned sloops. Neither side inflicted much damage on the other. Meanwhile, Saltonstall's Continental marine force of about 150 men under the command of Captain John Welsh seized small Nautilus Island, near where the British had anchored their sloops. This action had the effect of driving Mowat's ships up the river. It also allowed Lovell to land his main assault force on the rocky tip of the Bagaduce Peninsula. Saltonstall's ships would cover the landing. Unfortunately for the attackers, the British defended the beachhead and killed the senior Continental marine Captain Welsh and 14 soldiers. They then withdrew to their still unfinished fort.

Lovell pushed to within six hundred yards of the fort but suddenly stopped his forward momentum in order to wait for Paul Revere to bring up his artillery. This task proved easier said than done. Meanwhile, Saltonstall in *Warren* attacked the British sloops in the harbor. *Warren* received some minor damage from the lighter British ships but Saltonstall, like Lovell, elected not to press the attack. For the next several days the Americans dithered over what to do next. The assault had turned into a siege.

No one seemed to want the responsibility for ordering offensive operations. Saltonstall and Lovell held "frequent councils of war" where nothing got decided. Each commander demanded that the other engage the enemy first. American subordinate commanders, especially the privateers who accompanied Saltonstall, worried about a British relief force coming to the aid of Mowat. More days went by, and the "morale of the American force ashore nose-dived." Finally ordered into action by the "Naval Board of the Eastern District sitting in Boston," on August 13, Lovell and Saltonstall prepared to make their respective attacks, but they waited for a heavy fog to lift. When the fog cleared, the shocked Americans saw five enemy sails on the horizon. What they beheld was the long-feared British relief force led by Sir George Collier in the powerful 64-gun HMS *Raisonnable*. Consequently, the Americans now found themselves trapped between the sea and the British fort at Bagaduce.[40]

The following day Saltonstall's command tried to get under way. However, the British were ready for them. As the British naval force engaged the Americans, Saltonstall lost all semblance of control, and his ships fled pell-mell in every direction. Many blew up, caught on fire, or were beached and burned by their crews. Lovell noted that the scene was so awful that any "attempt to give a description to this terrible day is out of my Power, it would be a fit subject for some masterly hand to describe in its true colours, to see four ships pursuing seventeen sail of Armed Vessels, nine of which were stout ships, Transports on fire, Men of War blowing up."[41]

A tremendously lopsided fight, the Americans lost in killed, wounded, and missing 474 men to only 13 for the British. Saltonstall's entire fleet of forty-one total vessels was burned or captured. Saltonstall's flagship, the *Warren*, burned to the waterline. The ubiquitous sloop of war *Providence* ran up the river as far as it could go and it too was burned on the riverbank among other vessels. Captured was the New Hampshire state frigate *Hampden*. Paul Revere lost all his artillery. Without waiting for orders, Lovell's beached infantry struck out for home. Nearly the entire Massachusetts state navy had been destroyed. All in all, the British enjoyed a tremendous victory. The fort at Bagaduce remained "the last on United States soil to be abandoned by British forces in 1783."[42]

The year 1780 did not bode much better for the Americans. British commander Henry Clinton decided in 1779 to shift his efforts toward the southern colonies. Holding onto New York, Clinton ordered the evacuation of Newport, Rhode Island, and proposed to launch a major campaign against Charleston, South Carolina. Fortunately for the defense of this major southern port, South Carolina had already established a state navy—predominately galleys and smaller vessels designed to defend the local waters. Recognizing the new threat posed by Clinton's southern strategy, Congress ordered Abraham Whipple along with four Continental navy vessels, the frigates *Providence* (not to be confused with the sloop *Providence* burned in 1779 in the Penobscot expedition), *Queen of France*, *Boston*, and *Ranger* to assist in the defense of Charleston. On its way south, the decrepit *Queen of France* lost a mast and barely made it into port just before Christmas. The state of South Carolina put its small navy under Whipple's command.

Just a month later, a shocked Whipple viewed a massive British invasion force of 140 sails and at least 8,500 redcoats and Hessian infantry arriving off Charleston. Due to the disparity in firepower, Whipple decided that his best chance of success resided in bringing his ships into the Cooper River in order to cooperate with the powerful American land artillery at Fort Moultrie. Some of Whipple's men and naval ordnance were offloaded to reinforce the ground troops. Meanwhile the British made plans to land their ground forces at the mouth of the Edisto River, march overland, and cut the city off from its weaker landward side. At the time, approximately 5,000 Continentals and militia under the command of Major General Benjamin Lincoln stood ready to defend Charleston.[43]

While the British army used row galleys and barges to transport and defend its ground forces as they island-hopped their way toward Charleston, Admiral Marriot Arbuthnot, in command of Royal Navy forces, kept the city firmly blockaded from its seaward side. By the end of March 1780, the British land forces had crossed the Ashley River and began operations to cut off the Charleston Peninsula. Lincoln had seen this eventuality coming but likely felt he had little choice in choosing to remain in place. Consequently, Lincoln's army and Whipple's naval force were now caught between the British fleet just off the Charleston bar and the redcoats and Hessians digging traverses on the landward side that would enable them to bring up their siege artillery.

On April 8, 1780 (some accounts say it was April 9), Admiral Arbuthnot forced his way into Charleston harbor with a relatively small number of frigates and gunboats and passed by the guns of Fort Moultrie without suffering too much damage. Hessian observer Johann Ewald stated that it was "an entertaining spectacle." Arbuthnot was aboard the 44-gun HMS *Roebuck*. Two of Arbuthnot's lead frigates were the captured *Virginia* and the *Raleigh*, both 32 guns. According to Captain Ewald, a transport called *New Vigilant* "ran aground on a sandbank and was set on fire after the equipage had been saved. The rebels, having considered this place impassable, were so dumbfounded that they ceased firing."[44]

On May 12, 1780, Benjamin Lincoln surrendered. As described by Ewald, the American officers had their swords taken from them for shouting "Long Live Congress" the evening after they were captured. Besides taking Lincoln's entire force of between four and five thousand officers and men, Ewald noted:

> We captured 343 guns (including 21 brass cannon, 3 brass mortars, and several howitzers and coehorns), a great deal of ammunition, and stores of rum, rice, and indigo—all of which was an irreparable loss for the rebels. . . . Since all the inhabitants of the city are rebels and have been under arms we are liked about as well as a Prussian officer in Dresden after the Seven Years' War. The following twenty-seven vessels came into our possession: The *Boston* frigate (now called the *Charleston*), 36 guns, the *Providence*, 32 guns, the *Ranger* (now called the *Halifax*), 24 guns, *L'Aventure*, 24 guns, a polacre, 18 guns, and five three-masted ships as well as seventeen smaller ones. Then there were nine ships submerged, among them an old East Indiaman of 50 guns, the *Queen of France*, 32 guns, as well as two three-masted ships.[45]

Ewald may have exaggerated the number of ships actually captured. Some of the original American fleet had been scuttled or burned before the May 12 surrender. Captain Johann Hinrichs of the Hessian Jäger Corps only mentioned two ships in his diary, "the *Ranger* and *Providence,* which still had all their guns."[46] Perhaps Ewald was counting ships the British resurrected from their temporary watery graves or those left totally unarmed by the Americans. It does not seem plausible that the ships would be left for the British to capture. Nevertheless, the total defeat at Charleston surpassed even that of Penobscot. It was the largest capitulation of American combined arms in the history of the war. In a brilliant campaign of maneuver ashore by Henry Clinton's army forces and der-ring-do on the part of Admiral Arbuthnot, the British now controlled the largest American city in the South.

For the next fifteen months, a British field army under General Charles, Lord Cornwallis, created havoc in the Carolinas. Starting with another catastrophic defeat at Camden, South Carolina, of a second American army commanded by Major General Horatio Gates and after repeatedly engaging without much success Major General Nathanael Greene's rebuilt American southern army, an exhausted Cornwallis headed toward the Virginia tidewater where he hoped to be resupplied by the Royal Navy at a place called Yorktown. Thinking himself secure on the Yorktown Peninsula, Cornwallis did not know that, by August 1781, Washington and his French allies, commanded by the Comte de Rochambeau, were already starting to shift some of their forces south-ward to assist Greene and the Marquis de Lafayette. Moreover, by late March 1781, a large French fleet under the Comte de Grasse had left for the Caribbean as well. The British were aware of this and ordered a fleet under Rear Admiral Samuel Hood to reconnoiter the Caribbean and en-gage De Grasse if possible before he could do much harm in North America.

By late July, de Grasse had made it safely to the Caribbean, and his fleet sailed from Haiti for North America on August 5, 1781. De Grasse worked hard to conceal his destination as Hood searched in vain for him. Hood's faster vessels made it the Chesapeake on August 21 and, finding nothing amiss, moved up the coast to New York in order to concentrate British naval power in North America for a major showdown with the French. At that time, the British had little intelligence as to the exact whereabouts of de Grasse. Both Hood and his commander, Rear Admiral Thomas Graves in New York, believed that de Grasse was likely going

The Comte de Grasse (1722–1788), left, was a French naval commander during the American Revolution. He is most famously known for his command of the French naval forces when he successfully fended off a British relief fleet under Vice Admiral Samuel Graves (1725–1802), right, at the Battle of the Virginia Capes on September 5, 1781. Once the British were driven off, the British army under Lord Charles Cornwallis, then trapped at Yorktown, Virginia, was doomed. (*New York Public Library*)

to link up with a smaller French fleet then known to be at Newport, Rhode Island, under the Comte de Barras and possibly attack New York City. On July 2, 1781, Admiral Graves, now senior station commander in North America, wrote to Admiral George Rodney of his increasing concern that "a considerable force, expected from the French Commander in Chief in the West Indies, in concert with whom M. de Barras seems to act. . . . I shall certainly keep the squadron under my command as collected as possible, and so placed as to secure a retreat to New York, where our stand must be made; and will keep cruisers to the southward."[47]

Overleaf: "A Representation, of the sea fight, on the 5th of Sepr. 1781, between Rear Admiral Graves and the Count de Grasse," c. 1781. The Battle of the Virginia Capes was the most decisive naval engagement of the entire Revolution for the American cause. Fought exclusively between French and British naval forces, the Virginia Capes victory ensured that Lord Charles Cornwallis's British army, then trapped at Yorktown, Virginia, would be ultimately forced to surrender and thereby provided the catalyst for eventual American independence in 1783. (*Library of Congress*)

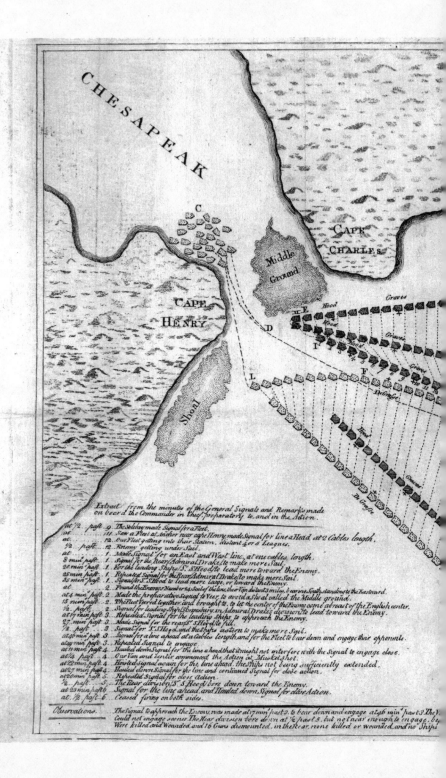

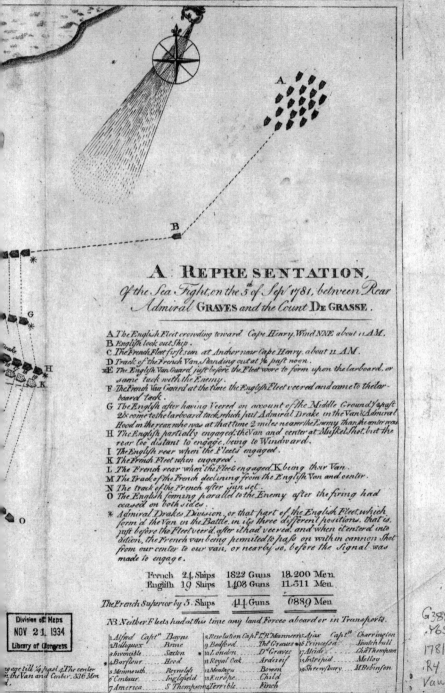

A

B

A REPRESENTATION,
Of the Sea Fight, on the 5ᵗʰ of Sepᵗ 1781, between Rear
Admiral GRAVES and the Count DE GRASSE.

A The English Fleet crowding toward Cape Henry, Wind NNE about 11 AM.
B English look out Ship.
C The French Fleet first seen at Anchor near Cape Henry, about 11 AM.
D Track of the French Van, Standing out at ¼ past noon.
E The English Van Guard just before the Fleet wore to form upon the larboard, or same tack with the Enemy.
F The French Van Guard at the time the English Fleet veered and came to the larboard tack.
G The English after having Veered on account of the Middle Ground ½ past 2& come to the larboard tack, which put Admiral Drake in the Van & Admiral Hood in the rear, who was at that time 2 miles nearer the Enemy than the center was.
H The English partially engaged; the Van and center at Musket Shot, but the rear too distant to engage, being to Windward.
I The English rear when the Fleets engaged.
K The French Fleet when engaged.
L The French rear when the Fleet engaged, K being their Van.
M The Track of the French declining from the English Van and center.
N The track of the French after gun set.
O The English forming parallel to the Enemy after the firing had ceased on both sides.
* Admiral Drakes Division, or that part of the English Fleet, which form'd the Van in the Battle, in its three different positions, that is, just before the Fleet veer'd, after it had veered, and when it entered into action, the French van being permitted to pass on within cannon Shot from our center to our van, or nearly so, before the Signal was made to engage.

French	24 Ships	1822 Guns	18,200 Men
English	19 Ships	1408 Guns	11,311 Men
The French Superior by 5 Ships		414 Guns	6889 Men

N.B. Neither Fleets had at this time any land Forces aboard or in Transports.

	Captⁿ			Captⁿ
1 Alfred	Bayne	8 Resolution Capt. F.L.R. Manners	15 Ajax	Charrington
2 Bellique	Brine	9 Bedford	The Graves	16 Princessa	Knatchbull
3 Invincible	Saxton	10 London	Dᵉ Graves	17 Alcide	Chaᵗ Thompson
* 4 Barfleur	Hood	11 Royal Oak	Ardesoif	18 Intrepid	Molloy
5 Monmouth	Reynolds	12 Montagu	Bowen	19 Shrewsbury	M Robinson
6 Centaur	Inglefield	13 Europe	Child		
7 America	S Thompson	14 Terrible	Finch		

G

*

G

*

H

K

O

...gage till ¼ past 4 The center
..., the Van and Center. 336 Men

Once the British had intelligence that de Barras had put to sea on August 25, 1781, both Graves and Hood correctly assumed that the destination of both French fleets was the Chesapeake Bay. Graves got his combined fleet under way on August 31. However, on August 30, De Grasse's fleet had already reached the bay and was in the process of landing reinforcements for Lafayette and blockading Yorktown.[48] The British army at Yorktown was now hemmed in by growing French and American forces on land and French frigates on the York River. Unless the Royal Navy could raise the blockade, Cornwallis's army was all but doomed.

While two previous Franco-American attempts at combined operations had turned into finger-pointing debacles (Newport, 1778, and Savannah, 1779), this time the French naval force had beaten the British to their objective. Rear Admiral Graves's fleet from New York arrived off the Virginia Capes on September 5, and the aggressive de Grasse immediately decided that he would engage this enemy just outside the entrance to Chesapeake Bay, despite having a considerable number of his men (approximately 1,500) still on shore foraging for provisions. Getting underway with a favorable tide around 2 p.m., both fleets adopted the classic "line ahead" battle formation. What occurred was a desultory battle that extended over several days and resulted in both fleets being drawn farther away from the mouth of the Chesapeake. The French, for once, seemed to get the better of their opponents and inflicted some amount of damage to a number of Royal Navy vessels that affected their ability to maneuver. While the British lost only a single vessel, the HMS *Terrible*, this drawn-out sea battle nevertheless proved to be fortunate for the French because during the interregnum de Barras's Newport fleet with Rochambeau's siege artillery aboard was able to enter the bay unmolested. This was exactly what de Grasse had hoped to accomplish. He quickly regrouped his forces inside the Virginia Capes.[49]

On September 12, 1781, the frigate HMS *Medea* reconnoitered the bay entrance and reported seeing a forest of French navy ships at anchor. Graves and Hood had no choice but to retreat to New York, make some quick repairs and, once accomplished, return for another engagement with de Grasse. The problem with this plan was that New York lacked at that moment "a proper dock yard" for such repairs. To make matters worse, a series of misunderstandings further delayed the departure of a rescue fleet. The British commander-in-chief, General Henry Clinton,

believed that Cornwallis could hold out until the end of October. However, the Royal Navy did not fully make their rescue attempt until it was
too late. On October 19, 1781, Cornwallis surrendered to Washington
and Rochambeau. While not known at the time, thanks to French sea
power the prospect of reconquering the erstwhile colonies was all over
for the British in North America.[50]

While the defeat and capture of a second British field army did not
end the war at sea, it was clear by 1782, at least for the Americans, that
activity was beginning to wind down. A good example of this trend is
apparent in the number of letters of marque issued by Congress. "In
1782, 300 letters of marque were granted . . . to private armed vessels;
in 1783, the number dropped to 22."[51] By 1781, American navy resources were totally exhausted. Most of its continental vessels had been
either captured or destroyed and the British rightfully focused on the
French threat to their valuable Caribbean possessions. In fact, the British
partially recouped their prospects in April 1782 when a fleet under Admiral George Rodney defeated that of de Grasse at the Battle of the
Saintes in the Caribbean. While American privateers and state navies
still operated against the British, the Royal Navy clearly had bigger fish
to fry.

The southern congressional delegates of 1775 had been proven pre-
scient. Trying to field a Continental navy was indeed costly and largely
ineffective in the long run. Nonetheless, American privateers and single
cruisers made shocking forays upon the British home islands, causing
maritime insurance rates to skyrocket. The Royal Navy was forced to detach precious maritime assets to guard their home waters against the likes
of John Paul Jones and Gustavus Conyngham. With their vaunted navy
spread out from India to Nova Scotia, Great Britain's naval power lacked
the capacity to provide adequate coverage in every critical theater. This
became apparent after the French openly allied themselves with America
in 1778. Their entry into the war complicated things for the Royal Navy.
The victory of de Grasse at the Chesapeake Bay in 1781 was a good example of this British conundrum. More worried about New York or their
valuable Caribbean possessions, the North American station commander,
Rear Admiral Thomas Graves, found himself temporarily outgunned at
the Battle of the Virginia Capes. When he foolishly allowed the fleet of
de Barras to join with de Grasse at the Virginia Capes, there was nothing
Graves could do about it and Cornwallis's fate was sealed.

Finally and perhaps most important, seaborne communication between France and America was never seriously affected by the British until it was too late. Throughout the war, neither the Americans nor the French seemed to have had much trouble crossing the Atlantic in either direction. This freedom to maneuver allowed the French to retain the strategic initiative at sea in 1781. While Admiral Sir George Rodney ended this prospect for France in 1782 at the Battle of the Saintes, his victory came too late. The British debacle at Yorktown had already ended Lord North's ministry and incredibly, thanks to French sea power decisively applied at the right time and place, was instrumental toward America gaining its independence in 1783.

As far as the Continental navy was concerned, the impact of the war at sea during the American Revolution was mixed. American blue water forces were simply too small and too inexperienced to make much of a dent against the mighty Royal Navy. As evidenced by the Penobscot Bay debacle, even a tiny British squadron was more than a match for the Continental navy. At Charleston in 1780, a massive British and Hessian invasion force backed up by dozens of men-of-war far exceeded the small squadron Abraham Whipple could muster in defense. The loss of Charleston was a foregone conclusion. Until the United States could create a fleet of similar size and armament to that of Great Britain (and this would not take place until nearly the end of the nineteenth century), the Royal Navy continued to dominate wars at sea.

However, on inland waterways, American naval power seemed to do better. Benedict Arnold's Lake Champlain defense (Valcour Island, 1776) delayed the British invasion of New York for nearly a year, and the stalwart performance of the Pennsylvania state navy on the Delaware River (1776–1777) in keeping the British out of Philadelphia for as long as they did was also noteworthy. Moreover, individual commerce raiders such as *Ranger, Revenge, Bon Homme Richard*, and swarms of American privateers did have an impact on the war. Their presence in British home waters caused the Admiralty to detach valuable men-of-war, leaving far-flung station commanders like Admiral Graves at the Battle of the Virginia Capes (1781) with insufficient naval strength needed to defend against the likes of the Comte de Grasse. Further, the mere presence of even a small Continental navy demonstrated American offensive resolve at sea. In order to protect their interests, many British merchant houses demanded that a significant portion of the Royal Navy stay in home waters if only to deal with the swarms of American privateers who harried the shipping lanes in and around the British Isles.

In the end, the war at sea convinced key decision makers in Congress that America's future resided in maintaining a robust maritime establishment. While the presence of the Continental navy did not substantially alter operations on land, it did, in combination with "brown water" state navies on American lakes and rivers and privateers on the open sea, cause enough damage that the British were eventually more than happy to let their former colonies go. This was especially true after their catastrophic defeat at Yorktown—a situation brought on by a French fleet working in concert with Franco-American forces ashore. Finally, the war at sea provided a wealth of combat experience for a new generation of seagoing officers such as Joshua Barney and especially Edward Preble. It was Preble who later established the aggressive fighting tradition of the early United States Navy, and he imparted this attitude to a coterie of newly commissioned officers such as Stephen Decatur, Thomas Truxton, William Bainbridge, and John Rodgers. These young officers later became famous for their skill and success against the Royal Navy during the War of 1812.

NOTES

INTRODUCTION

1. Nathanael Greene to Henry Knox, Dec. 7, 1780, in Dennis Conrad et al., eds., *Papers of General Nathanael Greene*, 13 vols. (Chapel Hill: University of North Carolina Press, 1976–2005), 6: 547 (hereinafter cited as *PNG*).

2. Nathanael Greene to Henry Knox, December 1780, and Greene to George Washington, Oct. 31, 1780, *PNG* 6:547, 448; Greene to Samuel Huntington, Dec. 28, 1780, *PNG* 7:9; Terry Golway, *Washington's General: Nathanael Greene and the Triumph of the American Revolution* (New York: Owl Books, 2006), chapter 11. For Greene's reconnaissance of the terrain, see Greene to Thaddeus Kosciuszko, Dec. 3, 1780, *PNG* 6:515.

3. Nathan Bailey, *Dictionarium Britannicum Or a More Compleat Universal Etymological English than Any Extant* (London: T. Cox, 1736), defines "the Theatre of War" as "the Country or Place where a War is carry'd On." *The American Military Pocket Atlas; being an approved collection of correct maps, both general and particular; of the British colonies; especially those which now are, or probably may be the theatre of war; taken principally from the actual surveys and judicious observations of engineers De Brahm and Römans; Cook, Jackson, and Collet; Maj. Holland, and other Officers* (London: R. Sayer and J. Bennet, 1776).

4. George Washington to Samuel Washington, July 20, 1775; and George Washington from Lieutenant Colonel Joseph Reed, March 23, 1776, in Philander D. Chase, ed., *Papers of George Washington*, Revolutionary War Series, 24 vols. (Charlottesville: University Press of Virginia, 1985–2016), 1:136 and 3:518–519.

5. Col. Martin Bladen, *C. Julius Caesar's Commentaries of his War in Gaul, and Civil War with Pompey* (London: T. Wood, 1737), Book 1, 228; Carl von Clausewitz, *On War*, ed. Michael Howard and Peter Paret (Princeton: Princeton University Press, 1989), Book 5, Part 2, 280.

6. Worthington Chauncey Ford, ed., *Journals of the Continental Congress, 1774–1789*, 34 vols. (Washington, DC: GPO, 1906), July 12, 1775, 2:175 and Feb. 13, 1776, 4:133 (quote); *Letters of Delegates to Congress, 1774–1789*, July 31, 1775, 1:690; Robert K. Wright, *The Continental Army* (Washington, DC: U.S. Army Center of Military History, 1983), 82–90.

CHAPTER ONE: THE NORTHERN THEATER

1. Secret Orders, Lord Dartmouth to Thomas Gage, Jan. 27, 1775, in Clarence E. Carter, ed., *The Correspondence of General Thomas Gage, 1763–1775*, 2 vols. (New Haven, CT, 1931–1933), 2:179–83. Many valuable accounts of the Lexington and Concord engagements exist. Good starting places include Nathaniel Philbrick, *Bunker Hill: A City, a Siege, a Revolution* (New York: Viking, 2013), 109–87; and David Hackett Fischer, *Paul Revere's Ride* (New York: Oxford, 1994).

2. James Kirby Martin, *Benedict Arnold, Revolutionary Hero: An American Warrior Reconsidered* (New York: NYU Press, 1997), 60–69. The Massachusetts Committee of Safety had earlier learned about the weapons at Ticonderoga from John Brown, a Pittsfield attorney who had traveled all the way to Montreal in March 1775 on a mission to contact British subjects there about possibly joining in the rebellion, if warfare broke out. For further details, see Mark R. Anderson, *The Battle for the Fourteenth Colony: America's War of Liberation from Canada, 1774–1776* (Hanover, NH: UPNE, 2013), 53–56.

3. For a critical appraisal of Ethan Allen and the Boys, see John J. Duffy and H. Nicholas Muller, III, *Inventing Ethan Allen* (Hanover, NH: UPNE, 2014).

4. Ethan Allen, *A Narrative of Colonel Ethan Allen's Captivity . . .* (Philadelphia, 1789), J. Kevin Graffagnino, ed., *Ethan and Ira Allen: Collected Works*, 3 vols. (Benson, VT: Chaldize, 1992), 2:3–4. See also Martin, *Arnold*, 67–72.

5. "By the King, a Proclamation, for Suppressing Rebellion and Sedition," London, August 23, 1775, Merrill Jensen, ed., *English Historical Documents, Volume IX: American Colonial Documents to 1776* (New York: Oxford, 1969), 850–51.

6. Benedict Arnold worked diligently to assure patriot control of the lake, including a raid in mid-May on St. John's on the Richelieu River in Canada. See Martin, *Arnold*, 74–75.

7. Benedict Arnold to Continental Congress, Crown Point, June 13, 1775, Peter Force, ed. *American Archives (AA)*, 4th ser., 6 vols. and 5th ser., 3 vols. (Washington, DC, 1847–1853), 4th ser., 2:1087. Ethan Allen sent a similar letter to Congress, also advocating an invasion of Quebec Province. Both Allen and Arnold hoped to obtain a command assignment. See Martin, *Arnold*, 92–93.

8. On this important British leader, see Paul David Nelson, *General Sir Guy Carleton, Lord Dorchester: Soldier-Statesman of Early British Canada* (Cranbury, NJ: Fairleigh Dickinson University Press, 2000).

9. Schuyler received his appointment on June 19, 1775, Worthington C. Ford et al., eds., *Journals of the Continental Congress, 1774–1789 (JCC)*, 34 vols. (Washington, DC, 1904–1937), 2:99.

10. Orders to consider attacking key points in Canada, June 27, 1775, *JCC*, 2: 109–10. Invading Canada appeared very inconsistent with the desire of most delegates to reconcile differences with the home government. However, military reality led to this kind of bold defensive action—by literally going on the offensive. For Congress's rationale in regard to defending hearth and home until hoped-for reconciliation took place, see the "Declaration of the Causes and Necessity of Taking up Arms," addressed to King George III and Parliament, July 6, 1775, *JCC*, 2:127–57. King George considered such rationales hypocritical nonsense, as shown in his August 23 "Proclamation, for Suppressing Rebellion and Sedition" in the thirteen colonies, cited above.

11. Montgomery received his appointment on June 22, *JCC*, 2:103. See also Hal T. Shelton, *General Richard Montgomery and the American Revolution* (New York: NYU Press, 1994).

12. On George Washington's initial impression of the New Englanders under arms, see George Washington to Lund Washington, Cambridge, Aug. 20, 1775, Philander D. Chase et al., eds., *The Papers of George Washington: Revolutionary War Series* (*GW, RWS*), 24 vols. to date (Charlottesville, VA, 1985–2016), 1:335. On getting Arnold's expedition organized, see Martin, *Arnold*, 104–23.

13. For additional details, see Anderson, *Battle*, 87–160. Important was the surrender of Fort Chambly, located about twelve miles north of Fort St. Johns, which netted much needed gunpowder and ball for Montgomery's siege operations. Controversial patriot Major John Brown received credit for being in command of this successful sortie against this weakly defended fort.

14. Martin, *Arnold*, 121–150. See also Thomas Desjardin, *Through a Howling Wilderness: Benedict Arnold's March to Quebec, 1775* (New York: St. Martin's, 2006), and Stephen Darley, *Voices from a Wilderness Expedition: The Journals and Men of Benedict Arnold's Expedition to Canada in 1775* (Bloomington: AuthorHouse, 2011).

15. Benedict Arnold to [James Clinton?], Nov. 25, 1775, in Kenneth Roberts, ed., *March to Quebec: Journals of the Members of Arnold's Expedition* (New York, 1938), 96–97; Benedict Arnold to [Philip Schuyler?], Nov. 27, 1775, ibid., 97–99. Dr. Isaac Senter, the expedition's doctor, coined the phrase "famine proof veterans." See his "Journal," Dec. 31, 1775, ibid., 232.

16. Richard Montgomery to Robert R. Livingston, Montreal, Nov. 1775, *AA*, 4th ser., 3:1638–39.

17. Martin, *Arnold*, 158–82. See also Charles Bracelen Flood, *Rise and Fight Again: Perilous Times along the Road to Independence* (New York: Dodd Mead, 1976), 5–80.

18. Don R. Higginbotham, *Daniel Morgan: Revolutionary Rifleman* (Chapel Hill: University of North Carolina Press, 1961), 27–54.

19. Montgomery's remains were returned to New York City in 1818, where they reside at St. Paul's Chapel in lower Manhattan. Governor Guy Carleton sent out small raiding parties from the walled city into the suburbs to get much needed firewood. Arnold responded by burning most of the suburbs, in other words using fire as a war tactic to get Carleton to surrender. See Martin, *Arnold*, 175–98, and Anderson, *Battle*, 259–89.

20. Details about the desperate rebel retreat may be followed in Martin, *Arnold*, 199–222, and Anderson, *Battle*, 290–315.
21. "Journal of a Physician [Lewis Beebe]," June 17, 1776, *Pennsylvania Magazine of History and Biography* (1935):335–36.
22. Minutes, June 17 and July 8, 1776, *JCC*, 5:447–48, 525–26. For details, see Jonathan G. Rossie, *The Politics of Command in the American Revolution* (Syracuse, NY: Syracuse UP, 1979), 101–111; and Don R. Gerlach, *Philip Schuyler and the War of Independence, 1775–1783* (Syracuse, NY: Syracuse UP, 1987), 160–66.
23. Many descriptions of the fleet and Arnold's defense of Lake Champlain exist. The following section relies on materials found in Martin, *Arnold*, 246–92; James Kirby Martin, "The Battle of Valcour Island," in Jack Sweetman, ed., *Great American Naval Battles* (Annapolis, MD: Naval Institute UP, 1998), 3–26; James L. Nelson, *Benedict Arnold's Navy: The Ragtag Fleet That Lost the Battle of Lake Champlain and Won the American Revolution* (Camden, ME: Ragged Mountain, 2006), 235–320; and Stephen Darley, *The Battle of Valcour Island: The Participants and Vessels of Benedict Arnold's 1776 Defense of Lake Champlain* (n.p., 2013).
24. Orders and Instructions, Ticonderoga, Aug. 7, 1776, *AA*, 5 ser., 1:826–27.
25. On the governor's more limited campaign objectives, see Governor Guy Carleton to Lord George Germain, Chambly, September 28, 1776, Kenneth G. Davies, ed. *Documents of the American Revolution, 1770–1783*, 21 vols. (Shannon, Ireland, 1972–1981), 12:232–34. Germain had hoped his generals would effect the Hudson Highlands strategy of cutting off New England by the end of 1776, but Carleton and William Howe, in their hesitancy and careful steps, left this overall objective far from complete.
26. Benedict Arnold to Philip Schuyler, Ticonderoga, Oct. 15, 1776, *AA*, 5 ser., 2:1080.
27. Horatio Gates, General Orders, Northern Army, Ticonderoga, Oct. 14, 1776, *AA*, 5 ser., 3:527; William Maxwell to Gov. William Livingston, Ticonderoga, Oct. 20, 1776, *AA*, 5 ser., 2:1143.
28. Alfred Thayer Mahan, *The Major Operations of the Navies in the War of American Independence* (Cambridge, MA, 1913), 25.
29. Burgoyne to Henry Clinton, Chambly, July 7, 1776, Burgoyne to Henry Clinton, Quebec, Nov. 7, 1776, and Burgoyne to Germain, Jan.1, 1777, Douglas R. Cubbison, ed., *Burgoyne and the Saratoga Campaign: His Papers* (Norman, OK: University of Oklahoma Press, 2012), 150–53, 157–61, 162–63. Burgoyne had a loving relationship with his wife, Lady Charlotte Stanley, who died in June 1776.
30. Lieutenant General John Burgoyne, "Thoughts on Conducting the War, From the Side of Canada," Hertford Street [London], Feb. 28, 1777, ibid., 178–86. Burgoyne wanted a force of 11,000, which would have included 2,000 Canadians and 1,000 Indians. Available Canadians and Indians fell well below these projections.
31. "Thoughts on Conducting the War," ibid., 184. Cubbison makes the point that Burgoyne's planning was detailed in regard to breaking through to the Hudson River but lacked clarity of purpose after reaching that geographic location in making final movements toward Albany. See ibid., 34–36.

32. "Thoughts on Conducting the War," ibid., 185–86.
33. For more information on Burgoyne's flamboyance, see Andrew Jackson O'Shaughnessy, *The Men Who Lost America: British Leadership, the American Revolution, and the Fate of the Empire* (New Haven, CT: Yale UP, 2013), 123–64.
34. Benedict Arnold to Horatio Gates, Valcour Island, Oct. 10, 1776, and Arnold to George Washington, Ticonderoga, Nov. 6, 1776, *AA*, 5 ser., 2:982, and 3:550. For details regarding the complex dealings involving Schuyler, Gates, and Arnold, see Martin, *Arnold*, 290–344; and Rossie, *Politics of Command*, 135–73.
35. Horatio Gates to Jonathan Trumbull, Ticonderoga, Oct. 22, 1776, *AA*, 5 ser., 2:1192.
36. George Washington to Richard Henry Lee, Morristown, March 6, 1777, *GW, RWS*, 8:523; and Washington to Arnold, Morristown, March 3, 1777, ibid., 8:493.
37. See Martin, *Arnold*, 316–23, for details about Governor William Tryon's raid to destroy the rebel supply base at Danbury, CT, April 25–28, 1777. For Arnold's belated promotion on May 2, 1777, see *JCC*, 7:323. John Adams thought Congress should recognize Arnold with a special medal, but the delegates refused. To do so would have embarrassed them, having so recently passed over him for a promotion. See Adams to his wife Abigail, Philadelphia, May 2, 1777, in Paul H. Smith et al., eds., *Letters of Delegates to Congress, 1774–1789 (LDC)*, 26 vols. (Philadelphia, 1976–2000), 7:12.
38. Board of War Report, May 15, 1777, and Minutes, May 22, 1777, *JCC*, 7:364, and 8:375. On this phase of Schuyler's career, see Martin, *Arnold*, 327–29.
39. March 25, 1777, and April 2, 1777, *JCC*, 7:202, and 217. See also John Hancock, President of Congress, to Horatio Gates, Philadelphia, March 25, 1777, *LDC*, 6:486–87. Wrote Hancock, using words almost implying that Gates was to assume overall command, "I have it therefore in charge to direct, that you repair to Saratoga immediately, and *take the command* of the army in that department." Italics in original. For a sympathetic presentation regarding Gates's ambitious behavior during the spring of 1777, see Nelson, *Gates*, 79–89.
40. Congress's Minutes for June 18, 1777, *JCC*, 8:476–79, do not mention Gates's appearance that day. See Gates's Notes for a Speech to Congress [Philadelphia, June 18, 1777], *LDC*, 7:213–15; James Duane to Philip Schuyler, Phila., June 19, 1777, ibid., 7:225; and William Duer to Philip Schuyler, Phila., June 19, 1777, ibid., 7:228–30.
41. Arthur St. Clair to Philip Schuyler, Ticonderoga June 13, 1777; Arthur St. Clair to Philip Schuyler, Ticonderoga, June 18, 1777; and Arthur St. Clair to James Wilson, Ticonderoga, June 18, 1777, William H. Smith, ed., *The St. Clair Papers*, 2 vols. (Cincinnati, 1882), 1:399–400, 1:401–2, and 1:402–4. For the futile, last minute preparations to hold the line at Fort Ticonderoga, see Martin, *Arnold*, 348–50; and Bruce Venter, *The Battle of Hubbardton: The Rear Guard Action that Saved America* (Charleston, SC: Arcadia, 2015), 19–30.
42. General William Phillips, quoted in Hoffman Nickerson, *The Turning Point of the American Revolution, or Burgoyne in America* (Boston, 1928), 144. For a first-

hand description of the British overrunning Ticonderoga, see Burgoyne to Germain, Skenesborough, July 11, 1777, *Burgoyne and the Saratoga Campaign*, 265–73.

43. Council of War Minutes, Ticonderoga, July 5, 1777, Smith, ed., *St. Clair Papers*, 1:420–21. For a full description of the Hubbardton engagement, see Venter, *Battle of Hubbardton*.

44. Manifesto Issued by Lieutenant General Burgoyne, June 24, 1777, *Burgoyne and the Saratoga Campaign*, 201–3.

45. Washington to John Hancock, President of Congress, Morristown, July 10, 1777, *GW, RWS*, 10:240–41.

46. Based on a muster roll dated July 20, 1777, Schuyler could claim 6,359 soldiers on paper, divided between 3,925 Continentals and 2,434 militiamen. More than 2,000 were either unfit for duty or absent, meaning that Schuyler's real numbers were actually 4,467, according to this muster role. See Martin, *Arnold*, 350.

47. Burgoyne to Germain, Fort Edward, July 30, 1777, *Burgoyne and the Saratoga Campaign*, 275–76. For more details on the wilderness challenges faced by Burgoyne's army, see Richard M. Ketchum, *Saratoga: Turning Point of America's Revolutionary War* (New York: Holt, 1997), 230–44, and Martin, *Arnold*, 350–53.

48. The original source of the McCrea story is Arnold to George Washington, Snook–kill, July 27, 1777, *GW, RWS*, 10:433–35.

49. Marvin L. Brown, Jr., trans., *Baroness von Riedesel and the American Revolution: Journal and Correspondence, 1776–1783* (Chapel Hill: UNCP, 1965), 55–56.

50. Burgoyne to Germain, Nearly Opposite to Saratoga, Aug. 20, 1777, *DAR*, 14:163–65. For the lack of coordination in the execution of overall British strategy in 1776 and 1777, see Ira D. Gruber, *The Howe Brothers and the American Revolution* (Chapel Hill: UNCP, 1972), 224–56.

51. As with Benedict Arnold, Congress passed over talented Stark, in his case during March 1777 in possibly promoting him from colonel to brigadier general. He resigned but then assembled a force of some 1,500 New Hampshire militiamen. They were headed northeast to attack Burgoyne's supply lines in the Skenesborough area when they engaged the Hessians in the Bennington battle. For details, see Ketchum, *Saratoga*, 285–308, and Michael P. Gabriel, *The Battle of Bennington: Soldiers and Civilians* (Charleston, SC: History Press, 2012).

52. Burgoyne to Germain, Nearly Opposite to Saratoga, Aug. 20, 1777, *DAR*, 14:163–65; and Burgoyne to Germain (Private), Nearly Opposite Saratoga, Aug. 20, 1777, *DAR*, 14:165–67.

53. Despite earlier intelligence received by St. Leger, the fort was in defensible shape and could not be easily reduced. The cannons his force brought along were 6-pounders, lacking the firepower to breach the walls. Inside the fort was the 3rd New York regiment under Colonel Peter Gansevoort. They had ample supplies, giving them the capacity to hold out against the siege for several weeks. On the Battle of Oriskany itself, see Joseph T. Glatthaar and James Kirby Martin, *Forgotten Allies: The Oneida Indians and the American Revolution* (New York, Hill and Wang, 2006), 149–78; and more generally, Gavin K. Watt, *Rebellion in the Mohawk Valley: The St. Leger Expedition of 1777* (Toronto: Dundurn, 2002).

54. The 900 Continentals belonged to Brigadier General Ebenezer Learned's brigade. Learned accompanied Arnold on the expedition. For more information regarding Schuyler's war council, including the accusation that he was purposely dividing his force to aid the enemy's advance, see Martin, *Arnold*, 361–64.

55. For more on Hon Yost Schuyler, possibly a distant relative of Philip Schuyler, see William L. Stone, *Life of Joseph Brant–Thayendanegea, Including the Border Wars of the American Revolution*, 2 vols. (New York, 1838), 1:258–60.

56. On September 15 Burgoyne reported a total force of 6,588, including women, children, and other hangers on, but not quite 5,000 effectives prepared to engage in combat. Intelligence reports had reached him that some 14 to 15,000 patriots were waiting to challenge him, an exaggerated number at this point in time. See Martin, *Arnold*, 373.

57. Minutes of Congress, July 29, Aug. 1, and Aug. 4, 1777, *JCC*, 8:585, 596, and 603–4. See also New England Delegates to George Washington, Phila., Aug. 2, 1777, *LDC*, 7:405; and Washington to John Hancock, Phila., Aug. 3, 1777, *GW, RWS*, 10:492–93.

58. Even Horatio Gates's sympathetic biographer, Paul David Nelson, admitted that the former British major treated Schuyler with indignity when assuming command, to wit that "Gates's accession to command was not his finest hour, either as a man or as a soldier." See Nelson, *Gates*, 107.

59. On Burgoyne's less than desirable choices, see Martin, *Arnold*, 374–78. See also Eric H. Schnitzer, "The Tactics of the Battles of Saratoga," in William A. Griswold and Donald W. Linebaugh, eds., *The Saratoga Campaign: Uncovering an Embattled Landscape* (Hanover, NH: UPNE, 2016), 40–43.

60. The Gates-Arnold dispute might be labeled the third battle of Saratoga. See Martin, *Arnold*, 370–71, for incidents igniting differences at Saratoga, which had deep roots going back to December 1776, as described above.

61. The debate about how extensive Arnold's role was in the September 19 battle has been a source of controversy all the way back to the battle itself. The Gates camp, featuring well known scoundrel James Wilkinson, actually claimed that Arnold had no involvement. Among those historians who diminish Arnold's role is John F. Luzader, *Saratoga: A Military History of the Decisive Campaign of the American Revolution* (New York: Savas Beatie, 2008), Appendix H, 380–93. Ketchum, *Saratoga*, 362–63, and Martin, *Arnold*, 375–83, have Arnold in the thick of the fighting. Surviving comments of those actually engaged in the Sept. 19 engagement support the latter position. Also informative is Appendix II in Willard M. Wallace, *Traitorous Hero: The Life and Fortunes of Benedict Arnold* (New York, 1954), 326–32, which calls into question Gates's judgment had he had not allowed Arnold to take the lead in the field that day.

62. Casualty numbers, Martin, *Arnold*, 381–82. For Burgoyne's description of the September 19 engagement, see Burgoyne to Germain, Albany, Oct. 20, 1777, *Burgoyne and the Saratoga Campaign*, 322–25.

63. On Clinton's less than supportive campaign up the Hudson River, with reflections on his cautionary temperament, see O'Shaughnessy, *Men Who Lost America*, 207–20.

64. For more details regarding Gates vs. Arnold at Saratoga, see Martin, *Arnold*, 383–91. See also Arnold to Gates, Camp Stillwater, Oct. 1, 1777, in James Wilkinson, *Memoirs of My Own Time*, 4 vols. (Phila., 1816; reprint, New York, 1973), 1:259–60.

65. The letter in question was apparently written on Oct. 9, 1777, two days after that battle. A New Hampshire militia adjutant, Nathaniel Bacheller, wrote to his wife, Suzanna, and claimed that he saw Gates and Arnold working together harmoniously in resisting the British reconnaissance in force that day. The problem is that there is no proof that Bacheller was doing more than repeating camp rumors or simply making up a story to impress his wife. Corroborating evidence must be found before the Bacheller letter is considered more than a misleading report, given the deep-rooted Gates-Arnold feud as described herein.

66. Martin, *Arnold*, 392–406. Arnold's mounting disillusionment with the patriot cause clearly festered during his lengthy stay (Oct. 1777–March 1778) in the Albany hospital.

67. For Burgoyne's casualty figures, see ibid., 401.

68. Congress recognized Gates by awarding him a gold medal on Nov. 4, 1777. At the same time the delegates resolved to commend Arnold and the officers "for their brave and successful efforts in support of the independence of their country." Nothing in the record states anything about Arnold's wound or that Gates was never near the actual fighting in either battle. See *JCC*, 9:861–62.

69. This particular anti-Arnold characterization appears in Dean Snow, *1777: Tipping Point at Saratoga* (New York: Oxford, 2016), 28, which offers a detailed day-to-day account of the battles. For other examples, see Ketchum, *Saratoga*, 350, and especially Luzader, *Saratoga*, xix–xx, which repeats tales about Arnold's alleged sordid youth while pointing out that "ambition, avarice, and vainglory" were his only motives in life. Unfortunately, demeaning Arnold does nothing to make Gates's less than spectacular performance at Saratoga look better than it was. For a summary of Luzader's pro-Gates, anti-Arnold approach, see "The Coming of the Revolutionary War Battles at Saratoga," in Griswold and Linebaugh, eds., *Saratoga*, 1–38.

70. For a dissenting analysis of the importance of the Saratoga victory that records the history of additional fighting in the northern region after 1777, see Theodore Corbett, *No Turning Point: The Saratoga Campaign in Perspective* (Norman, OK: University of Oklahoma Press, 2012).

CHAPTER TWO: THE MIDDLE THEATER

1. For balanced assessment of Washington as a commander, see Edward G. Lengel, *General George Washington: A Military Life* (New York: Random House, 2005), 365–71.

2. In fact, after he marched into Virginia, and ultimately to Yorktown, Cornwallis's important communications were almost exclusively with the ministry in London and with Clinton in New York. Having left the young Lord Rawdon in command in South Carolina, Lord Cornwallis never looked back. His fate, he knew, lay with events in the North, not below the Dan, and his correspondence with Rawdon was

scant indeed—the most important of which asked Rawdon to forward reinforcement expected to arrive at Charleston. There was never a serious mention of Cornwallis's moving south again. See Cornwallis to Lord Rawdon, Feb. 21, 1781, and Mar. 17, 1781, in Charles Ross, ed., *Correspondence of Charles, First Marquis Cornwallis*, 3 vols. (London: John Murray, 1859), I:84–85.

3. E.g., Peter O. Wacker, *Land and People: A Cultural Geography of New Jersey: Origins and Settlement Patterns* (New Brunswick, NJ: Rutgers University Press, 1975), 1–54, 409–12, details climatic and environmental conditions, as well as settlement patterns in New Jersey, where much (indeed most) of the war would be fought in the Middle Theater.

4. Johann Ewald, *Diary of the American Revolution: A Hessian Journal*, ed. Joseph P. Tustin (New Haven: Yale University Press, 1979), 8, 22, 51, 75, 80, 91.

5. John McCusker and Russell R. Menard, *The Economy of British America, 1607–1789* (Chapel Hill: University of North Carolina Press, 1991), 133, 136, 189, 198, 203; Jackson Turner Main, *The Social Structure of Revolutionary America* (Princeton: Princeton University Press, 1965), 25–28, 30–33, 42–43.

6. Entry of Jan. 8, 1781, *The Diaries of George Washington*, ed. Donald Jackson (Charlottesville: University Press of Virginia, 1978), III:356; Gregory W. Walsh, "'Most Boundless Avarice': Illegal Trade in Revolutionary Essex," in James J. Gigantino, ed., *The American Revolution in New Jersey: Where the Battlefront Meets the Home Front* (New Brunswick, NJ: Rutgers University Press, 2015), 32–53.

7. Alan Gilbert, *Black Patriots and Loyalists: Fighting for Emancipation in the War for Independence* (Chicago: University of Chicago Press, 2012), 95–115; Mark Edward Lender, *The War for American Independence* (Santa Barbara, CA: ABC-CLIO, 2016), 29, 117–18.

8. T. H. Breen, *American Insurgents, American Patriots: The Revolution of the People* (New York: Hill and Wang, 2010), 10–19, and especially chapters 3, 4, and 6.

9. Lender, *War for American Independence*, 3.

10. Lengel, *General George Washington*, 86–91.

11. Ibid., 126–27.

12. On the British decision to take the city, and the reasoning behind it, see Ira D. Gruber, *The Howe Brothers and the American Revolution* (New York: W.W. Norton, 1972), 82–83.

13. Charles Lee to George Washington, *The Papers of George Washington*, Revolutionary War Series [hereafter *PGW*, RWS], ed. Philander D. Chase (Charlottesville: University Press of Virginia, 1988), 3:339–41.

14. On the American fortifications, see Lengel, *General George Washington*, 131, 133–34.

15. Gruber, *Howe Brothers and the American Revolution*, 109–12; Willard M. Wallace, *Appeal to Arms: A Military History of the American Revolution* (Chicago: Quadrangle Books, 1951), 106–11.

16. Henry Clinton, *The American Rebellion: Sir Henry Clinton's Narrative of His Campaigns, 1775–1782, with an Appendix of Original Documents* (New Haven: Yale University Press, 1954), 44.

17. William Howe, *The Narrative of Lieut. General Sir William Howe, in a Committee of the House of Commons, on the 29th of April, 1779, Relative to his Conduct during His Late Command of the King's Troops in North America: to Which Are Added Some Observations upon a Pamphlet, Entitled Letters to a Nobleman*, 3rd ed. (London: R. Baldwin, printer, 1781), 5.

18. Lengel, *General George Washington*, 153–54.

19. The later chapters in Arthur S. Lefkowitz, *The Long Retreat: The Calamitous American Defense of New Jersey, 1776* (Metuchen, NJ: Upland Press, 1998), detail Washington's retreat across the state and the fact that American forces, no matter how battered, remained operational.

20. On the situation in New Jersey, see Mark Edward Lender, "The Cockpit Reconsidered: Revolutionary New Jersey as a Military Theater," in Barbara Mitnick, ed., *New Jersey in the American Revolution* (New Brunswick, NJ: Rivergate Books, Rutgers University Press, 2005), 45–60.

21. Joseph Reed to Charles Lee, Nov. 21, 1776, in William B. Reed, *Life and Correspondence of Joseph Reed* (Philadelphia: Lindsay and Blakiston, 1847), I:255–56; Reed to Lee, Nov. 21, 1776, in *Collections of the New York Historical Society for the Year 1872. The Lee Papers* (New York: New York Historical Society, 1873), II:293–94; Lee to Horatio Gates, Dec. 12–13, 1776, ibid., 348.

22. George Washington to John Augustine Washington, Dec. 18, 1776, *The Writings of George Washington from the Original Manuscript Sources, 1745–1799*, ed. John C. Fitzpatrick, 39 vols. (Washington, DC: U.S. Government Printing Office, 1931–1944), 6:397–98. A very similar letter is George Washington to his brother Samuel Washington, Dec. 18, 1776, *The Papers of George Washington Digital Edition* (hereafter *PGWde*), ed. Theodore J. Crackel et al. (Charlottesville: University Press of Virginia, Rotunda, 2007), Revolutionary War Series (RWS), 7:369–71.

23. Lefkowitz, *The Long Retreat*, 124, plate 14–15; Gruber, *Howe Brothers and the American Revolution*, 189–90.

24. Mark Edward Lender, "Small Battles Won: New Jersey and the Patriot Military Revival," *New Jersey Heritage* 1 (2002):34–35.

25. William S. Stryker, *The Battles of Trenton and Princeton* (Trenton, NJ: Old Barracks Association, 2001 [orig. 1898]), 187–88, 194–95.

26. Ibid., 264–66, 268–69. There is little evidence Cornwallis actually used the term, but it is clear enough he expected to find Washington in place behind the Assunpink in the morning; Don Higginbotham, *The War of American Independence: Military Attitudes, Policies, and Practice, 1763–1789* (New York: Macmillan, 1971), 169. Washington's account of the Assunpink and Princeton operations is in George Washington to John Hancock, Jan. 5, 1777, *PGWde*, RWS, 7:519–30.

27. On Morristown's role in the Revolution, see Bruce W. Stewart, *Morristown: A Crucible of the American Revolution*, New Jersey's Revolutionary Experience, No. 3 (Trenton, NJ: New Jersey Historical Commission, 1975).

28. Lengel, *General George Washington*, 208–9.

29. Howard H. Peckham, ed., *The Toll of Independence: Engagements and Battle Casualties of the American Revolution* (Chicago: University of Chicago Press, 1974),

29–32; David C. Munn, comp., *Battles and Skirmishes of the American Revolution in New Jersey* (Trenton, NJ: Bureau of Geology and Topography, Department of Environmental Protection, 1976), 127–28. Peckham's conservative count found 6 engagements in New York State (the section in the Middle Theater) and 35 in New Jersey, while Munn's more detailed survey found 49 in New Jersey alone.

30. George Washington to John Hancock, Sept. 2, 1776, *PGW*, RWS, 6:199–201; George Washington to John Hancock, Dec. 16, 1776, ibid., 7:351–53.

31. James Kirby Martin and Mark Edward Lender, *"A Respectable Army": The Military Origins of the Republic, 1763–1789,* 3rd ed. (Malden, MA: Wiley-Blackwell, 2015), 76–77.

32. Edward C. Papenfuse and Gregory A. Stiverson, "General Smallwood's Recruits: The Peacetime Career of the Revolutionary War Private," *William and Mary Quarterly*, 3rd ser., 30 (1973), 117–32; Mark Edward Lender, "The Social Structure of the New Jersey Brigade: The Continental Army as an American Standing Army," in Peter Karsten, ed., *The Military in America: From the Colonial Era to the Present* (New York: Macmillan, 1980), 27–44; John R. Sellers, "The Common Soldier in the American Revolution," in S. J. Underdal, ed., *Military History of the American Revolution: Proceedings of the Sixth Military History Symposium, USAF Academy* (Washington, DC, 1976), 151–61; Sellers, "The Origins and Careers of the New England Soldier: Noncommissioned Officers and Privates in the Massachusetts Continental Line" (unpublished paper, American Historical Association meeting, 1972).

33. Benjamin Quarles, *The Negro in the American Revolution* (Chapel Hill: University of North Carolina Press, 1961), 33–50, 182–200; Martin and Lender, *"A Respectable Army,"* 91.

34. Lender, *War for American Independence*, 30.

35. Lengel, *General George Washington*, 366.

36. Samuel Adams to James Warren, June 18, 1777, in *The Writings of Samuel Adams*, ed. Harry Alonzo Cushing (New York: G. P. Putnam's Sons, 1907), III:374; Samuel Adams to Nathanael Greene, May 12, 1777, in ibid., III:370–71.

37. Jared C. Lobdell, "Six Generals Gather Forage: The Engagement at Quibbletown, 1777," *New Jersey History* 102 (1984):35–50.

38. Lengel, *General George Washington*, 150.

39. On planning for the 1777 campaign, see Gruber, *The Howe Brothers and the American Revolution*, 199–201; Troyer Steele Anderson, *Command of the Howe Brothers during the American Revolution* (New York: Oxford University Press, 1936), 213–29; Andrew Jackson O'Shaughnessy, *The Men Who Lost America: British Leadership, the American Revolution, and the Fate of the Empire* (New Haven: Yale University Press, 2013), 143–44. On Burgoyne's communications with Howe (or lack thereof) see O'Shaughnessy, 152.

40. Robert K. Wright Jr., "Short Hills (Metuchen), New Jersey," in Harold E. Selesky, *Encyclopedia of the American Revolution*, 2nd edition (Detroit: Thomson Gale, 2006), 2:1057.

41. George Washington to William Heath, July 19, 1777, *PGWde*, RWS, 16:339.

42. On Washington's inability to discern Howe's intentions, see Lengel, *General George Washington*, 217–23.

43. The most recent treatment of the engagement is Michael Harris, *Brandywine: A Military History of the Battle that Lost Philadelphia but Saved America, September 11, 1777* (El Dorado Hills, CA: Savas Beatie, 2014).

44. For a full account of Paoli, see Thomas J. McGuire, *Battle of Paoli* (Mechanicsburg, PA: Stackpole Books, 2000).

45. John W. Jackson, *The Pennsylvania Navy, 1775–1781: The Defense of the Delaware* (New Brunswick, NJ: Rutgers University Press, 1974), 225–81.

46. George Washington to Henry Laurens, Dec. 22, 1778, *PGWde*, RWS, 12:669.

47. Joseph Lee Boyle, "Valley Forge Winter Quarters, Pennsylvania," in Selesky, *Encyclopedia*, 2:1186–87. The best overall study of the Valley Forge encampment is Wayne Bodle, *The Valley Forge Winter: Civilians and Soldiers at War* (University Park: Pennsylvania State University Press, 2002).

48. Lender, *War for American Independence*, 42.

49. Martin and Lender, "*A Respectable Army*," 131–32; George Washington to Lord Stirling, Mar. 21, 1778; to Stephen Moylan, Apr. 11, 1778; to John Banister, Apr. 21, 1778; all in *PGWde*, RWS, 14:262, 479–80, 573–74; Lengel, *General George Washington*, 269–71; Charles H. Lesser, ed., *The Sinews of Independence: Monthly Strength Reports of the Continental Army* (Chicago: University of Chicago Press, 1976), 53, 61.

50. On the work of the Committee and Camp, see Mark Edward Lender, "Logistics and the American Victory," in John Ferling, ed., *The World Turned Upside Down: The American Victory in the War of Independence* (New York: Greenwood Press, 1988), 106–7.

51. Greene's complaint is in a letter to Washington, Apr. 24, 1779, in Richard K. Showman, ed., *The Papers of General Nathanael Greene* (Chapel Hill: University of North Carolina Press, 1983), III:427.

52. For the rejuvenation of Continental logistics, see Lender, "Logistics and the American Victory," 106–7; Victor Leroy Johnson, *The Administration of the American Commissariat during the Revolutionary War* (Philadelphia: University of Pennsylvania Press, 1941), 136–37; Erna Risch, *Supplying Washington's Army* (Washington, DC: Center of Military History, U.S. Army, 1981), 46; Terry Golway, *Washington's General: Nathanael Greene and the Triumph of the American Revolution* (New York: Henry Holt, 2005,) 170–73.

53. Ricardo Herrera, "'The Zealous Activity of Capt. Lee': Light-Horse Harry Lee and *Petite Guerre*," *Journal of Military History* 79 (2015):16–17, 22–23.

54. For Steuben, we have relied on John M. Palmer, *General von Steuben* (New Haven: Yale University Press, 1937), especially the early chapters and pp. 122–23, and on Paul Lockhart, *The Drillmaster of Valley Forge: The Baron de Steuben and the Making of the American Army* (New York: Smithsonian Books, 2008).

55. Robert K. Wright, Jr., *The Continental Army* (Washington, DC: Center of Military History, 1989), 137–46; General Orders, May 4, 1778, *PGWde* RWS, 15:27.

56. Lesser, *Sinews of Independence*, 60–73.

57. This account of Knox has relied on North Callahan, *Henry Knox: George Washington's General* (New York: Rinehart, 1958), 142; Selesky, *Encyclopedia*, 2:592–94; and Berg, *Encyclopedia of Continental Units*, 24.

58. General Orders, May 5, 1778, *PGWde*, RWS, 15:38–39; Bloomfield, *Diary*, 134; Washington to the President of Congress, May 4, 1778, and to Horatio Gates, May 5, 1778, *PGWde*, RWS, 15:39.

59. Lengel, *General George Washington*, 273–74, 279–80; Ezra Selden to Samuel Mather, May 15, 1778, in "Letters from Valley Forge," Americanrevolution.org, http://www.americanrevolution.org/ vlyfrgeltrs.html; accessed Nov. 11, 2016.

60. On the new imperial strategy and the British evacuation of Philadelphia, see Clinton, *American Rebellion*, 85–87; William B. Willcox, "British Strategy in America," *Journal of Modern History* 19 (1947):97–102, puts Clinton's account in the wider context of imperial policy.

61. For the fullest account of the Monmouth campaign, see Mark Edward Lender and Garry Wheeler Stone, *Fatal Sunday: George Washington, the Monmouth Campaign, and the Politics of Battle* (Norman: University of Oklahoma Press, 2016). The battle itself is recounted in chapters 9–15, and the political implications of the battle, especially for Washington's position as commander-in-chief, are discussed in chapters 18 and 19.

62. George Washington to Nelson, Aug. 20, 1778, *PGWde*, RWS, 16:341.

63. Clinton, *American Rebellion*, 133.

64. Peckham, ed., *Toll of Independence*, 62–63; Robert K. Wright, Jr., "Paulus Hook, New Jersey," in Selesky, ed., *Encyclopedia*, II:876–79. For the best account of the Springfield campaign, see Thomas Fleming, *The Forgotten Victory: The Battle for New Jersey, 1780* (New York: Reader's Digest Press, 1973).

65. Ezekiel Cornell to Horatio Gates, Aug. 20, 1780, in *Letters of Delegates to Congress*, ed. Paul H. Smith (Washington, DC: Library of Congress, 1988), 15:607; Cornell to William Greene, Aug. 22, 1780, in ibid., 15:616; Henry Clinton to William Phillips, Apr. 26–30, 1781, in Clinton, *American Rebellion*, 515.

66. Peckham, ed., *Toll of Independence*, 57–58. During these years Peckham found no armed encounters at all in Maryland and Delaware, and only seven in Virginia, including three on Chesapeake Bay. Munn, comp., *Battles and Skirmishes in New Jersey*, 133–38; Todd W. Braisted, "A Nest of Tories: The American-versus-American Battle of Fort Lee, 1781," in James J. Gigantino, ed., *The American Revolution in New Jersey: Where the Battlefront Meets the Home Front* (New Brunswick, NJ: Rutgers University Press, 2015), 71–84.

67. Michael S. Adelberg, *The American Revolution in Monmouth County: The Theater of Spoil and Destruction* (Charleston, SC: History Press, 2010), 22, 24, 121–43.

68. George Washington to William Livingston, Feb. 4, 1778, *PGW*, RWS,13:450; John W. Jackson, *With the British Army in Philadelphia, 1777–1778* (San Rafael, CA: Presidio Press, 1979), 151–52, 163–54. However much he deplored illegal trade, Washington occasionally had agents posing as traders gather intelligence

about the British; see George Washington to William Livingston, Jan. 20, 1778, *PGW*, 13:297.

69. Walsh, "'Most Boundless Avarice': Illegal Trade in Revolutionary Essex," 32–53; Jackson, *British Army in Philadelphia*, 163.

70. Entry of Jan. 8, 1780, Washington, *Diaries*, III:370.

71. Lender, *War for American Independence* (Santa Barbara, CA: ABC-CLIO, 2016), 137–38.

72. E.g., Clinton, *American Rebellion*, 203, 209–10, 221.

73. Selesky, ed., *Encyclopedia*, II:1263; Clinton was convinced the failure of Arnold's plot was a real blow to British fortunes, *American Rebellion*,

74. E.g., entries of June 6 and 7, 4 Aug. 1781, Washington, *Diaries*, III:378–79, 405, 408.

75. On the war in Virginia, see John Selby's authoritative *The Revolution in Virginia, 1775–1783* (Williamsburg, VA: Colonial Williamsburg Foundation, 1988); and Michael A. McDonnell, *The Politics of War: Race, Class, and Conflict in Revolutionary Virginia* (Chapel Hill: University of North Carolina Press, 2007).

76. On the Yorktown campaign, especially Franco-American cooperation, see Lengel, *General George Washington*, 335–44; for an older but solid military account of the campaign, see Henry P. Johnston, *The Yorktown Campaign and the Surrender of Cornwallis* (New York: Da Capo Press, 1971 [1881]), especially Chapters 5–7.

CHAPTER THREE: THE SOUTHERN THEATER

1. William B. Willcox, "British Strategy in America, 1778," *Journal of Modern History* 19 (June 1947), 97–121, esp. 102.

2. Lord George Germain to Sir Henry Clinton, Aug. 5, 1778, Henry Clinton Papers, William L. Clements Library (hereafter WLCL).

3. Gerald Saxon Brown, *The American Secretary: The Colonial Policy of Lord George Germain, 1775–1778* (Ann Arbor: University of Michigan Press, 1963), 26, 30; Ira D. Gruber, "Britain's Southern Strategy," in *The Revolutionary War in the South: Power, Conflict, and Leadership*, ed. W. Robert Higgins (Durham, NC: Duke University Press, 1979), 206–7.

4. Sir James Wright to the Earl of Dartmouth, June 9, 1775, in K. G. Davies, ed., *Documents of the American Revolution, 1770–1783* (Colonial Office Series), (hereafter *DAR*), 21 vols. (Dublin: Irish University Press, 1972–1981), 9:167.

5. Thomas Fletchall to Lord William Campbell, Aug. 19, 1775, American Papers of the Second Earl of Dartmouth, microfilm, David Library of the American Revolution (hereafter DLAR); Campbell to Dartmouth, Sept. 19, 1775, in Davies, ed., *DAR*, 11:118.

6. John Richard Alden, *The South in the Revolution, 1763–1789* (Baton Rouge: Louisiana State University Press, 1976), 197.

7. Christopher Hibbert, *Redcoats and Rebels: The American Revolution through British Eyes* (New York: Avon Books, 1990), 101–2.

8. Jack M. Sosin, *The Revolutionary Frontier, 1763–1783* (New York: Holt, Rinehart and Winston, 1967), 5; John Stuart to Thomas Gage, March 27, 1775, and May

26, 1775, Thomas Gage Papers, WLCL; Alan Valentine, *Lord North*, 2 vols. (Norman: University of Oklahoma Press, 1967), 1:375.

9. Valentine, *Lord North*, 1:375; Edward J. Cashin, "'But Brothers, It Is Our Land We Are Talking About': Winners and Losers in the Georgia Backcountry," in Ronald Hoffman, Thad W. Tate, and Peter J. Albert, eds., *An Uncivil War: The Southern Backcountry in the American Revolution* (Charlottesville: University Press of Virginia, 1985), 250.

10. Alan Valentine, *Lord George Germain* (Oxford: Oxford University Press, 1962), 185; Germain to Patrick Tonyn, Dec. 23, 1775, Lord George Germain Papers, WLCL.

11. Alden, *The South in the Revolution*, 6, 9, 10; Rachel Klein, *Unification of a Slave State: The Rise of the Planter Class in the South Carolina Backcountry, 1760–1808* (Chapel Hill: University of North Carolina Press, 1990), 9.

12. John Adams, *Diary and Autobiography of John Adams*, L. H. Butterfield, ed., 2 vols. (Cambridge, MA: Belknap Press, 1983), Sept. 24, 1775, 2:182–83.

13. Jim Piecuch, *Three Peoples, One King: Loyalists, Indians, and Slaves in the Revolutionary South, 1775–1782* (Columbia: University of South Carolina Press, 2008), 40, 42.

14. Piecuch, *Three Peoples, One King*, 40–42.

15. Dartmouth to Sir William Howe, Oct. 22, 1775, Headquarters Papers of the British Army in America (Sir Guy Carleton Papers, hereafter BHQP), microfilm, DLAR.

16. Gerald Saxon Brown, *The American Secretary: The Colonial Policy of Lord George Germain, 1775–1778* (Ann Arbor: University of Michigan Press, 1963), 52; William B. Willcox, *Portrait of a General: Sir Henry Clinton in the War of Independence* (New York: Alfred A. Knopf, 1964), 76–77.

17. Willcox, *Portrait of a General*, 81; Eric Robson, "The Expedition to the Southern Colonies, 1775–1776," *English Historical Review* 67 (Oct. 1951), 544–45, 547–48, 553.

18. Piecuch, *Three Peoples, One King*, 49–52.

19. Marvin L. Cann, "Prelude to War: The First Battle of Ninety Six, November 19–21, 1775," *South Carolina Historical Magazine* 76 (Oct. 1975), 207–211; Robert Stansbury Lambert, *South Carolina Loyalists in the American Revolution* (Columbia: University of South Carolina Press, 1987), 44–45; Lewis Pinckney Jones, *The South Carolina Civil War of 1775* (Lexington, SC: Sandlapper, 1975), 77–79.

20. Alden, *South in the Revolution*, 196–97; Hibbert, *Redcoats and Rebels*, 103.

21. Don Higginbotham, *The War of American Independence: Military Attitudes, Policies, and Practice, 1763–1789* (Boston: Northeastern University Press, 1983), 135; Hibbert, *Redcoats and Rebels*, 103; Alden, *South in the Revolution*, 197–98.

22. Hibbert, *Redcoats and Rebels*, 101–2.

23. Quoted in Benjamin Quarles, *The Negro in the American Revolution* (Chapel Hill: University of North Carolina Press, 1996), 19.

24. Quarles, *Negro in the Revolution*, 20, 22–23, 28–29, 31; Alden, *South in the Revolution*, 194–95.

25. John Buchanan, *The Road to Guilford Courthouse: The American Revolution in the Carolinas* (New York: John Wiley & Sons, 1997), 5; Sir Henry Clinton, *The American Rebellion, Sir Henry Clinton's Narrative of His Campaigns, 1775–1782, with an Appendix of Original Documents*, William B. Willcox, ed. (New Haven, CT: Yale University Press, 1954), 29; Dartmouth to William Campbell, Nov. 7, 1775, and Germain to William Howe, Nov. 8, 1775, BHQP.

26. C. L. Bragg, *Crescent Moon over Carolina: William Moultrie and American Liberty* (Columbia: University of South Carolina Press, 2013), 45, 52–53.

27. Buchanan, *Road to Guilford Courthouse*, 10–11; Bragg, *Crescent Moon over Carolina*, 54–56, 58, 59, 64–65.

28. Buchanan, *Road to Guilford Courthouse*, 13.

29. Bragg, *Crescent Moon over Carolina*, 63, 73, 75–77, 81.

30. Bragg, *Crescent Moon over Carolina*, 81–82, 85.

31. Higginbotham, *War of American Independence*, 137.

32. Wilbur H. Siebert, *Loyalists in East Florida, 1774–1785: The Most Important Documents Pertaining Thereto with an Accompanying Narrative*, 2 vols. (Deland: Florida State Historical Society, 1929), 1:23–24; Martha Condray Searcy, *The Georgia–Florida Contest in the American Revolution, 1776–1778* (Tuscaloosa: University of Alabama Press, 1985), 37–38.

33. M. F. Treacy, *Prelude to Yorktown: The Southern Campaign of Nathanael Greene, 1780–1781* (Chapel Hill: University of North Carolina Press, 1963), 3–9, 58–59; Henry Lee, *The Revolutionary War Memoirs of General Henry Lee*, Robert E. Lee, ed. (New York: Da Capo Press, 1998), 36, 386.

34. Piecuch, *Three Peoples, One King*, 69–72.

35. Thomas Taylor to Mr. Morrison, Dec. 16, 1775, in Thomas Taylor, "A Georgia Loyalist's Perspective on the American Revolution," Robert Scott Davis, ed., *Georgian Historical Quarterly* 81 (Spring 1997), 125.

36. "Extract of a letter, dated on board the Brig Allerton, Cockspur, in Georgia," March 24, 1776, in Margaret Wheeler Willard, ed., *Letters on the American Revolution, 1774–1776* (Boston: Houghton Mifflin, 1925), 297; Kenneth Coleman, *The American Revolution in Georgia, 1763–1789* (Athens: University of Georgia Press, 1958), 70.

37. Searcy, *Georgia–Florida Contest*, 34–38, 43–44, 50, 54–56, 61, 68.

38. Searcy, *Georgia–Florida Contest*, 84–88; Edward J. Cashin, *The King's Ranger: Thomas Brown and the American Revolution on the Southern Frontier* (New York: Fordham University Press, 1999), 61–62.

39. Searcy, *Georgia–Florida Contest*, 89, 92–96; Charles E. Bennett and Donald R. Lennon, *A Quest for Glory: Major General Robert Howe and the American Revolution* (Chapel Hill: University of North Carolina Press, 1991), 62.

40. Searcy, *Georgia–Florida Contest*, 113; Patrick Tonyn to Sir William Howe, April 6, 1778, BHQP.

41. Harry M. Ward, *Between the Lines: Banditti of the American Revolution* (Westport, CT: Praeger, 2002), 195; Rawlins Lowndes to Henry Laurens, April 14, 1778,

The Papers of Henry Laurens, vol. 13, David R. Chesnutt, ed. (Columbia: University of South Carolina Press, 1992), 114; Robert Howe to Samuel Elbert, April 6, 1778, and Robert Howe to unnamed, April 13, 1778, Robert Howe Papers, Georgia Historical Society.

42. Robert Howe to unnamed, April 13, 1778, Howe Papers; John Fauchereau Grimke, "Journal of a Campaign to the Southward: May 9th to July 14th, 1778," *South Carolina Historical and Genealogical Magazine* 12 (July 1911), 120, 125; Thomas Brown to Tonyn, June 30, 1778, BHQP; Cashin, *King's Ranger*, 77–78; Searcy, *Georgia–Florida Contest*, 142, 144, 145–47; Augustine Prevost to Sir William Howe, June 13, 1778, BHQP.

43. Germain to Sir Henry Clinton, March 8, 1778, Germain Papers.

44. Piecuch, *Three Peoples, One King*, 127–28.

45. John Laurens Commonplace Book, Nov. 3, 1779, Historical Society of Pennsylvania, Philadelphia; Piecuch, *Three Peoples, One King*, 7.

46. Coleman, *American Revolution in Georgia*, 119, 120; Archibald Campbell, *Journal of an Expedition against the Rebels of Georgia in North America under the Orders of Archibald Campbell Esquire Lieut. Colol. of His Majesty's 71st Regimt. 1778*, Colin Campbell, ed. (Darien, GA: Ashantilly Press, 1981), 20–21; David K. Wilson, *The Southern Strategy: Britain's Conquest of South Carolina and Georgia, 1775–1780* (Columbia: University of South Carolina Press, 2005), 71, 73–74.

47. Campbell, *Journal*, 22–28; Wilson, *Southern Strategy*, 75–77.

48. Coleman, *American Revolution in Georgia*, 121.

49. Archibald Campbell to William Eden, Jan. 19, 1779, William Eden, First Baron Auckland Papers, microfilm, DLAR.

50. Quoted in Patrick S. Furlong, "Civil-Military Conflict and the Restoration of the Royal Province of Georgia, 1778–1782," *Journal of Southern History* 38 (August 1972), 422–23.

51. John Wilson, *Encounters on a March through Georgia in 1779: The Maps and Memorandums of John Wilson, Engineer, 71st Highland Regiment*, Robert Scott Davis, ed. (Sylvania, GA: Partridge Pond Press, 1986), 19, 42; Campbell, *Journal*, 54–56, 58–60, 64; James H. O'Donnell III, *Southern Indians in the American Revolution* (Knoxville: University of Tennessee Press, 1973), 81.

52. David S. Heidler, "The American Defeat at Briar Creek, 3 March 1779," *Georgia Historical Quarterly* 66 (Fall 1982), 318; John Dooly to Samuel Elbert, Feb. 16, 1779, Misc. Mss.— John Dooly, Library of Congress.

53. Edward J. Cashin, "George Walton and the Forged Letter," *Georgia Historical Quarterly* 62 (Summer 1978), 136–37; Proceedings of a Council of War, Jan. 14, 1779, in Robert S. Davis, ed., *Georgia Citizens and Soldiers of the American Revolution* (Easley, SC: Southern Historical Press, 1979), 64.

54. Campbell, *Journal*, 39, 66; Robert S. Davis and Kenneth H. Thomas, *Kettle Creek: The Battle of the Cane Brakes: Wilkes County, Georgia* ([Atlanta]: Georgia Department of Natural Resources, 1975), 31, 33–34, 36–39, 43.

55. Wilson, *Southern Strategy*, 91–96.

56. Alden, *Revolution in the South*, 291; Piers Mackesy, *The War for America, 1775–1783* (Lincoln: University of Nebraska Press, 1992), 269–70.
57. David B. Mattern, *Benjamin Lincoln and the American Revolution* (Columbia: University of South Carolina Press, 1995), 69.
58. Wilson, *Southern Strategy*, 93; Mattern, *Benjamin Lincoln*, 70.
59. Wilson, *Southern Strategy*, 108; Mattern, *Benjamin Lincoln*, 70–71.
60. Mattern, *Benjamin Lincoln*, 71–72.
61. Wilson, *Southern Strategy*, 111–12, 121; Mattern, *Benjamin Lincoln*, 71–72.
62. Wilson, *Southern Strategy*, 122–28; Mattern, *Benjamin Lincoln*, 73–74.
63. Wilson, *Southern Strategy*, 133, 135.
64. Philippe-Auguste Meyronnet de Saint-Marc, "Meyronnet de Saint-Marc's Journal of the Operations of the French Army at the Siege of Savannah, September 1779," Roberta Leighton, ed., *New York Historical Society Quarterly* 36 (July 1952), 272; Alexander A. Lawrence, *Storm over Savannah: The Story of Count d'Estaing and the Siege of the Town in 1779* (Athens: University of Georgia Press, 1951), 5; Mattern, *Benjamin Lincoln*, 81–82.
65. Lawrence, *Storm over Savannah*, 29, 49; Mattern, *Benjamin Lincoln*, 82–83.
66. Anthony Stokes to Mrs. Stokes, in Benjamin Kennedy, ed., *Muskets, Cannon Balls, and Bombs: Nine Narratives of the Siege of Savannah in 1779* (Savannah, GA: Beehive Press, 1974), 115; Augustine Prevost to Germain, Nov. 1, 1779, in "Papers Relating to the Allied Attack on Savannah," *Historical Magazine* 8 (Sept. 1864), 291; Lawrence, *Storm over Savannah*, 80–82, 157; Petition of William Hanscomb to Augustine Prevost, March 30, 1780, Clinton Papers, WLCL; Piecuch, *Three Peoples, One King*, 169; Wilson, *Southern Strategy*, 180–81.
67. Mattern, *Benjamin Lincoln*, 84–85.
68. Wilson, *Southern Strategy*, 158–59, 181; Mattern, *Benjamin Lincoln*, 85–86.
69. Mattern, *Benjamin Lincoln*, 86.
70. Germain to Clinton, Sept. 27, 1779, Germain Papers, WLCL; Clinton, *American Rebellion*, 151; Clinton to Germain, Aug. 21, 1779, Sept. 26, 1779, and Nov. 10, 1779, Clinton to unnamed, c. Oct. 26, 1779, Clinton Papers, WLCL.
71. Carl P. Borick, *A Gallant Defense: The Siege of Charleston, 1780* (Columbia: University of South Carolina Press, 2003), 23, 25–26, 28–29.
72. Borick, *Gallant Defense*, 42–43, 81–82, 97, 103, 121.
73. Borick, *Gallant Defense*, 129–30.
74. Borick, *Gallant Defense*, 133, 148–49, 158–59.
75. Borick, *Gallant Defense*, 161–62, 193, 196, 206, 219, 222.
76. Clinton to Germain, June 4, 1780, in Elizabeth R. Miller, ed., *The American Revolution, as Described by British Writers and the Morning Chronicle and London Advertiser* (Bowie, MD: Heritage Books, 1991), 14.
77. Piecuch, *Three Peoples, One King*, 179–80.
78. Piecuch, *Three Peoples, One King*, 185–86.
79. For a complete account of the Battle of the Waxhaws, including an analysis of the massacre legend and its use as propaganda, see Jim Piecuch, *"The Blood Be Upon*

Your Head": Tarleton and the Myth of Buford's Massacre (Lugoff, SC: Southern Campaigns of the American Revolution Press, 2010).

80. Buchanan, *Road to Guilford Courthouse*, 106–10.

81. Nisbet Balfour to Lord Cornwallis, June 27, 1780, and Lord Rawdon to Cornwallis, July 7, 1780, Papers of Charles, First Marquis Cornwallis, United Kingdom Public Record Office, microfilm, DLAR.

82. Buchanan, *Road to Guilford Courthouse*, 113–15.

83. Buchanan, *Road to Guilford Courthouse*, 132, 134–36.

84. Jim Piecuch, *The Battle of Camden: A Documentary History* (Charleston, SC: History Press, 2006, 13; Otho Holland Williams, "A Narrative of the Campaign of 1780," in William Johnson, *Sketches of the Life and Correspondence of Nathanael Greene, Major General of the Armies of the United States in the War of the Revolution*, 2 vols. (Charleston, SC: A. E. Miller, 1822), 1:488–89.

85. Buchanan, *Road to Guilford Courthouse*, 150; John S. Pancake, *This Destructive War: The British Campaign in the Carolinas, 1780–1782* (Tuscaloosa: University of Alabama Press, 1985), 100–101.

86. Josiah Martin to Germain, Aug. 18, 1780, in Banastre Tarleton, *A History of the Campaigns of 1780 and 1781, in the Southern Provinces of North America* (London: T. Cadell, 1787), 128–35; Cornwallis to Germain, Aug. 21, 1780, Cornwallis Papers, microfilm, DLAR.

87. Thomas Pinckney to William Johnson, July 27, 1822, in Robert Scott Davis, ed., "Thomas Pinckney and the Last Campaign of Horatio Gates," *South Carolina Historical Magazine* 86 (April 1985), 84–97; Cornwallis to Germain, Aug. 21, 1780, Cornwallis Papers, microfilm, DLAR.

88. Buchanan, *Road to Guilford Courthouse*, 161–65; Williams, "Narrative," 494–95.

89. Buchanan, *Road to Guilford Courthouse*, 167–69; Cornwallis to Germain, Aug. 21, 1780, Cornwallis Papers; Pancake, *This Destructive War*, 106–7; Tarleton, *History*, 102–10, 137–39, 151–53.

90. Buchanan, *Road to Guilford Courthouse*, 173–75.

91. Piecuch, *Three Peoples, One King*, 196–97; Buchanan, *Road to Guilford Courthouse*, 176–79, 184–85; Pancake, *This Destructive War*, 116.

92. Piecuch, *Three Peoples, One King*, 198–99, 209–10.

93. Pancake, *This Destructive War*, 118, 120–21; Piecuch, *Three Peoples, One King*, 199.

94. Pancake, *This Destructive War*, 109; Piecuch, *Three Peoples, One King*, 229–33; Nisbet Balfour to Cornwallis, Nov. 5, 1780, and Cornwallis to Alexander Leslie, Nov. 12, 1780, Cornwallis Papers.

95. Buchanan, *Road to Guilford Courthouse*, 171; Pancake, *This Destructive War*, 106–7, 127–28.

96. Pancake, *This Destructive War*, 130–31; Buchanan, *Road to Guilford Courthouse*, 294–95; Nathanael Greene to Daniel Morgan, Dec. 16, 1780, in Richard K. Showman, ed., *The Papers of General Nathanael Greene*, vol. 6 (Chapel Hill: University of North Carolina Press, 1991), 588.

97. Lawrence E. Babits, *A Devil of a Whipping: The Battle of Cowpens* (Chapel Hill: University of North Carolina Press), 1998, 9; Tarleton, *History of the Campaigns,* 207–8, 210–12.

98. Babits, *Devil of a Whipping,* 52–55, 61–65, 150; Buchanan, *Road to Guilford Courthouse,* 316–17.

99. Babits, *Devil of a Whipping,* 30–42, 150–51; Tarleton, *History of the Campaigns,* 215–17.

100. John Eager Howard to [John Marshall], c. 1804, Bayard Family Papers, Maryland Historical Society, Baltimore; Tarleton, *History of the Campaigns,* 217; Babits, *Devil of a Whipping,* 119–20, 151–52.

101. Tarleton, *History of the Campaigns,* 219, 222–23; Buchanan, *Road to Guilford Courthouse,* 337–40; Pancake, *This Destructive War,* 161.

102. Jim Piecuch and John Beakes, *"Cool Deliberate Courage": John Eager Howard in the American Revolution* (Charleston, SC: Nautical & Aviation Publishing, 2009), 73–78; Cornwallis to Germain, March 17, 1781, in Tarleton, *History of the Campaigns,* 264.

103. Henry Lee to Greene, Feb. 20, 1781, and Andrew Pickens to Greene, Feb. 26, 1781, in Showman and Dennis M. Conrad, eds., *Papers of Greene,* vol. 7 (Chapel Hill: University of North Carolina Press, 1994), 324, 355; Pancake, *This Destructive War,* 173; Tarleton, *History of the Campaigns,* 231–33; Lee, *Memoirs,* 256–58.

104. Lee, *Memoirs,* 588; Tarleton, *History of the Campaigns,* 233–34; Pancake, *This Destructive War,* 175, 177; Buchanan, *Road to Guilford Courthouse,* 369; Greene to Samuel Huntington, March 16, 1781, in Showman and Conrad, eds., *Papers of Greene,* 7:433–34.

105. Cornwallis to Germain, March 17, 1781, in Tarleton, *History of the Campaigns,* 305–6; Greene to Huntington, March 16, 1781, in Showman and Conrad, eds., *Papers of Greene,* 7:435; Howard to Johnson, [c. 1822], Bayard Papers; Lawrence E. Babits and Joshua B. Howard, *Long, Obstinate, and Bloody: The Battle of Guilford Courthouse* (Chapel Hill: University of North Carolina Press, 2009), 118–27, 148–56.

106. Babits and Howard, *Long, Obstinate, and Bloody,* 223–24; Tarleton, *History of the Campaigns,* 280.

107. Pancake, *This Destructive War,* 190; Greene to George Washington, March 29, 1781, in Showman and Conrad, eds., *Papers of Greene,* 7:481.

108. Tarleton, *History of the Campaigns,* 283–85; Pancake, *This Destructive War,* 189–90.

109. Lord Rawdon to Cornwallis, April 26, 1781, Cornwallis Papers.

110. Rawdon to Cornwallis, April 26, 1781, Cornwallis Papers; Greene to Huntington, April 27, 1781, in Conrad, ed., *Papers of Greene,* vol. 8 (1995), 156; Pancake, *This Destructive War,* 196, 198.

111. Tarleton, *History of the Campaigns,* 470; "Return of the Killed Wounded & Missing" at Hobkirk's Hill, April 25, 1781, Cornwallis Papers; Rawdon to Corn-

wallis, May 24, 1781, Cornwallis Papers; Lee, *Memoirs*, 330–32; Marion to Greene, April 23, 1781, in Conrad, ed., *Papers of Greene*, 8:138–39.

112. Thomas Sumter to Greene, May 11, 1781, Marion to Greene, May 12, 1781, Greene to Henry Lee, May 13, 1781, in Conrad, ed., *Papers of Greene*, 8:244, 246, 249; Lee, *Memoirs*, 352.

113. Cashin, *King's Ranger*, 132–36; Lee, *Memoirs*, 360–66; Lee to Greene, June 4, 1781, in Conrad, ed., *Papers of Greene*, 8:346.

114. Pancake, *This Destructive War*, 209–11; Rawdon to Cornwallis, June 4, 1781, Cornwallis Papers; Greene to Lee, May 22, 1781, in Conrad, ed., *Papers of Greene*, 8:291–92.

115. Rawdon to Cornwallis, June 5, 1781, Cornwallis Papers; Pancake, *This Destructive War*, 212–14; Thomas Sumter to Greene, June 13, 1781, Greene to Sumter, June 15, 1781, and June 18, 1781, in Conrad, ed., *Papers of Greene*, 8:388, 390, 404.

116. Greene to Huntington, June 20, 1781, in Conrad, ed., *Papers of Greene*, 8:421; Rawdon to Cornwallis, Aug. 2, 1781, Cornwallis Papers.

117. Greene to Thomas McKean, July 17, 1781, in Conrad, ed., *Papers of Greene*, vol. 9 (1997), 27–29; Rawdon to Cornwallis, June 7, 1781, Cornwallis Papers.

118. William Washington to Greene, July 30, 1781, Lee to Greene, Aug. 8, 1781, Greene to Lee, Aug. 9, 1781, Lee to Greene, Aug. 10, 1781, Lee to Greene, Aug. 13, 1781, Greene to Lee, Aug. 14 and 20, 1781, in Conrad, ed., *Papers of Greene*, 9:118, 151, 153, 162, 177, 181.

119. Alexander Stewart to Cornwallis, Sept. 9, 1781, Cornwallis Papers; "Return of the Army under the Command of Lieutenant Colonel Alexander Stewart . . . before the Action at Eutaws," Sept. 8, 1781, Colonial Office Transcripts, Library of Congress, Washington, DC; Jim Piecuch, "The Evolving Tactician: Nathanael Greene at the Battle of Eutaw Springs," in Gregory D. Massey and Jim Piecuch, eds., *General Nathanael Greene and the American Revolution in the South* (Columbia: University of South Carolina Press, 2012), 226–27.

120. Stewart to Cornwallis, Sept. 9, 1781, and Sept. 26, 1781, Cornwallis Papers; Lee, *Memoirs*, 466.

121. Stewart to Cornwallis, Sept. 9, 1781, and Sept. 26, 1781, Cornwallis Papers; Greene to Thomas McKean, Sept. 11, 1781, in Conrad, ed., *Papers of Greene*, 9:329.

122. Stewart to Cornwallis, Sept. 9, 1781, Cornwallis Papers; Greene to McKean, Sept. 11, 1781, in Conrad, ed., *Papers of Greene*, 9:331–32; "Battle of Eutaw. Account furnished by Colonel Otho Williams, with additions by Colonels W. Hampton, Polk, Howard, and Watt," in Robert W. Gibbes, ed., *Documentary History of the American Revolution, Consisting of Letters and Papers Relating to the Contest for Liberty Chiefly in South Carolina*, 3 vols. (New York: Appleton, 1857), 3:151–55.

123. Stewart to Cornwallis, Sept. 9, 1781, Cornwallis Papers; "Return of the Killed, Wounded and Missing of the Southern Army," Sept. 25, 1781, in Walter Clark, ed., *The State Records of North Carolina*, vol. 15 (Winston: State of North Carolina,

1898), 637; "Return of the Killed, Wounded, and Missing in the Action at the Eutaws," Sept. 8, 1781, Colonial Office Transcripts, Library of Congress.

CHAPTER FOUR: THE WESTERN THEATER

1. Claudio Saunt, *West of the Revolution: An Uncommon History of 1776* (New York: W.W. Norton, 2014), 25.

2. Tenuous as Iroquois claims south of the Ohio were, they made the cession partially in hopes to take Anglo-American settlement pressure off of their central homelands in upper and western New York; that is, the Iroquois wanted white settlers moving south, not north. Colin G. Calloway, *The American Revolution in Indian Country: Crisis and Diversity in Native American Communities* (New York: Cambridge University Press, 1995), 161, 189.

3. Michael Toomey, "Daniel Boone (1734–1829)," *The Tennessee Encyclopedia of History and Culture*, http://tennesseeencyclopedia.net/entry.php?rec=111, accessed Nov. 13, 2016; John Mack Faragher, *Daniel Boone: The Life and Legend of an American Pioneer* (New York: Holt, 1992), 374–76; John E. Kleber, ed., "Harrod, James," *The Kentucky Encyclopedia* (Lexington: University Press of Kentucky, 1992), 413–14.

4. Cameron's transcription of Dragging Canoe's speech is in John P. Brown, *Old Frontiers: The Story of the Cherokee from Earliest Times to the Date of Their Removal to the West* (Kingsport: Southern Publishers, 1938). Cameron was agent to the Cherokees for fifteen years until his death in 1781. In August 1779 Britain appointed him superintendent of Indian affairs for the entire Southwest. As such Cameron was influential in Cherokee affairs (he had three children with Cherokee consorts) and worked unceasingly to keep the tribe allied to the British cause. How close his version of Dragging Canoe's speech is to the chief's actual words is unknown, but it certainly captured Dragging Canoe's sentiments. On Cameron, see Tara Mitchell Mielnik, "Alexander Cameron," *The Tennessee Encyclopedia of History and Culture*, Dec. 25, 2009, http://tennesseeencyclopedia.net/ entry.php?rec=175; accessed Feb. 10, 2016.

5. Henry Stuart to John Stuart, Aug. 25, 1776, *Colonial Records of North Carolina*, ed. William L. Saunders, 10 vols. (Raleigh, NC: Josephus Daniels, 1886–1890),10:778.

6. Cornstalk quoted in Gary B. Nash, *The Unknown American Revolution: The Unruly Birth of Democracy and the Struggle to Create America* (New York: Penguin, 2006), 260.

7. Ethan Schmidt, *Native Americans in the American Revolution: How the War Divided, Devastated, and Transformed the Early American Indian World* (Santa Barbara: Praeger, 2014), 143.

8. Captain Thomas Cook quoted in Saunt, *West of the Revolution*, 4.

9. Hamilton was one of Quebec's five lieutenant governors. For a concise biography, see Elizabeth Arthur, "Hamilton, Henry," *Dictionary of Canadian Biography*, IV (1771–1800), http://www.biographi.ca/ en/bio/hamilton_henry_4E.html; accessed Feb. 29, 2016.

10. Ibid., 143–45.

11. On the British Indian agents generally, see Colin Calloway, *The American Revolution in Indian Country*. For specific individuals, see Richard A. Colbert, "James Logan Colbert of the Chickasaw, The Man and the Myth," *North Carolina Genealogical Society Journal* 20, no. 2 (1994):82, http://www.angelfire.com/ ok3/greybird7/genealogy.html, accessed Mar. 7, 2016; Consul Willshire Butterfield, *History of the Girtys: Being a Concise Account of the Girty Brothers, Thomas, Simon, James and George . . . .* (Cincinnati, OH: Robert Clarke and Co., 1890); R. Douglas Hurt, *The Ohio Frontier: Crucible of the Old Northwest, 1720–1830* (Bloomington: Indiana University Press, 1996), 73–75; Larry L. Nelson, *A Man of Distinction among Them: Alexander McKee and the Country Frontier, 1754–1799* (Kent, OH: Kent State University Press, 1999); Tara Mitchell Mielnik, "Alexander Cameron," *The Tennessee Encyclopedia of History and Culture*, Dec. 25, 2009, http://tennesseeencyclopedia.net/ entry.php?rec=175, accessed Feb. 10, 2016; John Walton Caughey, *McGillivray of the Creeks* (Columbia: University of South Carolina Press, 2007).

12. A. B. Brooks, "Story of Fort Henry," *West Virginia History* 1, no. 2 (1940):110–18; Otis Rice, *West Virginia: A History*, 2nd ed. (Lexington: University Press of Kentucky, 1993), 43; "History of Fort Randolph," *First Biennial Report of the* [West Virginia] *Department of Archives and History, 1906*, 236–39, http://www.wvculture.org/HiStory/settlement/fortrandolph04.html, accessed Apr. 14, 2016.

13. Daniel Boone thought a few settlers held out at the Falls of the Ohio around modern Louisville, although there is little evidence of this. Michael A. Lofaro, *Daniel Boone: An American Life* (Lexington: University Press of Kentucky, 2003), 83; John Filson, *The Discovery, Purchase, and Present State of Kentucky: and an Essay towards the Topography and Natural History of That Important Country . . .* (Wilmington: Printed by James Adams, 1784), 9, 48, An Online Text Edition, Paul Royster, ed. (Lincoln: DigitalCommons@University of Nebraska), http://digitalcommons.unl.edu/cgi/ viewcontent.cgi?article=1002&context=etas, accessed Feb. 14, 2016.

14. Brown, *Old Frontiers*, 162–63; William Anderson and James A. Lewis, eds., *A Guide to Cherokee Documents in Foreign Archives* (Metuchen, NJ: Scarecrow Press, 1995), 160.

15. Greg O'Brien, "Southeastern Indians and the American Revolution," *Encyclopedia of Alabama*, http://www.encyclopediaofalabama.org/article/h-1133, accessed Feb. 14, 2016.

16. Robert K. Wright, Jr., *The Continental Army* (Washington, DC: Center of Military History, United States Army, 1989), 151; Fred Anderson Berg, *Encyclopedia of Continental Army Units: Battalions, Regiments, and Independent Corps* (Harrisburg, PA, Stackpole Books, 1972), 97, 129. Because of its assignment to the Western Department, the 9th Virginia (it was originally the 13th Virginia, and occasionally appears as such in accounts of the war in the West) was the only Virginia regiment to escape the surrender of the rest of the Virginia Line at Charleston in 1780; ibid., 129. "Military History of William Irvine," The State Society of the Cincinnati of

Pennsylvania, www.pasocietyofthecincinnati.org/Names/WilliamIrvine. html, accessed Apr. 14, 2016.

17. Charles H. Lesser, ed., *The Sinews of Independence: Monthly Strength Reports of the Continental Army* (Chicago: University of Chicago Press, 1976), 104, 141, 145, 154, 164, 169, 192.

18. Brady J. Crytzer, "Allegheny Burning: George Washington, Daniel Brodhead, and the Battle of Thompson's Island," *Journal of the American Revolution*, May 12, 2015, https://allthingsliberty.com/2015/05/ allegheny-burning-george-washington-daniel-brodhead-andthe-battle-of-thompsons-island/#_edn18, accessed Apr. 14, 2016; William Irvine to George Washington, Dec. 2, 1781, Founders Online, National Archives, http://founders.archives.gov/documents/Washington/99-01-02-07473, accessed May 3, 2016.

19. On Fort Crawford, see Louise Phelps Kellogg, ed., *Frontier Advance on the Upper Ohio, 1778–1779* (Bowie, MD: Heritage Books, 1994 [orig. 1916]), 164; and C. W. Butterfield, *An Historical Account of the Expedition against Sandusky under Col. William Crawford in 1782* (Cincinnati: R. Clarke & Co., 1873), 107. A detailed description of Fort McIntosh is in Frank Camer, National Register of Historic Places Nomination Form [Form 10-300], Fort McIntosh (National Park Service, 1973), http://www.dot7.state.pa.us/ CRGIS_Attachments/SiteResource/H001274_01H. pdf, accessed Apr. 17, 2016; Joseph Henderson Bausman and John Samuel Duss, *History of Beaver County, Pennsylvania and Its Centennial Celebration* (New York: Knickerbocker Press, 1904), 1320.

20. Daniel Brodhead to Archibald Lochery, Apr. 16, 1779, "Instructions to Officers on Different Commands and at Different Posts," 1779–1781, Box 1, Vol. 1, Daniel Brodhead Papers, 1779–1781, DAR.1925.04, Darlington Collection, Special Collections Department, University of Pittsburgh (hereafter cited as Brodhead Papers). Brodhead's papers reveal a virtually constant concern with issues of logistics and supply as well as manpower shortages, especially at smaller outposts any distance from Fort Pitt; e.g., Brodhead to Lochery, Apr. 25, 1779, ibid.

21. The best account of Fort Pitt during the Revolution is Brady J. Crytzer, *Fort Pitt: A Frontier History* (Charleston, SC: History Press, 2012). See also Daniel Barr, *The Ends of the American Earth: War and Society on the Pittsburg Frontier* (Kent, OH: Kent State University Press, 2007); William Irvine to George Washington, Dec. 2, 2016, Founders Online, National Archives, http://founders.archives.gov/ documents/Washington/99-01-02-07473, accessed May 3, 2016.

22. Daniel Brodhead to John Clark, Apr. 4, 1779, "Instructions to Officers," Brodhead Papers; Brodhead to Clark, July 27, 1779, ibid.

23. Hurt, *The Ohio Frontier*, 68–69.

24. The Indians with Bird were Delawares, Wyandots, and Mingos. Thomas Pieper and James B. Gidney, *Fort Laurens, 1778–1779: The Revolutionary War in Ohio* (Kent, OH: Kent State University Press, 1976).

25. John Grenier, *The First Way of War: American War Making on the Frontier, 1607–1813* (New York: Cambridge University Press, 2005), 10; Peter Silver, *Our*

Savage Neighbors: How Indian Warfare Transformed Early America (New York: W.W. Norton, 2007); Patrick Griffin, *American Leviathan: Empire, Nation, and Revolutionary Frontier* (New York: Hill and Wang, 2007), 171.

26. Mark Edward Lender and James Kirby Martin, "Liberty or Death! *Jus in Bello* and Existential Warfare in the American Revolution," Conference paper, presented at "Was the American Revolution a Just War?" Agora Institute, Philadelphia, Oct. 31, 2015.

27. On the interplay between fears of Indian conspiracies and republican ideology during the Revolution, see Robert M. Owens, *Red Dreams, White Nightmares: Pan-Indian Alliances in the Anglo-American Mind, 1763–1814* (Norman: University of Oklahoma Press, 2015), 59–70.

28. Saunt, *West of the Revolution*, 27.

29. Resolution of June 11, 1778, *JCC*, 11:588–90; Andrew Lewis to George Washington, Aug. 8, 1778, *PGWde*, RWS, 16:272; George Gibson to Washington, Nov. 13, 1778, *PGWde*, RWS, 18:134–36; Philip Schuyler to Washington, *PGWde*, RWS, 18:351; Washington to Thomas Jefferson, Dec. 28, 1780, Founders Online, National Archives; http://founders.archives.gov/documents/Washington/99-01-02-04360.

30. George Gibson to George Washington, Nov. 13, 1778, *PGWde*, RWS, 18:134–36; Washington to Thomas Jefferson, Dec. 28, 1780, Founders Online, National Archives; http://founders.archives.gov/documents/Washington/99-01-02-04360.

31. Consul Willshire Butterfield, *History of George Rogers Clark's Conquest of the Illinois and the Wabash Towns, 1778–1779* (Columbus, OH: F. J. Heer, 1903), 88–89.

32. Filson, *Discovery of Kentucky*, 31–37. In summer 1776 Captain George Gibson led 20 men on the Fort Pitt to New Orleans journey under Virginia authority. They conducted no raid, but did sound out the Spanish on their reactions should the Americans attack the British on the Mississippi and in Pensacola—proposals that met only a diplomatic coolness. (Washington knew nothing about any of this.) Gibson, however, did make the return trip with 10,000 pounds of gunpowder for the patriot cause; and he clearly demonstrated the practicality of commercial links to Spanish Louisiana. See David Narrett, *Adventurism and Empire: The Struggle for Mastery in the Louisiana-Florida Borderlands, 1762–1803* (Chapel Hill: University of North Carolina Press, 2015), 70–71.

33. Michael A. McDonnell, *Masters of Empire: Great Lakes Indians and the Making of America* (New York: Hill and Wang, 2015), 289–90.

34. The 8th Foot deployed to North America in 1768. Its ten companies were dispersed as follows: Fort Detroit, 3 companies; Fort Michilimackinac, 2; Fort Niagara, 4; Fort Oswego, 1; J. A. Houlding, *Fit for Service: The Training of the British Army, 1715–1795* (New York : Oxford University Press, 1981), 17; on the composition of the expedition, see "Henry Hamilton's Journal," Oct. 7, 1778, Indiana Historical Bureau, http://www.in.gov/history/3013.htm, accessed Mar. 7, 2016.

35. "Henry Hamilton's Journal," Dec. 10 and 17, 1778, ibid., http://www.in.gov/history/3011.htm; accessed Mar. 7, 2016.

NOTES TO PAGES 162–169

36. For a full account of Sullivan's expedition, see Glenn F. Williams, *Year of the Hangman: George Washington's Campaign Against the Iroquois* (Yardley, PA: Westholme Publishing, 2005).

37. Daniel Brodhead to Frederick Vernon, Apr. 28, 1779, "Instructions to Officers," Brodhead Papers.

38. A concise account of Brodhead's expedition is in Crytzer, "Allegheny Burning," https://allthingsliberty.com/2015/05/allegheny-burning-george-washington-daniel-brodhead-andthe-battle-of-thompsons-island/#_edn18, accessed Apr. 14, 2016.

39. General Orders, Oct. 18, 1779, John C. Fitzpatrick, ed. *Writings of George Washington* (Washington, DC: United States Government Printing Office, 1936), 16:480–81.

40. David A. Armour, "De Peyster, Arent Schuyler," *Dictionary of Canadian Biography*, IV (1821–1835), http://www.biographi.ca/en/bio.php?id_nbr=2831, accessed Feb. 16, 2016.

41. Larry L. Nelson, *A Man of Distinction among Them: Alexander McKee and the Ohio Country Frontier, 1754–1799* (Kent, OH: Kent State University Press, 1999).

42. Willing's expedition receives thorough treatment in David Narrett, *Adventurism and Empire: The Struggle for Mastery in the Louisiana Borderlands, 1762–1803* (Chapel Hill: University of North Carolina Press, 2015), 79–88.

43. Arent S. De Peyster to Frederick Haldimand, Mar. 8, 1780, *Collections and Researches Made by the Pioneer Society of the State of Michigan* [various titles, hereafter *MPHC*] X (1908):378–79.

44. Arent S. De Peyster to Frederick Haldimand, Mar. 8, 1780, *MPHC* X (1908):379.

45. At Detroit, De Peyster did notify Sinclair of his plans to seize the falls while Sinclair's expedition was moving south, but that was the extent of their coordination. Neither man seems to have been in touch in West Florida with Campbell, who in any case was already on the defensive. Arent De Peyster to Patrick Sinclair, Mar. 12, 1780, *MPHC* IX (1908):580–81.

46. Arent S. De Peyster to Sinclair, May 18, 1780, *MPHC* IX (1908):582.

47. Alexander McKee to Major [Arent] De Peyster, July 8, 1780, Haldiman Papers, NG21, Add. Mss. 21760 (B-100), National Archives of Canada, http://www.frontierfolk.net/ramsha_research/mckee.html; accessed Feb. 5, 2016; Frederick Haldimand to Arent De Peyster, Feb. 12, 1780, *MPHC* IX (1908):634.

48. J. Winston Coleman, Jr., *The British Invasion of Kentucky* (Lexington, KY: Winburn Press, 1951), http://www.walthertree.com/BritishInvasionofKentucky.html, accessed Feb. 5, 2016. Coleman's account is grotesquely anti-Indian, but it provides an accurate account of Bird's expedition based on primary sources.

49. R. E. Banta, *The Ohio* (Lexington: University Press of Kentucky, 1998 [orig. 1949]), 159.

50. John Hancock to George Washington, Oct. 12, 1777, *PGWde*, RWS, 11:492–93.

51. Bradley J. Birzer, "French Imperial Remnants on the Middle Ground: The Strange Case of August de la Balme and Charles Beaubien," *Journal of the Illinois*

State Historical Society 93, no. 2 (2000):135–154; Harvey Lewis Carter, *The Life and Times of Little Turtle: First Sagamore of the Wabash* (Urbana: University of Illinois Press, 1987).

52. Thomas Jefferson to William Fleming, Aug. 7, 1779, Founders Online, National Archives, http://founders.archives.gov/documents/Jefferson/01-03-02-0068; George Washington to Jefferson, Dec. 28, 1780, Founders Online, National Archives; http://founders.archives.gov/documents/Washington/99-01-02-04360; Thomas Jefferson to Daniel Brodhead, Feb. 13, 1781, editor's note, Founders Online, National Archives, http://founders.archives.gov/documents/Jefferson/01-04-02-0745. Brodhead never sent the troops to Virginia; on Arnold's threat to the state, see Mark Edward Lender and James Kirby Martin, "A Traitor's Epiphany: Benedict Arnold in Virginia and His Quest for Reconciliation," *Virginia Magazine of History and Biography* (2017), forthcoming.

53. Entry of June 7, 1781, *The Diaries of George Washington*, ed. Donald Jackson (Charlottesville: University Press of Virginia, 1978), III:379.

54. Daniel Brodhead to John Clark, Oct. 11, 1779, "Instructions to Officers," Brodhead Papers; Louise Phelps Kellogg, ed., *Frontier Retreat on the Upper Ohio, 1779–1781* (Madison: Wisconsin Historical Society, 1917), 376–77.

55. Calloway, *American Revolution in Indian Country*, 228–333. Fort Carlos was also known as Post Charles III.

56. Schmidt, *Native Americans in the American Revolution*,147–48.

57. After the war South Carolina authorities arrested Bates and sentenced him to hang. Instead, a Gowen's Fort survivor entered the jail and shot him to death; and South Carolinians lauded the vigilante avenger as a hero. Edward McCrady, *The History of South Carolina in the Revolution, 1780–1783* (New York: Macmillan, 1902), 477–479.

58. At different times other Indians suspected the Gnadenhutten Lenapes (Delawares) were in sympathy with the Americans. Williamson didn't care. His men had a reputation for wanton barbarity, and learning of the militia commander's target, at Fort Pitt Continental colonel John Gibson actually tried to warn the Delawares of the impending assault, for which whites threatened his life. Banta, *The Ohio*, 160–61; Rob Harper, "Looking the Other Way: The Gnadenhutten Massacre and the Contextual Interpretation of Violence," *William and Mary Quarterly*, 3rd ser., 64, no. 3 (2007):633–42.

59. Peckham, *Toll of Independence*, 94–96; Ted Franklin Belie, "Crawford's Sandusky Expedition," in *The American Revolution, 1775–1783: An Encyclopedia*, ed. Richard L. Blanco (New York: Garland, 1993), 1:416–20.

60. George Washington to William Irvine, Aug. 6, 1782, John C. Fitzpatrick, ed., *The Writings of George Washington from the Original Manuscript Sources* (Washington, DC: U.S. Government Printing Office, 1931–44), 24:474.

61. E. M. Sanchez-Saavedra, *A Guide to Virginia Military Organizations in the American Revolution,1774–1787* (Westminster MD: Heritage Books, 1978).

62. Bessie Taul Conkright, "Estill's Defeat; or, The Battle of Little Mountain, March 22, 1782," *Register of Kentucky State Historical Society* 22, no. 66 (1924):311–22;

Michael C.C. Adams, "An Appraisal of the Blue Licks Battle," *Filson Club History Quarterly* 75, no. 2 (2001):181–203.
63. David Curtis Scaggs, ed., *The Old Northwest in the American Revolution: An Anthology* (Madison: State Historical Society of Wisconsin, 1977), 132.
64. William Irvine to George Washington, Dec. 2, 1781, Founders Online, National Archives, http://founders.archives.gov/documents/Washington/99-01-02-07473, accessed May 3, 2016.
65. Arent De Peyster to Patrick Sinclair, Mar. 8, 1780, *MPHC* 9 (1908):378–79.
66. Narrett, *Adventurism and Empire*, 129; Richard L. Forstall, comp. and ed., *Population of the States and Counties of the United States: 1790–1990* (Washington, DC: U.S. Department of Commerce, Bureau of the Census, 1996), 4.
67. E.g., Harold E. Selesky, ed., *Encyclopedia of the American Revolution*, 2nd ed. (Detroit: Charles Scribner's Sons, 2006), 2:1257.
68. Jonathan R. Dull, *A Diplomatic History of the American Revolution* (New Haven: Yale University Press, 1985), 159–64.

CHAPTER FIVE: THE NAVAL THEATER

1. Worthington C. Ford, ed., *Journals of the Continental Congress [JCC]*, vol. III, (Washington, DC: Government Printing Office, 1906), 274–75.
2. William Bell Clark, ed., *Naval Documents of the American Revolution*, vol. 2, "Journal of the Continental Congress, 5 October 1775" (Washington, DC: Government Printing Office, 1966), 308n2.
3. L. H. Butterfield, ed., "Notes on the Debates in the Continental Congress," October 7, 1775, *Diary and Autobiography of John Adams* (Cambridge, MA: Harvard University Press, 1962), 198; Clark, ed., *Naval Documents of the American Revolution*, vol. 2, 308r9n2.
4. Jonathan R. Dull, *American Naval History, 1607–1865: Overcoming the Colonial Legacy* (Lincoln: University of Nebraska Press, 2012), 8–9.
5. Tim McGrath, *Give Me a Fast Ship: The Continental Navy and America's Revolution at Sea* (New York: Penguin Random House, 2014), 13–14.
6. Isaac J. Greenwood, *Captain John Manley: Second in Rank in the United States Navy, 1776–1783* (Boston: C. E. Goodspeed, 1915), 23–25; William James Morgan, *Captains to the Northward: The New England Captains in the Continental Navy* (Barre, MA: Barre Gazette, 1959), 9.
7. Greenwood, *Captain John Manley*, 26–27.
8. "Captain George Vandeput, Commanding Officer, HMS *Asia* to the Mayor of New York City," quoted in McGrath, *Give Me a Fast Ship*, 18.
9. Clark, ed., *Naval Documents of the American Revolution*, vol. 2, "George Washington to John Hancock, 5 October 1775," 301.
10. *JCC*, 13 October 1775, http://www.constitution.org/uslaw/contcong/03_journals_continental_congress.pdf, accessed September 27, 2016.
11. Charles Francis Adams, ed., *The Works of John Adams*, vol. 3 (Boston: Little and Brown, 1851), 12.
12. McGrath, *Give Me a Fast Ship*, 27.

13. James L. Nelson, *George Washington's Secret Navy: How the American Revolution Went to Sea* (New York: McGraw-Hill, 2008), 264.

14. Nathan Miller, *Sea of Glory: A Naval History of the American Revolution* (Annapolis, MD: Naval Institute Press, 1974), 92–93.

15. Nelson, *George Washington's Secret Navy,* 283–84.

16. Ibid., 304–6.

17. Miller, *Sea of Glory,* 99, 107–9.

18. Charles R. Smith, *Marines in the Revolution: A History of the Continental Marines in the American Revolution, 1775–1783* (Washington, DC: USMC History and Museums Division, 1975), 53–55.

19. Tim McGrath, *John Barry: An American Hero in the Age of Sail* (Yardley, PA: Westholme Publishing, 2010), 74–75.

20. McGrath, *John Barry,* 88.

21. Nicholas Biddle to James Biddle, May 10, 1776, quoted in William Bell Clark, *Captain Dauntless: The Story of Nicholas Biddle of the Continental Navy* (Baton Rouge: Louisiana State University Press, 1949), 113.

22. William M. Fowler, Jr., *Rebels Under Sail: The American Navy During the Revolution* (New York: Charles Scribner's Sons, 1976), 269; Abraham Whipple to Esek Hopkins, April 30, 1776, in *The Correspondence of Esek Hopkins* (Providence: Rhode Island Historical Society, 1933), 42–43.

23. Robert Armistead Stewart, *The History of Virginia's Navy of the Revolution* (reprint, Baltimore: Genealogical Publishing, 1993), 11.

24. http://founders.archives.gov/documents/Washington/03-05-02-0022, accessed September 16, 2016.

25. Esek Hopkins to Nathanael Shaw, Jr., May 22, 1776, in *Letter Book of Esek Hopkins, 1775–1777* (Providence: Rhode Island Historical Society, 1932), 63.

26. Frank Clement Mevers III, "Congress and the Navy: The Establishment and Administration of the American Revolutionary Navy by the Continental Congress, 1775–1784," Ph.D. dissertation, University of North Carolina at Chapel Hill, 1972, 104–5.

27. Fowler, *Rebels Under Sail,* 246; Samuel Eliot Morison, *John Paul Jones: A Sailor's Biography* (Boston: Northeastern University Press, 1959), 89.

28. John W. Jackson, *The Pennsylvania State Navy, 1775–1781* (New Brunswick, NJ: Rutgers University Press, 1974), 123–24.

29. Ibid., 195–99.

30. McGrath, *John Barry,* 136.

31. E. Gordon Bowen-Hassell, Dennis Conrad, and Mark L. Hayes, *Sea Raiders of the American Revolution: The Continental Navy in European Waters* (Washington, DC: Naval Historical Center, 2003), 18.

32. Ibid., 22–23, 28.

33. Ibid., 28, 30, 32, 36, 38.

34. James C. Bradford, "The Battle of Flamborough Head," in Jack Sweetman, ed., *Great American Naval Battles* (Annapolis, MD: Naval Institute Press, 1998), 41.

35. Morison, *John Paul Jones,* 232–35, 237–39; Bradford, "The Battle of Flamborough Head," 39.
36. Morison, *John Paul Jones,* 246.
37. McGrath, *Give Me a Fast Ship,* 273; Editor's Notes, "The Journal of the Siege of Penobscot," *Magazine of History,* 11 (1910), 295.
38. McGrath, *Give Me a Fast Ship,* 274; John E. Cayford, *The Penobscot Expedition* (Orrington, ME: C&H Publishing, 1976), 9.
39. G. W. Allen, *A Naval History of the American Revolution,* vol. II (Boston, 1913), 424; Henry I. Shaw, "Penobscot Assault—1779," *Military Affairs,* 17, no. 2 (Summer 1953), 87.
40. Shaw, "Penobscot Assault—1779," 92–93.
41. "The Original Journal of General Solomon Lovell kept During the Penobscot Expedition, 1779," *Proceedings of the Weymouth Historical Society for 1879–80* (Weymouth, MA: Weymouth Historical Society, 1881), 105; Shaw, "Penobscot Assault—1779," 93.
42. James M. Volo, *Blue Water Patriots: The American Revolution Afloat* (Westport, CT: Praeger, 2007), 91.
43. John W. Gordon, *South Carolina and the American Revolution* (Columbia: University of South Carolina Press, 2003), 72–73.
44. Bernard A. Uhlendorf, ed., "Diary of Captain Johann Ewald, 8 April 1780," in *The Siege of Charleston* (Ann Arbor: University of Michigan Press, 1938), 53.
45. Uhlendorf, ed., "Diary of Captain Johann Ewald, 12 May 1780," 87.
46. Bernard A. Uhlendorf, ed., "Diary of Captain Johann Hinrichs, 12 May 1780," in *The Siege of Charleston,* 295.
47. French Ensor Chadwick, ed., "Thomas Graves to George Rodney, 2 July 1781," in *The Graves Papers and Other Documents Relating to the Naval Operations of the Yorktown Campaign* (New York: Arno Press, 1968), 18–19.
48. Brendan Morrissey, *Yorktown 1781: The World Turned Upside Down* (Oxford, UK: Osprey Publishing, 1997), 52–53.
49. Ibid., 55–57.
50. Ibid., 58.
51. Allen, *A Naval History of the American Revolution,* vol. 2, 63.

ACKNOWLEDGMENTS

T he editors wish to express their thanks to several individuals and institutions for the support they provided to the Revolutionary War Symposium: the Henry and Jenny Johnson Endowment; The Citadel Department of History; Alan Stello, Michael Coker, and the Colonial Charleston Consortium; and the General Mark W. Clark Distinguished Visiting Chair of History. In addition, we would like to thank The Citadel History Department Chair, Katherine H. Grenier, and Professors Kyle S. Sinisi and Paul Johstono for their active involvement. Christina Bowman of The Citadel History Department accomplished virtually all of the logistical support for the symposium, and the editors remain especially grateful to her for her herculean efforts.

We also would also like to express our gratitude to Bruce H. Franklin, publisher at Westholme, for his enthusiasm and wise counsel in encouraging and supporting the development of this volume. In addition, the editors greatly appreciate the good work of copyeditor Noreen O'Connor-Abel, mapmaker Paul Dangel, and designer Trudi Gershenov.

INDEX